Christel Ahrens, Ebise Ashana (Eds.)

# In Memory of Them

# Beiträge zur Missionswissenschaft / Interkulturellen Theologie

herausgegeben von

Dieter Becker und Henning Wrogemann

Band 48

LIT

# In Memory of Them

Women witnessing to Christ in Ethiopia
(1870 – 2019)

edited by

Christel Ahrens and Ebise Ashana

LIT

Cover images: from left to right
Elizabeth Karorsa, Sr Hilma Olsson, Abeba Kifleegzy,
Rev. Sudi Gote, Qanaatuu Karorsaa, Elsabet Gulti


This book is printed on acid-free paper.


**Bibliographic information published by the Deutsche Nationalbibliothek**
The Deutsche Nationalbibliothek lists this publication in the Deutsche
Nationalbibliografie; detailed bibliographic data are available in the Internet at
http://dnb.dnb.de.

ISBN 978-3-643-91156-8 (pb)
ISBN 978-3-643-96156-3 (PDF)


A catalogue record for this book is available from the British Library.


© LIT VERLAG GmbH & Co. KG Wien,
Zweigniederlassung Zürich 2020
Flössergasse 10
CH-8001 Zürich
Tel. +41 (0) 76-632 84 35
E-Mail: zuerich@lit-verlag.ch    http://www.lit-verlag.ch
**Distribution:**
In the UK: Global Book Marketing, e-mail: mo@centralbooks.com
In North America: Independent Publishers Group, e-mail: orders@ipgbook.com
In Germany: LIT Verlag Fresnostr. 2, D-48159 Münster
Tel. +49 (0) 2 51-620 32 22, Fax +49 (0) 2 51-922 60 99, e-mail: vertrieb@lit-verlag.de

I just can't tell you how much I enjoyed reading the piece of work you have produced, especially as it lifts the contributions of our mothers and sisters to the life and ministry of the Church. Thank you for trusting me to take part in polishing it.

**Rev. Dr. Debela Birri**, Principal Mekane Yesus Seminary, 1996–99
Director of Ethiopian Graduate School of Theology, 2000–07

There is no human history without the participation of women. However, history mostly deals with patriarchs of those societies; and such sources continue to be quoted over generations. That is why women's stories of faith journeys, resilience and leadership remain untold. In this book the noble contributions of some women are brought to light. It is my hope that this humble work will motivate many others to do more to unfold the great stories of brave women.

**Aberash Dinssa**, EECMY, Women's Ministry Coordinator, 2000–07

I am so impressed! I have been looking for such initiatives.

**Rev. Dr. Lalissa Daniel,** EECMY,
Director of Department of Mission and Theology (DMT) Dircetor, 2017

Travelling to Ethiopia I was very impressed how strongly women in the Lutheran Church are committed to live our faith and tradition. I am very grateful that their history, witness and contribution are valued in this book.

**Dr. Margot Käßmann,** Bishop of the Evangelical Lutheran Church of Hannover, 1999–2010

# Preface

## 150 years of Women Witnessing to Christ in Ethiopia[1]

Scholars are predicting an unprecedented growth of Christianity in the global south. Philip Jenkins has reaffirmed that *"there can be no doubt that the emerging Christian world will be anchored in the Southern continents."*[2] Among the Lutheran churches in Africa that are exhibiting unprecedented growth, the Ethiopian Evangelical Church Mekane Yesus (EECMY) stands tall; she symbolizes the shift in the center of gravity of the Lutheran Church.

In the 1960s the leadership of the EECMY gave to Rev. Gustav Arén the assignment to write about the origins and history of the church. Arén did careful research in the archives of Ethiopia, Eritrea, Sweden, Norway, Switzerland, Germany and Great Britain and two volumes were published: The Evangelical Pioneers (1978) and The Envoys of the Gospel in Ethiopia (1998). His excellent work illustrates the historical background in this book.

*"In Memory of Them"* covers the long journey of the Evangelical Movement in the Horn of Africa over a century and half (1870–2019). Committed and selfless women who sacrificed their comfort and life took part in building and orchestrating this movement. The Evangelical movement in Ethiopia is full of women of ardent passion to bring the "Gospel to the whole person" as intercultural missionaries either from outside or inside the country. Women unarguably have a lion's share in evangelism, language development and literacy, Bible translation, diakonia work and several humanitarian ventures carried out by the EECMY. A plethora of untold stories with underlying immense wisdom is yet to be told. The fact that these pioneering women rose to their level of influence against all odds continues to shine as a beacon of hope.

The last 150 years have brought to the scene heroines of faith whose legacy can be inspirational. It is unfortunate that their decisive role in God's

---

[1] 1870 is the year Gustava Lundahl, one of the first Swedish women missionaries, arrived at the Red Sea coast. Her vision was a school for girls.

[2] Jenkins, Philip: *The Next Christendom: The Coming of Global Christianity,* Oxford University Press, 2002, p 14.

mission has never attracted a great deal of academic attention. Some powerful stories and contributions of these unsung heroines are now readily available to continue inspiring and shaping the dreams of those who follow a greater goal. Though they are still few, the contemporary female pastors and emerging women theologians among us deserve recognition and appreciation.

Presumably, this is the beginning. It is my hope and prayer that many more initiatives will follow to unearth the untold stories of thousands of Ethiopian women who have proclaimed Jesus Christ in word and in deed and continue to do so.

As we are celebrating the 60th anniversary of the EECMY as a nationally recognized institution, this important piece of work is pointing to the enormous and untapped historical treasure and heritage of the EECMY which is begging for attention.

Rev. Dr. Lalissa Daniel Gemechis (PhD)
EECMY, Director of Department of Mission and Theology

# Acknowledgement

The idea of this book was born in 2017, the year marking 500 years of Reformation. The Lutheran World Federation (LWF) had asked partner churches for stories of women reformers. Names from Ethiopia did not come up easily. Were there no 'her-stories' in the EECMY?

More than 50 individuals from three continents have made contributions about pioneer women of the EECMY. We are grateful to everyone who helped to preserve their lives.

Special thanks go to Sarah Wall in the UK for polishing up the English and to Dr. Hartwig Harms in Germany for proofreading much of the content of the book.

*In Memory of Them* helps fill the gap in literature. The book will be translated into Amharic and Oromo, so that people in Ethiopia can discover more of their own spiritual roots.

The editors

# Contents

## Mekane Yesus – The Mother Church

## Envoys of the Gospel

**The ministry and visions of women today**

# List of Abbreviations

| | |
|---|---|
| AAMYC | Addis Ababa Mekane Yesus Church |
| AIDS | Acquired Immune Deficiency Syndrome |
| ALERT | All African Leprosy Research Institute |
| AUPM | American United Presbyterian |
| BCMS | Bible Church Mission Society |
| CBE | Commercial Bank of Ethiopia |
| CLWR | Canadian Lutheran World Relief |
| DERG | Provisional Military Government of Socialist Ethiopia |
| EECMY | Ethiopian Evangelical Church Mekane Yesus |
| ELCA | Evangelical Lutheran Church in America |
| EOC | Ethiopian Orthodox Church |
| GHM | German Hermannsburg Mission |
| GTF | Gudina Tumsa Foundation |
| HIV | Human Immune deficiency Virus |
| LASS | Lalo Aira Secondary School |
| LWF | Lutheran World Federation |
| MYS | Mekane Yesus Seminary |
| MAF | Mission Aviation Fellowship |
| NGO | Non Government Organisation |
| NLM | Norwegian Lutheran Mission |
| OSSA | Organisation of Social Services for AIDS |
| PHC | Primary Health Care |
| SEM | Swedish Evangelical Mission |
| SIM | Sudan Interior Mission Now named Serving in Mission |
| TWR WHO | Trans World Radio Women of Hope |
| UNICEF | United Nations Children's Fund |

# Introduction

Names of women rarely appear in history books. This is true for most countries. Yet they are the ones who sustain life and pass it on to the next generation.

This book is about women who lived in the last 150 years in an area that is now Eritrea and Ethiopia. In 1870 Gustava Lundahl, one of the first Swedish women missionaries, arrived at the Red Sea coast. Her vision was a school for girls.

The lives of the women have to be understood in the context of the culture, the economics and politics of their time and place.

All of them heard about Jesus Christ. The first generation was exposed to missionaries, people with biblical values and a language and culture of their own; hence the relevant mission history was included.

Some women were the first Evangelical Christians in their areas and it was the Bible in their mother tongue that influenced their personal development. As members of a religious minority quite often they experienced opposition and persecution. Yet they were heralds of a new age.

Later generations of women witnessed about Jesus after the Ethiopian Evangelical Church Mekane Yesus (EECMY) was established in 1959. Lastly, a few women leaders of our days are mentioned as examples of many others.

Until today very little has been written about these women, their dedication and their courage. They brought the gospel to new generations. They have something else in common: They did beautiful things for Jesus. Here the sacred and the secular come together.

Their names are now documented and their deeds can be read, talked and preached about. This book will preserve memories of their lives and their legacy in the line with what Jesus said about the woman who anointed him: *She has done a beautiful thing to me! Wherever the gospel is preached throughout the world, what she has done will also be told, in memory of her.*[1]

It is the hope of the editors that the book may trigger further research into the lives of many more women and the beautiful things they did and do in the church and to the benefit of human kind.

---

[1] Mk, 14, 6+9, NIV Bible

# Early Pioneers (1832–1916)

Twenty years before the Swedish missionaries reached the Horn of Africa, a young woman from that part of Africa had been taken to Germany. She became a Christian. Though she died very young she had been well connected in Christian circles and her life inspired future mission work.

## 1.  Ganame Fathme Pauline: The ambassador

In 1832 a girl was born in the Kingdom of Guummaa[2], in West Ormania[3]. She was named Ganame[4] (1832–1855), meaning the one born in the morning. Ganame was the only child of her father Yaa'ii Shaseedaa Odaa; nothing is known about her mother. The father put much effort into her education and instructed her in traditional wisdom. His love and care provided Ganame with a strong foundation for life.

Yaa'ii was a well-to-do leader of the local people. Ganame remembered that he loved the poor and shared with them from his wealth; he prepared traditional medicines and treated the sick. In the Oromo religion there is only one God. He feared God and taught his daughter to pray. Before she reached the age of six years, her father died during a local conflict.

Ganame regularly went to his grave and cried much. One day while visiting his grave she was kidnapped. The resistance and begging of the nine-year-old girl did not help, Ganame was deported by slave hunters.

She was taken to Sudan, which was at that time ruled by Egyptians. At Sennar, a town at the Blue Nile River 280 km south of Khartoum, Ganame was sold at a market. Before a sale the purchaser would enquire about the background of each slave. Slaves were bought for domestic work and for farming. Women slaves were often destined to live in a harem. Female slaves of Oromo origin were known for their beauty and many used traditional substances to make their skin look ugly and infectious in order to escape that fate. Ganame asked God not to let her end up in a harem. She was sold 12 times and finally reached Cairo, where she became

---

[2]   The Kingdom of Guummaa is one of the five Kingdoms in the Gibbe region, a historic region in modern southwest Ethiopia.

[3]   Ormania was the name given to the land of the Orma in the 18th century in German literature. The name was an invention of Germans and encompassed all countries of Oromo peoples, most of which were annexed in the late 19th century.

[4]   The orthography of names and places shows a great diversity, depending on the European language into which African words were transcribed. The book used mostly the spelling that is common in today's' English literature, unless the authors preferred a different spelling.

*Ganame, known as Pauline Johanne Fathme*

the property of Ali Mohammed Pasha. Ganame became a Muslim and was named Fatima. She learnt to prepare tasty food and served in the kitchen of his palace.

In 1847 or 1848 Baron von Müller, an aristocrat from Baden-Württemberg, Germany, came to Egypt and visited Ali Mohammed. The Pasha wanted to give him a present and chose Fatima. The Baron took her to Germany and finally gave her into the care of his mother in Stuttgart. Fatima had an open mind and learnt German.

When the mother of the king of Württemberg heard about Fathme, the name by which she was known in Germany, she wanted to see her too.

She enjoyed the conversation with her and suggested the girl should receive Christian education. Thereafter Baron von Müller arranged for her to go to Korntal, near Stuttgart. On 12.7.1852 she was baptized with the name Pauline Johanne. A number of people of high standing were her guardians.

She prayed much that her people might get the same chance to study and find the Christian faith as she had. Korntal was the place where she met Johan Krapf who had spent a few years in Ankober, Shawa. Prior to him embarking again to East Africa, Pauline sent him a letter:

*I would love to go with you, but it is the will of God that I stay here. I wait patiently until he calls me. May God prepare me, so that one day I can tell my fellow country people the great mercy He had on me. Meanwhile I am glad that you and Mr. Deimler go to the dark country to preach the gospel. I ask God daily that he may be with you and help you always. I beg you to take a gift to the Galla[5]; pictures for children who love the Lord and the needlework for missionary women. Greet all souls who are with me in the Lord.*[6]1854

Krapf had the clothes Pauline had made in his luggage.

Pauline had become a believer with equal rights but she was without official papers. However, the King's mother and Baron von Müller intervened and she was allowed to live in Korntal. In 1853 she gave all her possessions, mainly her jewelry to Basel Mission.

Pauline was integrated in the Christian fellowship and at the same time she longed for her native country. She would cover her face with a veil, because she could not stand the people staring at her. Pauline was full of child-like joy and prayed a lot on her knees. She gave advice to people who crossed her way. Those who came to know her were amazed at her genuine love for all people, big and small. They appreciated her pure heart and her sense of justice and loved her too.

In 1855 she accepted an invitation by Spittler, one of her godfathers, to participate in a conference in Basel, Switzerland. She went, but she became sick and was diagnosed with tuberculosis of the lung. Deaconesses nursed her and they were surprised at her firm faith.

Some months later on September 11th 1855 she died and was buried in Riechen near Basel. She had become dear to the people in Riechen and many tears were

---

[5]   Galla is an expression given by the Abyssinians and Arabs to the Oromos in East Africa. It means immigrants, while their self designated name Oromo is translated strong and courageous men. The term *galla* was the general term used – with no pejorative meaning – in the literature of that time, be it German, French or English.

[6]   Galla Büchlein – Aus dem Leben der Galla-Negerin Pauline Johanne Fathme, K. Fr. Ledderhose, Verlag von EF Spittler, Basel 1867 (3. Auflage), pp 33–34.

shed. Her gravestone has her name and Ps 68, 31: The Ethiopians will raise their hands in prayer to God.

## Her legacy

St Chrischona, the mission near Basel, started a Mission to the Oromo after Pauline died. Years later a Swiss missionary bought a slave called Ruufoo, freed him and sent him to St Chrischona, to assist Krapf as translator.[7] The first Oromo translation of the New Testament was written in Latin script. Due to political circumstances the books had to be transcribed to Saba and reached Ethiopia only in 1870.

After Ganame was laid to rest in 1855, Hiikaa Awaajii (Onesimos Nasib) was born in 1870 and Ganno Salban (Aster Ganno) was born in 1874. Both were enslaved as children and sold several times. They became Christians, translated the Bible and spread the gospel among their people. Ganame's innermost wish and prayers were fulfilled.

The short biography on her life[8] became a bestseller and was reprinted several times from 1855 to 1927. The book was translated into French, English, Dutch and Swedish and served as material to prepare missionaries for their service. The income from its sale was invested in the foundation of a mission station among the Oromo.[9]

Thus the Oromo people became known in Germany and other European countries. Ganame can be called their ambassador and prepared the soil for future mission activities in the Horn of Africa.

**Kulani Gudina**

---

[7]    The Oromo Mission constituted another branch of the Pilgrim mission of St. Chrischona, Switzerland. Among German missionaries there existed the dream to turn the entire country of 'Ormania' Protestant. A small number of Oromos were invited to Germany to receive education. One of them, called Christian Ludwig Paulus Rufo by the Germans, embarked upon the significant task of translating the Bible into Oromo; today there are among the Oromo peoples several million Protestants.

[8]    Ledderhose: Galla Büchlein: Aus dem Leben der Galla-Negerin Pauline Johanne Fathme, 1857, see footnote 5

[9]    The sale of the book on Pauline Fathme's life had brought, together with some other contributions, around 500 Swiss Francs. This sum was to be invested in the foundation of a missionary station among the Oromo.

Wolbert Smith wrote on the role of the former Oromo slave Pauline Fathme in the foundation of the Protestant Oromo mission.[10]

*An interesting often overlooked factor in the development of the growing German interest in the Oromo people was the visit of a few Oromo individuals to Germany in the 19th century. Pauline Fathme was certainly the first to come to Germany. An entire small biography was dedicated to her after her death in 1855. It was published in the form of a small brochure, reprinted several times and translated into a number of languages including English. This literature was highly influential in missionary circles in Germany, Switzerland and England. The project of a mission among the Oromo soon found important sponsors in England.*

*In her biography she is mainly depicted as an extremely pious young woman who converted to Protestant Pietism. Her missionary zeal, which she even showed in daily conversations with people she met, made her a 'real child of God' in the eyes of the Pietist circles of Württemberg and Northern Switzerland. Soon her presence in Europe was interpreted as a sign from God.*

*She received a Christian education in Korntal, Württemberg, visited missionary festivals and was prepared for a role in the mission, possibly as a deaconess. The fact that she went through quite diverse religious backgrounds and finally stayed with the South-German Pietists might have contributed to the importance that was given to her.*

*The history of her names illustrates the dramatic changes in her life, and an interesting set of conflicting identities. First her name was written in Oromo, then it was changed into Arabic, and later Germanized after her baptism – her names thus all relate to dramatically different cultural and religious backgrounds (from the Waaqaa-religion via Islam to Protestant Christianity).*

*A decade after Pauline Fathme's death there were further 'signs': it is remarkable, that in the moment when the 'Galla-Mission' was to be started seriously, there were two important signs of God seen that encouraged them to go forward without any fear. The first was the fact that British Protestant missionaries had reached southern Oromo groups near the East-African mission station of Ribbe; the second was the arrival of the young Ruufoo in Europe to assist the Bible translation of Krapf.[11]*

---

[10]  Smidt, Wolbert: Ethiopia and the Missions, Historical and Anthropological Insights, LIT Verlag, Münster, 2005.

[11]  Smith, Wolbert, The Unknown First Bible Translator Christian Rufo (Ruufoo), Some Insights from Private Missionary Archives, Seminar paper, Asien-Africa-Institute, University of Hamburg, 2001

# Swedish Mission and missionaries in female education[12]

## The Swedish Evangelical Mission and its first venture

The Swedish Evangelical Mission (SEM) was founded in 1856 and had grown out of a revival movement within the Church of Sweden. Studying the Scriptures was a prominent feature of the awakening.

The board of the SEM sought guidance in selecting a mission field. Many areas were considered. Their supporters were familiar with writings by Louis Harms and his vision of sending out groups of pastors and lay missionaries to the Oromos. They had read reports by Johan Krapf, who had been a missionary in Abyssinia (1837–42) and was sent by the Church Mission Society, an Anglican mission organisation. The board of the SEM consulted Krapf who strongly urged the SEM to start a mission in East Africa. Eventually the Oromo people living beyond the Abyssinian highlands became the target of the SEM's first mission enterprise.

Undeterred by the failure of two Hermannsburg groups to reach the Oromo in 1854 and 1858, the Swedes were taking up the challenge. It was unforeseeable that it would take the SEM thirty-two years to reach Oromo country through indigenous missionaries. Working through indigenous people became a distinctive feature of the SEM.

The story of the first mission venture of the SEM is a striking example of the significance of ecumenical contacts and the sharing of spiritual and missionary insights across national borders.

When their Swedish missionaries arrived at the Red Sea port of Massawa in 1866, they were inexperienced and knew little of what to expect. They committed their enterprise to God's gracious guidance.

A significant aspect was the availability of the Scriptures and a catechism in Amharic. The young missionaries believed that though preaching

---

[12]  See Arén, Gustav: *Evangelical Pioneers in Ethiopia*, 1978, chapter 5, 6, 9 & 11; and Lundstroem, Karl J. & Ezra Gebremedhin: *Kenisha,* 2011, chapter 7 & 9.

was the primary means of initiating mission work, reading the Bible was the most important vehicle for the spread of the Gospel.

Unable to travel to Oromo territory, because Abyssinia did not allow them to pass their area the Swedes started to work among the Kunama, who shortly afterwards became victims of a border conflict between two imperial powers, Egypt and Ethiopia. In addition there was fighting among clans; hence mediating peace was a major feature of their early missionary activity.

The heaviest pressures upon the Swedish pioneers were undoubtedly those of the hot climate and tropical diseases as well as conflicts between different population groups. All missionaries were sick with fevers, five of them died prematurely and two were murdered.

The arrival of the Swedes coincided with a time of political changes. The opening of the Suez Canal in 1869 ended the isolation of Egypt and Ethiopia. The empire of Tewodros II (1855–68) was crumbling. Egypt pushed forward into the Ethiopian territory and established border posts. Britain, Italy and France were at the borders and their colonial interests threatened the independence of Ethiopia. These were the years of the Scramble for Africa (1870–1914), when European countries were acquiring colonies in Africa.

After the death of Emperor Tewodros II in 1868 a Tigrean ruler emerged supreme and ascended the imperial throne as Emperor Yohannes IV (1868–89). The new Negusa Nagast[13] regarded religious conformity as a prerequisite for national unity and initiated a religious policy denouncing Western missionaries, advocates of reform and other readers of the Bible.

From Kunama the missionaries eventually retreated to Massawa, which was under Egyptian rule. They initiated an educational programme and made teaching an instrument of evangelism as they were unable to travel inland. Knowing how important it is for a Christian to be able to read the Bible in the mother tongue, they felt this was equally applicable to life on the mission field. The availability of Amharic Bibles facilitated their new work.

---

[13]   Negus 'king, ruler, chief, head, commander' is the traditional title of the Ethiopian monarch, negusa nagast 'king of kings'

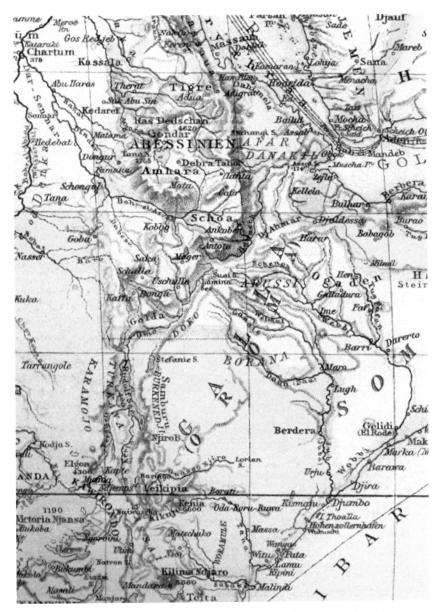

*European view on East Africa as seen in a map printed before 1900 AD*

The Swedes targeted three groups of people: poor refugees, exiled reformers and liberated slaves. The group of refugees was the largest, as there was a constant flow of people coming from the lowlands.

The exiled reformers were Bible reading Orthodox Christians who, under the edict of Emperor Yohannes IV, were banned from living within the territory of his empire. The reformers played an important role in the development of the mission by providing them with Ethiopian leaders.

When the Swedish missionaries settled in Massawa, the Egyptian authorities along the Red Sea Coast promised to send them freed slaves to receive education, but they got only very few, among them Onesimos Nasib.

From 1890 onwards the Red Sea coast was under Italian jurisdiction and was then called Eritrea. Slaves were set free and many young people were admitted to the boarding school run by the SEM missionaries.

The missionaries were fully occupied with work among these three categories of people.

### Bengt Peter Lundahl

Bengt Peter Lundahl (1840–85) went to Africa in 1868 as pastor and mission pioneer. He would become almost identified with the SEM because of his leadership over many years.

After an initial failed start among the Kunama, Lundahl recommended two main lines of action: the training of evangelists and the promotion of Bible study in the vernacular. He urged that promising young men should be sent abroad for better training than he himself could offer. The board supported his policy and resolved to receive four Ethiopians for training in Sweden. He promoted the translation of hymns, order of worship and portions of Scriptures. Lundahl had major influence on the mission policy, which had to adapt to the situation faced in the mission field. He encouraged repeated expeditions to the land of the Oromo bypassing Abyssinia.

In 1870 Lundahl opened a primary school for freed male slaves, as they had nowhere to go and nothing to do. He based his hopes on converted slaves and saw the chance to educate the youngsters and one day send them as missionaries to their homelands. His school started with five students.

Onesimos was his very first student and later the first Oromo to be educated in Europe. He was counted among the Swedish missionaries with whom he had his training. The SEM supported Onesimos by providing missionaries, money and moral support until his end. Evangelical Christianity struck root and spread in modern western Ethiopia as a result of indigenous enterprise and leadership.

Lundahl's wife Gustava had a dream of a school for girls, but passed away early in childbirth. The widower returned to Sweden, married Emelie and returned to the mission field.

Lundahl died of smallpox[14] in December 1885. Lundahl's hope of obtaining further freed slaves became a reality four months after his death, when a group of girls was admitted to the girls' boarding school. His wife Emelie survived him and worked in female education until she returned to Sweden in 1894.

## A living Christian community in Imkullu

The missionaries settled in Imkullu close to Massawa and their compound became the centre of the education and literature work as well as a place for refugees.

The multi-ethnic composition of the Evangelical community made use of one common language necessary. Lundahl felt this had to be Amharic; the most widely used Ethiopian language within the evangelical community. The Bible was already translated and Amharic was the easiest medium for contacts with the political and scholarly elite on the highlands. The language of the ordinary man and woman on the Eritrean highlands, however, was Tigrinya.

Rohlfs, a German traveler and scholar, undertook a journey to Abyssinia in 1880–81 and wrote about the life he saw on the mission compound in Imkullu.

*At the institution that was led by Mr. Lundahl, his wife and five other married missionaries 150 Abyssinian children are being taken care of at present. It is a joy*

---

[14]  Smallpox was a frequent pandemic in the Horn of Africa, one of the great killer diseases and eradicated in Ethiopia in the late 1960s by continuous vaccination campaigns.

*to see how the small creatures, ranging in age from infants to 12–15 years of age, are prospering and growing.*

*Among them there are all varieties of colour and skin, from yellow to black. Apart from learning to write, read and count each child must learn a practical skill. Here one sees girls learning to knit, do crochet and sew and, over there, one sees boys making shoes, doing carpentry etc.*

*All are smartly dressed, in European fashion. One need hardly add that their diet is good and that it takes local climatic conditions into consideration. Services are held in the chapel which is located in a mission building and is supplied with a small organ.*[15]

Within a relatively short period, the missionaries built up a remarkable interracial and intertribal congregation. Among the members of this congregation there were the educated and the illiterate, the sick and the recovering, people who had been sold into slavery and those who could trace their birth back to distinguished families in Sweden, Germany, Austria and Italy.

On Sunday afternoon they had so called 'forums for the free world' that were discussions where the native Christians could vent their feelings and opinions.

The congregation had the mark of *koinonia*, a fellowship of faith and life. It practiced *diakonia*, a reciprocal fellowship of service in which all members had a responsibility not only for each other's spiritual but also bodily wellbeing. The congregation practiced *leitourgia*, a fellowship of worship in which the Eucharist, the fellowship of Holy Communion, was decisive. And as a community born of mission, it practiced *martyria*, a fellowship that witnessed to Christ in its surroundings. The father and apostle of this community by the Red Sea was Pastor Bengt Peter Lundahl.

Prince Oscar Bernadotte (1872–1953), son of King Oscar II of Sweden who reigned from 1872–1907, visited Imkullu on a round-the-world journey. His diary entry for February 22, 1885 reads:

*What I saw in M'kullo (Imkullu) gave me, then a young man, much to ponder. There, God gave me one of the nudges forward, through which he wants to help*

---

[15]   Lundstroem, Johann and Ezra Gebremedhin: Kenisha, 148; words taken from Nils Dahlberg's book Under HögreBEfäl (Under higher Command) 1953, 28

*us, human beings, to come into the path of Life. I did not understand it then, but before long I realized that God had met me.*[16]

While working at Imkullu the missionaries were sending out one expedition after another by different routes to reach non-Christian Oromo areas. Many strenuous efforts did not succeed until, at the turn of the century, Bodji in Wollega became a centre of evangelical witness to the Oromo and, in fact, the cradle of the Ethiopian Evangelical Church Mekane Yesus (EECMY).

The Swedish missionaries studied the culture and the language of the people with the expectation that the history of every nation is an Old Testament, a witness of an experience with God. Every nation has a holy history, a history linked with God.

Literacy played a key role and the question of spiritual literature in African languages arose. Lundahl bought a small printing press in 1883 and recruited a qualified printer. Many people worked on translation and languages in Imkullu. The entire Bible had already been translated into Amharic in 1818 and published in 1840; whereas the New Testament had been translated into the Oromo language by a team around Krapf and was printed in 1876[17]. The translation of both the New and the Old Testament by Onesimos, Aster and a team of 12 people was ready in 1893 and printed in 1899 in Chrischona, Switzerland. In the absence of travel permissions, books were sent with traders and reached the inland areas. Other missionaries and teams at Imkullu were translating the Bible into Tigrinya and Tigre.

Linguistic pioneering and the production of vernacular literature turned out to be one of the most important activities of the Evangelical group over a long period of years. By transforming oral languages into written ones missions preserved the cultures of different peoples and made an important contribution to nation building.

Among the indigenous coworkers, Onesimos had a special gift for translation work.

---

[16]   Kenisha, 148; Gerhardt Rohlfs 1883, 117–118, quoted in Hofgren 1956, 170 (Ed)
[17]   Gütl, Clemens, Johann Ludwig Krapf, LIT Verlag, 2001, 173, footnote 564

## Onesimos Nasib (1856–1931)

Onesimos[18] was a four-year-old boy when he was enslaved. He was sold many times until he was freed at the age of fourteen.

His birth name was Hiikaa[19] Awaajii. When he was baptized he received a biblical name. Onesimos had been a runaway slave boy who ministered to Paul's needs when the latter was in prison. As for his second name, Nasib, that was the name of the man who had purchased Onesimos at Massawa and treated him well enough so that Onesimos kept his master's name.

In 1874 while Lundahl was in Sweden Onesimos wrote him a letter:

*Beloved Father Lundahl, Grace and peace from God be with you; Amen. My father, I have long been waiting for you to return. For this reason I have not written earlier. I have not had any peace in my heart because of my longing for you. All the time since you left I have not had any joy. There is no one who understands my heart and my thoughts as you do.*[20]

Lundahl in turn had a fatherly relationship with him. He knew Onesimos' talents and limitations and wrote in 1876:

*We have now started to learn the Galla language. It is Onesimos who has urged me to it through his earnest desire to return to his people to proclaim the gospel to them. That his desire is sincere has been proved to me several times. At times he may weep half the night praying for his country and his people pleading with the Lord, 'How long, O Lord, how long will it be until you send a preacher of the Gospel there?'*

*But I am afraid of sending him with the narrow views he has. The instruction he has received here is rather one sided. I have thought of sending him home (to Sweden) for some time with a view to learning some craft like carpentry and lifting his eyes higher up. Onesimos is very firm of mind and free from squeamishness and I trust he will suffer no harm from undertaking such a journey. But you must see to it that our friends at home do not spoil him.*[21]

---

[18]   Onesimos was born in 1856 in Hurrumuu, Illubabor the year the SEM was founded in Stockholm, Sweden

[19]   Hiikaa is an Oromo name meaning translator, problem solver and liberator.

[20]   Mission Tidining 1874: 152; Onesimos to Lundahl, Massawa, October 20, 1874

[21]   EFS Archives, Lundahl to Pettersson, Massawa 1876.3.18

1876 Onesimos was sent to Sweden and returned after five years. He studied theology, made contacts with congregations related to the SEM and formed close relationships with his fellow students, some of whom were later sent to the Red Sea Coast on his request.

On returning to Massawa Onesimos married Mehret, the daughter of Alaqa[22] Hailu who had been the secretary to Emperor Tewodros. After the king had died Alaqa Hailu entrusted his daughter to the missionaries. She worked in the house of the Lundahls, learnt Swedish and became a believer.

## A new form of fellowship on the second Oromo Expedition

Onesimos and Mehret[23] got married just before the second expedition to the Oromo (1881–82). Hailu, a young highlander and commissioned evangelist married Sematu, a girl from Aksum Tsion in the same age as Mehret and this young couple also joined the expedition. One of the two participating missionaries wrote:

*We are an odd group of people, bewildering to the world. This was in particular the case on board. Onesimos could hardly explain our situation. Muslims keep their wives carefully secluded. No outsider is allowed to look at them. But we all joined around our coffee pot at dusk. The authorities at Massawa could not find out who of us is servant and who is master[24].*

European travelers in this part of the world would usually be accompanied by a number of retainers to look after their personal comfort. Not so in this case. As a matter of principle nobody enjoyed special privileges. All were equals, whatever the outward difference. The two women could associate with their male companions in an unconstrained and natural manner. No wonder that the Muslim passengers aboard stared at the party in bewilderment. If they had followed the highland customs, Mehret and Sematu would not have mingled with the general company but would have been sitting in seclusion for the whole of their first year of marriage. For their part this was unthinkable.

---

[22]  Alaqa: Ecclesiastical title given to the head of an important church
[23]  Mehret was the 19-year-old daughter of Lundahl's first teacher Alaqa Hailu, Mehret and Onesimos had known each other since 1871
[24]  MT1882:3–4, G.E. Arrhenius, Suakin, 11.11.1881

Their education at the Månssons' School for Girls[25] had not merely widened their horizon; it had given them a new dignity. By their very appearance they foreshadowed a new type of Ethiopian woman, educated, well-mannered, on a par with men. Their daily devotions and the sociable gathering around the coffee pot were the manifestation of a deep inner community.

Mehret and Sematu were both brought up by the missionaries. They had shared in the spiritual awakening of 1878 at the girls' school in Imkullu and became communicant members of the Bethel congregation in 1879. It was a genuine commitment to Christ that from the very beginning bound the seven companions together in a unique fellowship, uniting indigenous people and foreigners, men and women.

The outcome of this expedition was tragic: Arrhenius, the Swedish leader of the expedition and a young Oromo named Filipos died. The other five returned back without reaching their destination, having all been extremely sick with fever.

### Female emancipation

Initially, owing to the hardship of pioneering, the mission vocation was regarded as a male prerogative. Women were not sent out except as future wives of missionaries, but they were qualified teachers and nurses; hence both men and women had equal education and their own jobs.

When the Italian authorities proclaimed religious tolerance in 1890, the Swedes left Imkullu and moved up to the highland. The boarding school for girls moved to new premises at Beleza. A school for women was established as an extension. It was run by Indrias, Haile-Ab's widow, and was presumably the first example of adult education for women in Eritrea and Ethiopia.

Advocating female literacy was revolutionary. Little had changed since the 1830s when Gobat[26] observed that "... *though there were few ladies*

---

[25]  Rosa and Ola Månssons began the first school for girls in 1876, also called the Månssons' School for Girls

[26]  Samuel Gobat (1799–1872) from Switzerland was one of the early missionaries sent by the Christian Mission Society to Abyssinia.

*who could read and write, women in general learnt nothing but spinning and running the household."* Orthodox schools were for boys and not for girls.

By admitting women to rural Bible schools and calling their attention to new ideas, these places became important instruments for female emancipation. The Bible schools were spiritual and cultural lighthouses which dispelled ignorance and prejudice, diffused gospel truth, and offered literacy and the prospect of further education even to the women in rural areas. Education was a vehicle for women's emancipation.

This development was a result fully consistent with the spirit of the gospel and was obviously expected in Evangelical circles, since a special branch for work among women was established in 1896 in conjunction with the programme for evangelism in the highlands of Eritrea.[27]

The fact that many of the missionaries were women and that the missionary wives were educated, was very important for the women they met. They were looked upon as role models. Gustava Lundahl, Rosa Månsson and Emelie Lundahl were the first female missionaries dedicated to educating girls.

---

[27]  Arén 1978, 318

# 1.  Gustava Lundahl: Her legacy – a girls' school

## A long journey and a difficult start

Gustava von Platen (1839–72), a teacher by profession followed Lundahl, her future husband. She, one of the first SEM female missionaries, was travelling with three young men. They left Sweden towards the end of 1869 and reached the Red Sea Coast early in April 1870.[28] It was Gustava who put fresh heart into her companions when they met with adversities and disappointments on their long journey to the mission field. After eight months she reached Lundahl and found him very weak. He and three other missionaries had escaped from Kunama, where four of them had died earlier. When she heard of the tragedy, while still on the way, she wrote:

*I have received the sad news of the murders of our brothers Kjellberg and Elfblad. In the history of missions, however, this is nothing exceptional and cannot prevent anyone whom the Lord has called and who is His from going out. If God is for us, who can be against us? May Jesus be glorified through our life and our death!*[29]

When Gustava got married; both were in poor health. Lundahl's health improved gradually. Gustava, however, contracted fever which developed into rheumatism.

The Lundahls spent the following months in the cool climate of the highland in Hamasen. They felt refreshed and decided to devote their time to study Amharic. A baptized Ethiopian Jew from Gondar was able to give them some lessons.

In September Mr. Ahlborg, a newcomer, decided to move to Massawa to set up a commercial agency for the mission. The political situation in Hamasen was taking a turn for the worse. Humanly speaking the first Swedish mission enterprise on African soil seemed thus to have failed. Gustava lost her usual optimism and confided to her journal on 6.10.1870:

*My poor heart was almost breaking from sorrow, anxiety and loneliness. I had to cry my heart out on my bed and cry to the Lord for calm and help."*[30]

---

[28]  Ingrid Kågedal "Gustava och bröderna i Ostafrika" (Gustava and the brothers in East Africa), Sweden 2019

[29]  Arén 1978, 158; Lundstroem, Gebremedhin 201q, p 150

[30]  Arén 1978, 161

*Gustava, later married to Rev Lundahl, courtesy EFS Archive*

Towards the end of the year the Lundahls moved from the highlands to the coast to celebrate Christmas.

## From her diary and letters

Gustava's diary notes and letters tell us something about her prayer, her experiences and her vision while she was in Massawa.

*Ahlborg, Lundahl and I have begun to think that it might be useful if we stayed in Massawa and started a small school. I was so happy when Ahlborg suggested this and Lundahl seemed to listen. Maybe the Lord has heard my silent prayer, which I almost did not dare to pray: I would rather stay down here than in the Abyssinian highland! I think Lundahl is best suited as a teacher. We both have taught children earlier. New Year's Eve 1870*

Gustava's rheumatism could stand the desert heat better than chilly highland fog. She wrote a few months later: *We have already begun teaching two boys from the Oromo people, our servant Nasib and Hassan's servant Gulla.*

*Four months ago, I got a little Abyssinian girl to take care of,* Mehret*. I teach her to speak and write Swedish and to sew and wash her clothes. I teach both boys and girls here to sew and just got a girl who will learn sewing. Her name is* Therese Zander*. Her father, Eduard Zander, was German and employed by Abyssinia's King Tewodros. His wife was a beautiful Oromo woman whom the Prince chose for him. Zander has been dead for three years and the family now lives in Massawa. Nov. 3rd, 1871*

By Nov. 1871 the school was growing, Lundahl was too weak to work or study. Gustava and a newly appointed Abyssinian teacher had to take his lessons. A letter to the mission leadership in Stockholm reports:

*In April 1872 there are nine children who get food, clothes and education. Unfortunately, we had to send home two of the earlier students who were weakly talented, which meant that we could accommodate Wolde Mariam from the Oromo people, and Adahano, the Abyssinian boy who had been with Hedenström. Our Nasib, who got Onesimos as his name when he was baptized, has always been educated in Arabic. He has also quickly learned Amharic so that he could read the Bible. He has, according to what you can understand, a fairly good understanding of the most important issues of the Christian faith. Nov. 1872*

## Her death and last wish

In December 1872 Gustava organized the household with the ten children. Each of the five older girls had her special task. It seems she was preparing for her coming absence. Gustava was pregnant and left for Alexandria to give birth with medically experienced people, accompanied by a friend to the Lundahl family. After a couple of days on the Red Sea the passengers were forced to get off the ship. It was the rule that passengers had to stay in quarantine for ten days before they could go ashore if they came from another country. Gustava was very ill, but she also had to go into quarantine in a tent with no food or water. She told her accompanying friend: *In this tent I will die* and she did. She was buried at Ayn Musa near Suez, close to the Red Sea.

In the letter in which Lundahl announced his wife's death, he wrote something that Gustava longed to see done.

*I would also like to convey a pronounced wish of my dear wife, namely that something should be done for the women here. For your information, there are three different groups of women here. Firstly large groups of slaves, who have been severely beaten and barely get any food, but have to work as creatures. We are always asked if we can accept slave children, even girls; secondly Abyssinian women who became prostitutes in order to survive and thirdly there are Muslim women. When listening to the men it gives you an understanding of their status. The woman is created for the men, not to be blessed. She dies like the animals. They are treated accordingly.*[31]

The mission board decided to send out female missionaries, so that a school could be opened for girls, *'otherwise there would be no educated Christian girls for converted men to marry!'*

For the first years after Gustava's death there were few missionaries in Massawa. Possibly nobody had time to deal with the decision until 1876.

---

[31]  Arén 1978, 216

## 2. Rosa Månsson: Her talented and strong women

### Background and journey to East Africa

In 1875 Rosa von Hagen (1841–1885) arrived in Massawa. Born in Germany, she was the daughter of an officer but early fatherless. However, she was given a careful education in Switzerland. Through the unfairness of her guardian she was deprived of a sizable legacy left to her by a rich grandfather. She went to England to become proficient in English while teaching French in a boarding school for girls.

During a visit to a friend in Sweden she was urged to stay and tutor a number of high-born girls at different manor houses. A profound spiritual experience turned her thoughts to foreign missions. She prepared for her career by taking a course at the Stockholm Institute for Deaconesses.

Rosa sailed to East Africa in 1875 with Bengt and Emelie Lundahl and two deaconesses: <u>Beata Andersson</u>, later Karlson and <u>Bengta Nilsson</u>, later Lager. Bengta, a trained nurse, opened a clinic at Bet Mekha in August 1875, one of the very first medical institutions in this part of East Africa. In 1875 Bengta sent the first diagnostic report on 325 patients who suffered from 52 different ailments, mainly sicknesses of the eye. In November 1875 Bengta married Per-Eric Lager who was killed in July 1876 during a conflict of two groups of the same clan. Following her husband's death she returned to Sweden, gave birth to a daughter, who died the same year. In 1880 Bengta migrated to America and settled in Chicago, where she qualified as a medical doctor in 1885, the first Swedish woman who did so. She died in Chicago in 1913.

### The Månsson Girls' School

Rosa married Rev. Ola Månsson, who had already spent a year on the mission field. The newly-weds were commissioned to open a school for girls and young women. In January 1876, the first girl was accepted in what was to become 'The Månsson Girls' School'.

In a letter to the board[32] Rosa Månsson mentioned two girls:

---

32   EFS Archives: Three letters from Rosa Månsson, 1876.01.25

*Swedish messengers of the Gospel: The Lundahls, Rosa von Hagen, Bengta Lager and Beata Anderson, who arrived in Massawa in 1875, courtesy of EFS Archive.*

*Mehret had been taught by Gustava at her father's request. She had got permission to visit him in Abyssinia and she had not returned when the school started. I trusted that the father would keep his promise and let her come back to the school and Mehret did return.*

*Ayani was a 14-year-old girl that had been a slave of a high-ranking man in Adua. He ordered her to follow one of his relatives, a woman with a baby, on her journey to Jerusalem. In Massawa, the woman got a free place on an Egyptian steamer and Ayani was sent to us.*

Within a few months, Rosa had also taken care of several Abyssinian girls who had come as refugees from the famine in Hamasen. Owing to the difficult times there the school was soon filled with girls of Orthodox background. Twenty were enrolled in 1877, thirty-one a year later, and thirty-five in 1879, when there were almost ninety girls in the school. It was impossible to take more, because the building was cramped and in poor condition.

The Egyptian authorities did not permit the mission to acquire a site for building at Massawa, and houses to be hired for rent were unsuitable for a boarding school. After several efforts to get a new site for a bigger school, Gordon, the British General who took over the post as Governor, bought land. On New Year's Day 1878 he gave the title deed to the SEM.

Rosa became the one who in practice was responsible for running the girls' school. The curriculum combined elementary education with training in domestic skills such as needlework and traditional crafts like spinning and basket work. The aim was to make the girls '*good Christian housewives, the only meaningful vocation an agrarian society could then offer a young woman*'. The school gave new life to all girls who were educated there.

Mehret, who had come to Gustava when she was 10 years old, made a list of everything she had learnt at the school.[33] Soon after this letter she got married to Onesimos.

---

[33]   Meheret wrote in Swedish, see EFS Archives

## Mamma Rosa's girls

Rosa suffered a lot under the hot climate and was in service up to her sudden death in 1885.

Emelie Lundahl, her fellow missionary, gave credit to Rosa for her skill in training girls to become talented, strong women. Rosa set an outstanding example of service and self-denial, challenging the students to do the same. Through her teaching and her personality she exerted a lasting influence. Many of her girls developed into attractive and capable women, who became known for their alert and open minds and good manners, which made them conspicuous among their sisters. *'Mamma Rosa's girls'* turned out to be an expression connoting no little esteem in Evangelical circles, as Emelie was able to observe many years later. The gospel changed the social condition of these women and moulded them in Christian character.

# 3.  Emelie Lundahl: Her memories of 1875–1895

Emelie Cassel (1842–1929) wrote her autobiography[34]. Brought up by her widowed mother in rural Sweden with four siblings, Emelie had to earn money by sewing and embroidering while at school. She became a teacher and taught at the Institute for Lady Teachers until she married Bengt Peter Lundahl as his second wife.

## First Impressions

The couple went to Massawa and in the company of three female missionaries, who were to join their future missionary husbands. On the long way Emelie started learning Amharic. Upon their arrival Emelie wrote:

My husband and I were taken over in a boat and met the brother missionaries and school children. There was joy that cannot be described. My husband has during the last days almost become ill from longing and now he was in their midst. They greeted me in Swedish and I greeted them in Amharic.

---

[34]  From ancient days and past years, Memories by Emelie Lundahl, 1922 translated to English by Lars Hofgren in 2018

Our living room was upstairs; it was also a classroom and a church on Sundays. In the evenings after prayer, the boys liked to stay with us for a while. They had so many questions to ask. It became especially lively when the globe was put on the table. They cannot get enough information about different countries, but it often ends with the conclusion that their Africa is anyhow the best.

The European way of being in a hurry, you had to learn to get away from. If you wanted to live according to it, you would not get anywhere. *"Why are you in such a hurry?"* they asked and *"What is the purpose of that?"*

Massawa was a small and insignificant place, but its bazaar had a lot to offer. The merchants' caravans came from the inner parts of East Africa with ivory, gold, coffee, musk, hides, butter, spices etc. and bought fabric, pearls, salt etc, bartering instead of using money. Many languages were being spoken. These merchants were invited to our prayer meetings, and several of them were glad to come. They came also in their free time and talked about spiritual matters and sought clarification about matters that seemed unclear to them.

### Merchants bring the gospel to Jimma

At that time we had in our home a merchant from Jimma, named Negusie. It was not the first time he had come to the mission. Five years ago he and his brother had come to ask for a Bible, and they had been given a New Testament each. "I read and read", he said, "and I did not become filled up or tired, but how can I become such as the word of God says? Maybe if I became a monk, but even the monks don't live in accordance with the word of God". With these questions on his mind he came now for the second time and asked to stay as a student in the school. My husband refused to admit him for a long time.

He was about 40 years old, and difficult to fit in among the school boys, but finally my husband gave in to his persistent begging, with the condition, that he would be willing to give himself to the Lord, and, if a way was opened, go where we would send him. He promised this, and through his quiet way of living, his unusual talent and his zeal to gather his countrymen to hear God's word, he became a real help to the mission.

The time came that he should go to Jimma. Emanuel joined him. Emanuel was once a Moslem and had even been to Mecca. When he was sick no one helped him except Lager who took care of him. Before Emanuel left he married Elisabet, one of the first students at the girls' school. And from our boys' school, John went with them. John was a poor eunuch, and this influenced his mind and hindered his development. His homeland, Kaffa, was close to Jimma. He could be a good help with the teaching.

They were dedicated by prayer and the laying on of hands after they had confessed their faith and promised to remain close to the word of God and his teachings and Luther's catechesis.

They travelled as merchants among merchants, but their donkeys were mostly loaded with books and school material and bartering goods.

Then they were on their way, but in this country, which at least at that time was so full of fighting, the road did not go straight to the goal. Sometimes they had to go forward and then backward, from one province to another, but they did not lose hope and taught the people along the way, especially the children.

In one place they spent such a long time that the children learned to read and write. That was at Gojjam; from there we had the joy to receive small letters from six of them. They called us mother and father and thanked us for sending teachers to them. From another place we got letters from no less than 15 pupils.

On 8<sup>th</sup> November 1877 they had left Massawa, and not until January 1885 did we receive a letter from them that they had reached Jimma.

## At the boys' school

In 1878 my husband got very ill. It was decided that he should go home and that I should stay with the children and the native teacher Kes Terfu and the eldest of our boys as my assistants. The children were unusually kind and obedient.

Only once somebody tried to break the respect. A woman is not very respected in this country, and in the beginning, when I came there, they asked when some of the boys were called, "Is it him that is calling or is it her?" If it was *him*, you had to obey, if it was *her*, they meant that it was not so important.

Now they were going to test if *she* could uphold the respect. One of them went to the bazaar without permission, which was totally prohibited. Both Kes Terfu and Hapte Mariam said that he needed a beating and that I should do it to show my power. Otherwise, they said, another day we could have them all in the bazaar.

The boy was taller than I, but confessed that he had been disobedient and should be punished. On my command he dropped his trousers, knelt down and accepted the flogging with a leather belt.

Meanwhile, the other boys were standing down in the yard listening to what was happening. After this I had no difficulties to get them to obey, and I felt especially grateful to my two assistants.

That boy, called Keffele, showed his affection in many ways after this. Just at that time I had a bad toothache. The more I worked during the day, the more painful it was at night. Then he used to come up in the mornings and ask, "Isn't it better?" Affection, won in this way, can do a lot of good!

## A new station in Imkullu

Imkullu is located one hour away from Massawa between two big villages at the border with the desert. The heat is the same as at Massawa, but the air is much nicer. We could dig wells so we did not have to buy water, and we could have a bigger area for schools and for the persecuted.

My husband had the plans ready for the building work at Imkullu. The Swedish architect who made the drawings while Lundahl was in Sweden was also a music composer. He used to put his sketches on the piano and play to get ideas. My husband heard him play over our plans and he thought that it would be something wonderful. And in a country where there are no care homes, this became a wonderful house, where the sick got care, the persecuted a home, the hungry bread and the defenseless protection. In March 1879 the house was ready for us to move in.

*Imkullu mission station established in 1879, courtesy of EFS Archive*

## Life at the school

The first lesson in all classes is about Christianity. We can feel how inadequate we are in the language, but the children are very patient and meet us half way. The best times were when God's Spirit warmed the heart; then it was much easier to speak the difficult language, and then we understood each other totally.

The second lesson is Swedish, Mathematics, Writing or Reading. We only have one table and four desks for the writing practice, otherwise the teacher sits on a chair and the pupils sit on the floor in a half circle around him/her. The livelier the teaching is, the closer the circle becomes.

After the lessons, each one goes to his/her chores and at 12 we have lunch. Rice is the main food for all of us; the children eat it with red pepper sauce, we with ordinary Swedish meat sauce. The children get meat twice a week. We are strict about the midday rest; it must be a calm moment. That is also the hottest time of the day; the thermometer shows from 42 degrees up to 45 degrees Celsius in the shade during the hot season. When the children go out, they jump as lightly as they can on their bare feet over the burning hot sand.

## Our greatest treasure

It is a common practice in our congregation that the Bible is read a lot and they know it. The word of God is our authority, and everybody bows to it. I have seen unforgiving hard faces become mild and smiling when hearing the words '*God wants us to forgive*'. When travelling, the Bible is kept close; it has its special leather pouch on the belt.

I remember how one day a man came and asked for a Bible. We had then recently moved to Imkullu and the Bible depot was still at Massawa. I was a bit afraid when I looked at my New Testament which I had received on my way out in London, and which was lying by the window. My husband's eyes followed mine. "*Yes*" he said, "*you can have another one later on.*" The man who received my New Testament was Kes Gebre Ewostateos, who later became a missionary to the Oromo. Even if it felt like I became separated from a good friend when I gave away my book, later I regarded it as an honour that he, through this book, had got life and light and later went out to spread it among others.'

## A painful year (1885)

Death often visited us. The year started with the death of our little eight-month-old Hanna after she had been sick for weeks. The next to pass were Gebre Kristos and Gebre Amlak. Gebre Kristos had been untouched by the word of God when he was healthy, and we could not see any heart pain or heart joy during his illness. It was a heavy burden when he was buried.

The whole summer, Rosa Månsson, who suffered much from the heat, had been very weak. She was also affected by the dangerous disease, and the end came so quickly that we could not understand that she had left us. The last morning she rang out her girls as usual. They always used to be dressed and were just waiting for the bell to open the door and spread out like pigeons to their morning chores. The next morning she died after a painful night with great difficulties to draw breath. We could not understand how it was possible that she would be lowered into the grave with all her rich gifts and her great sense of duty. Many people cannot bear to hear about the mission. She lived her life for it, in a climate that daily made her health worse, and still in her young age she was bedded down in the earth of Africa, in a desolate place, where she had done what she could to spread the knowledge of God on earth.

Along with the typhoid fever, smallpox came. There was hardly a single house where you would not hear mourning and crying. My husband got sick on Dec. 1st, four months after Rosa's death. When I came home, he said: *"Don't you think that I may die and go away?" "Oh no!"* I answered, *"I believe that you will live for a long time and see our little Josef, whom you have been longing so for."* He did not reply, but said after a while: *"It is good to be in the hands of God."* Just at that time, our doctor had been called up to the highlands by a chief, Ras Alola, to care for his injured soldiers.

The day before he died, Lundahl said to one of our boys: *"Behil, I am not delirious, and this is no dream, I see a wonderful house built of shining gold, filled with blessed people, and I see wonderful vegetation. But when do you think that all this will end"?* he said and pointed to his pocks. *On Saturday,* said the boy, *"then they will start to dry up and then you will be well." "No, Behil,"* he replied. *"Tomorrow I will be free."* When Behil told me about this, he asked me not to cry. *"He is in the blessed home with our God, may we all follow him there."*

On December 11th he was 'set free'. It was at 7 p.m. and the message that Father Lundahl had died, soon spread, and everybody who heard it came and participated in the mourning. Otherwise I did not like that crying, it sounded that it just came out of habit, but this evening it felt like it lightened my heart's sorrow. The children were very kind and helpful in every way.

When the coffin was carried in and put in front of the altar we sang one of my husband's favorite hymns: The great doctor is here, the loving Jesus. He comforts sad hearts, so hurry on to Jesus. At the grave we sang: O blessed home with our God, all in Amharic.

And again we had to leave the graveyard more lonely then before. Feeling like this I did not know where to go, and I felt like I did not have a home any more. Then one of our native sisters came, she was a recent widow of our teacher Hapte Georgis, and she took my arm so very kindly under her arm, and took me to her hut, where she had prepared a coffee table, which was waiting for me.

On the last day of the year we had to follow our boy Burro to his last resting place, and then we gathered in the church for the wedding of one of our girls with the guard of the girls' school. Brother Rodén then said, comfortingly: *Anyhow we got to end of the year with a joyful occasion!*

Close by Lundahl's grave our three small girls are buried. While he still was living, he had planned to put up four pillars and a roof over their graves, so that a tired wanderer could get a shady place to rest for a while. Now we did it over his grave and built a bench at each long side.

This place was a refuge, where you felt you were in another world. The sombreness of the place itself and the calmness of the desert-like area around contributed to the feeling. I liked to take a book with me, like "Light in your way" or Thomas à Kempis. That was and that is like a drink of fresh water for a desert wanderer to hear deep, true, warning and comforting words and thoughts about death and judgement, about eternity and heaven. They also fitted so well with such an environment. I returned strengthened and refreshed from such a restful moment at the Imkullu graveyard.

### At the girl's school (1886–1894)

Lundahl had been working on a commentary on the Gospel of St John. Emelie completed the manuscript, revised it with Taye and Onesimos and saw it through the press.

She wrote: The mission board decided the girls' school had become my task. The number of girls had risen to 41. They were aged from 10 to 30 years; some had been taken from husband and children, others from parents and other relatives.

Some came from very fertile areas. Yes, most of them did not know that there was such a desert area as where they now had arrived. When they read about God creating the world, they objected, *"But not this area and the people who brought us here"*. They had different languages, different characters and appearances.

After having been taken from their country, they had been led through desolate areas only during the night. In the day time they stayed hidden in bushes. If during the night they saw any camp fire, they moved away to other hills. When they got close to Massawa, the slave caravan was divided; small groups would move more easily get past the feared white people and reach the coast and be taken over to Arabia, where the slave hunters got the best profit. During such trips they could be sold many times.

The Italian government fought the slave trade. Their steamers followed the coast to look for traders, and when they were discovered they were severely punished. For example a ship was lying to the north of Massawa and it was said that it was loaded with salt, but when it was searched, it was discovered that at the bottom there were female slaves; these were freed and sent to us.

According to the customs of the country, the only future of a girl was to get married. If she did not get married, she would become a slave. Therefore the girls longed to get married and some of our girls ran away from us. A thirteen year old girl could sit and cry over the fact that she was not yet married. So you had to get them to turn their minds onto something else and get them interested in working.

We had a request from some Italian generals and soldiers to take care of their laundry. Mrs. Else Winqvist joined the workers. We washed, mangled and ironed all the time and mended what was torn. We started early in the morning, to do most of the things before the sun was too hot. There was no complaining and the work was being done better and better. We had managed to get some joy into the work among our girls. And our work contributed some extra income, so we were happy to give 420 kroner to the hospital building work.

The school was divided into a study area and a work area. We had the two native teachers Kes Sera Zion and Onesimos. When the latter started to use all his time for Bible translation, we appointed one of the older girls to be teacher in reading and writing for the beginners. After a while we could leave to the more responsible ones the supervision of the daily work, like taking care of the baking of bread, the laundry, the mending of clothing, the kitchen and the table. All the missionaries at the station had a joint household. One of our girls was the helper of Dr. Winqvist in the health care, and one was Sister Hulda Lindstom's help in the boys' school. My sister <u>Mimmi</u> had died already in March 1887, and Sister Hulda came after her.

Soon afterwards six of the Galla girls came and asked to be baptized. Among them was a girl with the name <u>Ganno</u>, who got the name Aster at the baptism; she later went with Onesimos and his wife to Oromoland as a Bible woman. She is still working there.

One Christmas already before she was baptized, Onesimos put a full Bible in my room with the note "*present for Ganno*". He said that she had made him happy so many times with her replies; now he wanted to make her happy.

She went around so silently with her secret that she wanted to give her life to God. But her friends teased her and said: "*Aster will never get married.*"

The last Christmas at Massawa in 1889, even the Sudanese girls came and said that they wanted to become new persons and get new names.


### Our Patroness

I have several times told about the freed slave children, who we received at our schools, and we were very happy about this; but at the same time we had difficulties to cater for them all. In a wonderful way, just at that time, we got to know a person who was warmly interested in fighting the slave trade. That was <u>the Countess de Noailles</u>, who at the time was living at Eastbourne in England. After she heard about our work in Imkullu she sent us 300 pounds sterling.

When I was at home during the summer of 1886, after my husband's death, she invited me to come and see her on my way out. I arrived at Eastbourne, where the Countess de Noailles had her villa close to the sea. I went up the pathway to the house with a pounding heart. Everything around pointed to the fact that I was in the middle of the distinguished world, among richness and luxury.

But there I would find a heart which sighed under the futility of everything and tried to satisfy her soul's hunger by helping in other people's needs. The Countess de Noailles had this whole time followed our work with great interest. When we built our huts and later the living quarters, she sent us generous contributions, and when she heard about the famine, she wrote and asked how she could help. When I read this to the girls, they shouted; *"Ask her to give us milk!"* You could not get this after the rinderpest. It did not take long for us to get money to buy cows.

In the summer of 1894 I had to go to Alexandria after a difficult chest illness. The Countess de Noailles had moved down to southern France and asked me to come to her as soon as possible and stay that winter with her. At the same time she sent me money for the journey.

With her I got the rest I so much needed. She had a big villa, almost a castle, Montclair, where she stayed during the winters, and a smaller one, St Vincent, which was situated close to the Mediterranean Sea, cool and nice, where she stayed during the summers. When in the morning you opened the big French windows, from your little balcony, you had the most wonderful picture, which I cannot describe, it was so wonderfully beautiful.

She had met sorrows early in her life. She became motherless early, and was given to relatives. She was very rich, but she did not get enough food, and malnourished from her childhood, she became weak and vulnerable all her life. When after a short marriage she became a widow, she started to live as she herself liked, separate from the world and the life there. She longed for love, in vain, and in her loneliness she used to bang her head against her iron bed, to get the outer pain to lessen the inner.

I really wanted to remain with her, as she wished, but I felt that if I were to stay in Europe, it was for the sake of Josef. Otherwise my home and my work would be in Africa.

## Back in Sweden

After arriving home in spring 1895, I got work at the SEM office as the secretary's assistant.

I have had the joy of being part of the mission friends and their sewing circles. Yes, that is happiness! I am so happy walking to these meetings, when you walk home, your feet are light. You cannot compare the best dinner party or something like that, with a small coffee gathering which the sewing circles invite you to! It refreshes your mind to hear something *from out there!*

At Malmo I went to a children's club, which is called the Circle, and I was surprised to find only grown people. "I thought it was a children's club", I said. "Yes," they answered, "we were children when we started". They had continued, and now some were pharmacists, others nurses, some teachers etc. And they are still working for and praying for the mission.

People work like in a bee hive, and for every item that is brought, we are as happy as children. When the selling of things begins, it does not look much, and the buyers are often few, but when evening comes and each one brings his or her cash box, the result is bigger than we dared to hope for, and our joy is great.

Yes, more than we dared to hope for, because it is not our work, it is God's like a little girl once said, "It is not because *we* are so kind, it is because *God* is so kind."

# Evangelical women pioneers bring the gospel

This part introduces the stories of three women who shared the same fate.[35] Born free in different areas located to the south-west of Abyssinia, they were kidnapped and enslaved while still children. In 1886 their ways crossed and they were liberated. From then onwards their lives continued in parallel. They became Christians and chose new names at baptism[36]. They spent eighteen years in different places along the Red Sea coast, named Eritrea by the Italian colonizers (1890–1941). In 1904 they joined a dangerous expedition to their homeland and reached Nedjo and Naqamte where they lived and taught for several decades.

In those days hundreds of thousands of young girls were captured and sold to foreign countries, but it is not known if any were freed and returned home apart from these three women. Their biographies are histories of violence, liberation and becoming messengers of God in the early 20th century. These factors and their contributions as educators and missionaries made them unique in the history of slavery and Evangelical mission.

## 1. Aster Ganno: Writer, translator and missionary

### Her journey from girl to slave to free woman

Ganno Salban (1874–1964) was born and brought up at Limmu, a rural district near Jimma. People at her time lived from livestock and crop production. Her area was known for its milk and honey. Ganno spoke Afaan Oromo. With no other languages around she obtained an excellent command of her mother tongue.

The king of Limmu once ordered his people to build him a residence. Many people refused to do so. All who did not obey were sold into slavery. Ganno was one of them, captured and sold at the age of ten. Being a slave

---

[35] Hirphoo, Tasgaraa (Rev Dr h.c.): Short biographies of Oromoo Women Evangelical Pioneers, 2013, translated by Margarsaa Guutaa (Rev Dr), masterprint addis, 2014

[36] In those days anyone who had a Christian (or Muslim) name was not considered a slave for sale.

means losing one's family and home, one's language and identity and it often means losing one's confidence.

Ganno was taken to Abyssinia and served a master for two years. Then she was sold to slave traders who took her to Massawa, from where she would cross the Red Sea to be taken to the Arab world.

At that time the coast was controlled by Italians who fought slavery. Ganno and twenty-one girls were freed by Italian soldiers who handed them over to the Swedish Evangelical Mission (SEM). The Swedes admitted them to their girls' boarding school. One of their teachers was Onesimos Nasib. He taught them in their mother tongue. Her mind and spirit were quite healthy despite what she had gone through.

Interested girls could attend confirmation classes and Ganno took that opportunity. She wanted to become a Christian. On the day of her baptism she chose a new name: Aster. The name is the Ethiopian version of Esther. The biblical Esther was greatly concerned for her people, the Jews, while she was in exile in Babylon. Likewise, Aster Ganno had great zeal for the liberation of her people, the Oromo.

### Aster's literature work

Aster completed five years of schooling. The missionary Nils Hylander wrote:

*The Oromo girl Aster is making an excellent contribution. Her work is of the greatest importance to our mission. She has a profound knowledge of her language and is extraordinarily qualified for this work. She labours all day long with her pen and traces all the words which are derived from one and the same root. Both she and Onesimos are from the interior of Oromo land and are preparing a wordbook in pure Oromo avoiding all dialect forms.* [37]

*She is filling the gaps. She finds the words as she knows the language better than anyone else. She has been assigned a new task of composing a dictionary of Galla. Although she is young she is unusually steady and has a genuine character. Her face bears evidence of intelligence and energy. She looks so earnest and skilful that even in the beginning I had due respect for her, being ashamed of my own poor language.*

---

[37]   Nils Hylander, Geleb 25.9.1891 to SEM Board

*Aster Ganno Salban in Eritrea, courtesy of EFS Archive*

By the time she was seventeen years old the SEM employed her and paid her a salary. At the age of twenty her first book was published: *The Primary Reader – the book that helps in learning the Oromo language.* Her prime reader, printed and published in Imkullu greatly facilitated literacy. The items of Oromo folklore in her book appealed to popular sentiment and stimulated reading.

Aster translated Dr Barth's Bible stories.[38] The title page says: by Aster Ganno with assistance from Onesimos. As she assisted him with translation work, so he did for her[39].

Aster and Onesimos translated John Bunyan's small treatise, *Man's Heart,* and gave it another title in their language: *Man's heart: Either God's temple or Satan's abode.*

Aster wrote down a great number of indigenous riddles, fables, proverbs, cradle songs and other songs. She copied, corrected and systemized some five-hundred vernacular songs, riddles and proverbs. Hylander copied all of them for his own use, as he regarded it as a very precious treasure from the linguistic and etymological point of view.

The Oromo translation team consisted of fifteen to twenty members and Aster was linguistically the most gifted team member. She had a big share in the revision of the New Testament. For the translation of the Old Testament there was no literature to refer to regarding sayings, words and idiomatic expressions. Therefore Aster prepared a collection of these items. The whole Bible was finally printed in Chrischona, Switzerland in 1899.

---

[38] Dr Barth's Bible Stories contain 52 illustrated stories from each the Old and the New Testament. The book is known in Amharic as *Hamsa Hulet Tarik.* Many knew the narratives by heart and they became an essential part of their faith, moulded them in Christian character and gave them an idea of what discipleship implies. Aster's translation was first printed in St. Chrischona in 1899 together with the whole Bible in Oromoo. Her translation influenced Emmanuel Abraham, who later served as president of the EECMY.

[39] The British and Foreign Bible Society published Aster's translation of the two times fifty-two Bible stories but attributed the translation to Onesimos Nasib, Swedish Missionary. The British might not have thought that African women could do such great work. Perhaps this is the reason behind ascribing the authorship to Onesimos.

The literature in general and the translation of the Bible in particular were crucial in spreading the gospel among the Oromo. The books travelled with merchants and were highly appreciated by the people.

Onesimos wrote in 1902: *Nowadays no Oromo wants to be an Oromo, i.e. pagan. They want to be either Christians or Muslims. Aster and I do what we can to make them literate.*

## Missionary to her people

Aster worked for over ten years as translator, writer and educator. By 1903 the political climate had changed and a new plan came up to send yet another expedition to the Oromo people. There had been several unsuccessful trials before. Onesimos made the necessary preparations for the departure of ten people including his three children. Aster was a member of the team. The Evangelical Church at Asmara, who supported the enterprise financially, commissioned each of them as a missionary and prayed for God's protection on the way.

The route they had chosen was from Massawa to Djibouti by ship, afterwards by land via Hararghe to Addis Ababa and from there to proceed to Leeqaa in western Wollega. With a permit from Emperor Menilek II in Addis Ababa and a provisional pass they were able to continue to Naqamte through the territory he had conquered. Menilek had also told them his wish that schools be built in his country. In addition they had a letter from the Archbishop, saying they should teach and not be hindered as long as their teaching did not deviate from that of the Orthodox Church.

Prior to their arrival, news of their coming had already spread throughout the town and the government of Wollega accorded them a warm welcome. They found out that the Dajjazmach[40] Gebre-Igziabeher was about to transfer his residence to Nedjo. The Dajjazmach invited Onesimos and his group to come with him and provided them with land for housing and a school in Nedjo. The first school at Nedjo opened in September 1904. People were hungry for education. Onesimos reported to the SEM: *If there were enough space and teachers, hundreds could have been enrolled.*

---

[40]   High military title, governor

Aster started teaching. Sixty-eight students were enrolled and fifty learnt to read and write. The school met opposition from the priests of Nedjo Kidane Mehret Church. Those priests had come from Gojjam and neither knew the language of the people nor were they willing to learn it, thus they were dissociated from the life of the people they were supposed to teach. On the other side the Onesimos' school used the local language and became popular among the people.

Soon later in November 1905 Dajjazmach Gebre-Igziabeher left Nedjo again for Naqamte and Onesimos went with him. The school they had started functioned for another six months.[41]

Moti Kumsa, the king of Naqamte looked upon them favourably, but the Orthodox priests opposed them, so that Onesimos was not allowed to work in public. The king sent five of his servants to be educated at the home of Onesimos. Aster visited and taught women at their homes.

In 1906 a local church council excommunicated Onesimos accusing him to be a Roman Catholic heretic. The Emperor permitted Onesimos to stay in Naqamte and allowed him to support himself by farming and trade. With the silent consent of the king Onesimos and Aster gave instruction in the Bible to successive groups of youth who were kept as domestic servants and workers on the small holdings of Onesimos.

Onesimos, Aster and Gebre-Sillase kept in close contact with the other evangelists supported by SEM. In the autumn of 1907 they held a conference in Naqamte to discuss a common policy. One by one the evangelists reported on the work at the seven places they came from. They realized that their evangelistic ministry had to be independent and free from every mission from abroad if it was to prosper and avoid the charge of unorthodox beliefs. They were determined to go ahead with their ministry and gave each other fresh courage in God's name.

---

[41] Twenty-five years after their departure the school at Nedjo was re-opened under the leadership of Gammachu Onesimos, who continued his father's work.

## From letters and annual reports[42]

Since Onesimos and Aster were Swedish missionaries Onesimos reported regularly to the SEM in Stockholm.

**1908:** *We work in several places, including Jimma. Aster and I work at Naqamte. We read our Bibles in our homes to anybody who comes to visit. I am allowed to sell and give away both the Bible and spiritual books.*

**1909:** *All the students who have been to our schools dislike marrying ignorant (= uneducated) women.*

**1910:** *We cannot gather for public worship services. We must be careful because of the priests. We can however talk to individuals. Although very few are literate, we have sold more Bibles than in any previous year. Students in Orthodox Church Schools come to us and buy books in Amharic and Oromo. They are not satisfied with only studying Geez. Morning and evening devotions in my home are conducted in the vernacular.*

**1915:** *Men and women, children and slaves are eager to learn the word of God. Our diligent Aster visits her women almost daily. They hunger and thirst for the word of the gospel. Every home to which she comes with the message of joy receives her with greatest gratitude. She has drawn a number of girls and women to our savior with the net of the gospel both in Leeqaa and Wollega. Aster has taught the governor's wife so that she is able to read and write. A great number of men are anxious that their wives shall learn to read.*

*Light and darkness are engaged in a bitter struggle all over the land. As soon as the servants of darkness find that either Aster or I have been in a home for a time in order to give them the word of life, the enemies turn up in disguise and frighten the poor sheep. They say that they will be bound by the high priest if they accept our teaching. They have not dared to attack us because our future king appears to be indifferent to religious matters. Ignorant people who cannot but be afraid of their father confessors often act contrary to their own conviction. Yet it seems as if the time of liberty is not far away.*

---

[42]   Unpublished, translated from Swedish to English by Gustav Arén for Tasgaraa Hirphoo

Because of the war in Europe, giving to the mission decreased and Aster and Onesimos did not receive any allowance for 1914 and 1915.

Rev Karl Cederqvist, the first Swedish missionary in Addis Ababa, kept in close contact with Onesimos and wrote about new perspectives for their work:

**1916:** *It is worth much that we have been able to obtain permission to work so that our people in the provinces may labour in peace. Both Onesimos and I (Cederqvist) consider it such a big step forward that we have resolved to start a couple of schools for girls also. In countries where people live in ignorance, dirt, superstition and fanaticism it is just as important to educate women as men if there are to be good and pleasant Christian homes. There are prospects that here in Addis Ababa we may have as a teacher a woman who belongs to a half European family, and in Naqamte Lidia and Aster will have to make a start.*

**1919:** Aster had been forced to abstain from teaching women in their homes to prevent her from being seized on charges of heresy. There were people who sneaked around their compound both late and early to spy on them and their visitors.

Cederqvist wrote: *As far as Aster is concerned, no accuser has ever been able to get away with her and if she is accused she will have to come here (to Addis Ababa) and be acquitted, and if she is jailed there, a telegram from the Ras will set her free. A congregation at Naqamte has not yet been formed.*

Onesimos told how the persecution in Naqamte cooled down:

**1922:** *There was a wealthy Gurage in Naqamte. He was in prison and requested to learn. So I taught him to read and write. Later at a church festival he heard the priests referring to me as a weed. He said: "It is unfair to call an evangelist a weed. Preach in your manner but let that man work in peace among his people. We know for sure that he is a man of God who is zealous for his people." With these words he tempered the clergy's fearful hatred against me and the evangelists. From that moment on Aster and I have been able to work in peace – late and early – for the sake of the gospel, though we are forced to be as shrewd as snakes and as innocent as doves.*

## Arrival of Swedish missionaries

In 1923 Dr Erik Söderström and his co-workers were the first Swedish missionaries to reach Wollega. Their arrival was a source of great joy and the opening of a new chapter for the work. The hard work of Onesimos, Aster and others over twenty years continued to gain momentum through those co-workers. Dr Söderström was given a house by Dajjazmach Gebre-Igziabeher and he was one of his first patients too. Fitawuraarii Dibaabaa donated a piece of land outside the village for gospel ministry and for building a hospital. One year later more missionaries and families came to Naqamte. The church building for Evangelical Christians in Naqamte was completed. On the day of inauguration hundred-fifty people attended the service. Soon a school building for grades 1–3 was completed and inaugurated. Thirty students both males and females were admitted and fifteen of them were boarders. Their subjects were Christian education, Oromo and Amharic language. The teachers were Onesimos, Feben Hirphe, who came from Bodji, Aster Ganno and Lidia Dimboo.

Dajjazmach Gebre-Igziabeher died and in his will he stated that the people should follow in his footsteps by honoring and protecting the missionaries.

In 1931 Onesimos passed away aged seventy-five. His widow, Lidia and Aster continued their ministry in Naqamte. Aster Ganno taught many women to read and write.[43]

Aster remained single. In Emelie's memories there is a hint that Aster decided to stay single because she wanted to give her life to God. As it was unsafe for an unmarried woman to live alone, she joined Lidia and Onesimos and lived with them on their compound.

Aster Ganno died aged 90 in Naqamte. The inscription on her tomb reads: Aster Ganno, Envoy of the Gospel. Praise the LORD, o my soul Psalm 146, 1.

---

[43] One of them was Desise Abaku, who spread the gospel at the time when all Swedish missionaries had left Naqamte. Desise taught her husband to read and write and founded one of the first congregations near Naqamte.

The Aster Ganno Literature Society was instituted at Aira in 1998 in memory of her life and work. She was an outstanding woman, but not yet recognized for her translations and other work.[44]

## 2. Lidia Dimboo: Envoy of the gospel and wife of Onesimos

The life of Lidia is presented as an autobiographic narrative.

I, Lidia Dimboo Garbaa (1872–1941) was born many generations ago. Life was different then from what it is today. My parents were farmers. They gave me the name *Dimboo*, because I was as pretty as a little bird called *Dimbiiti*. I grew up in the western highland. My country is called Sayyoo which is also the name of my clan.

One day, I was ten years old, my parents sent me to my aunt. On the way to her house I had to cross a little river. Suddenly men jumped out of the bushes and caught me. I cried, but no-one came to my help. The kidnappers forced me to go with them and sold me to local merchants. I was not the only one; there were other abducted children like me and we were taken away from our country by travelling caravans.

Can you imagine what it means to be sold? I was sold several times. And I worked hard for my master's family. Everyone was my boss, even the children of the master, who were younger than me. That was my sad life for the next four years. The last master sold me for a high price. When slave girls were sent to far away countries their owners got a lot of money for them. My master did good business while my life was in danger again.

Many female slaves were sent to Arabia. We had to walk for weeks in the heat lacking food and water. Some died on the way. Then the slave traders became angry because they had lost their money. The dead bodies were left behind; no one cared. But we, the survivors, were scared. Which of us would be the next?

Some slave girls spoke my language. Though we were strangers to each other, we had gone through similar experiences. Whenever I hear my lan-

---

[44] No paper has been written about Aster Ganno's life and contribution to the church. Her original writings are in Sweden and wait to be transcribed and made available to the public.

guage I am happy and I am reminded of my family and the days of my childhood. Everything was taken away from me, but my language and my memories no one can take away.

We reached Massawa. The place was crowded with people. Some carried big iron weapons that could kill more people than a spear. We were even more scared of the white people, because the slave traders told us they eat human beings. No one had ever seen such people before. How could we trust them? Some of us expected the worst to happen.

The soldiers chased the slave traders away. They did not eat us; they did not take us as slaves either nor did they sell us. They liberated us; we did not have to go to Arabia. But we had nowhere to go, not even a family whom we could serve and who would give us shelter. We were homeless. What is freedom if there is no place to go to?

## My liberation

The soldiers took us to a place where white people were living. They talked to each other in a language I had never heard before. At the end of their discussion we were told to stay there.

These white people were from Sweden. A number of people like us were already living with them on their big compound. One of them was Onesimos. He translated for the Oromo speaking girls. Had it not been for him, we might have run away because of our fear of the men eaters.

The Kunama girls from our group disappeared on the first evening. The next morning they were found at two hours distance from where we were, suffering from hunger, thirst and heat. They had been scared after the questioning the day before and were afraid of being sold again. That is why they had escaped. These girls had no one to translate for them or to communicate with them.

Later I saw the list of names and details about each girl in our group.

**A list of the recently arrived girls[45]**

| Nr | Name | Place of birth | Language |
|----|------|----------------|----------|
| 1. | Bakita Muhamed, 30 | Arab | - |
| 2. | Trango Shono, 30 | Illu/Galla | Oromo |
| 3. | Bakita Araddo, 28 | Boneia/Galla | Oromo |
| 4. | Bashene Jijo, 25 | Leqa | Oromo |
| 5. | Midina Hagena, 25 | Kunama | Kunama |
| 6. | Midina Hagen, 1 | Kunama | Kunama |
| 7. | Laitu Medina (mother), 23 | Kunama | Kunama |
| 8. | Medina Halima, 3 | Kunama | Kunama |
| 9. | Hirphe Abbamagal, 22 | Jimma/Galla | Oromo |
| 10. | Trungo Walu, 20 | Limma/Galla | Oromo |
| 11. | Macka Ali, 20 | Kunama | Kunama |
| 12. | Asha Ahmed, 19 | Dafus/Sudan | Arabic |
| 13. | Backale Shuka, 18 | Muchichu/Galla | Oromo |
| 14. | Bakita Ali, 18 | Galabat | Oromo |
| 15. | Ayantu Backina, 17 | Gobbo/Galla | Oromo |
| 16. | Bakita, 16 | Gallabat | Oromo |
| 17. | Lansu Tullu, 16 | Limmu/Galla | Oromo |
| 18. | Dimbo Garba, 14 | Sayo/Galla | Oromo |
| 19. | Berille Yarotchi, 14 | Kaffa | Sidama |
| 20. | Salama Ahmed, 1 | Kardofan/Sudan | - |
| 21. | Halima Kabon, 13 | Kunama | Kunama |
| 22. | Ganno Salban, 12 | Limmu/Galla | Oromo |
| 23. | Bakila Masso, 11 | Kunama | Kunama |
| 24. | Dasta Ahmed, 10 | Arab | - |

They asked us about our background and how we had become slaves. For many these were painful memories to touch. Everyone had her own story. And that was also recorded:

Trungo was married and living in Ilu Galan when Abyssinian soldiers kidnapped and sold her. She had been a slave for three years, one year in Abyssinia. Baketa was born as a slave. After the death of her mother she was brought to Barka and from there to Massawa. Bashene was kidnapped during a war between two Oromo chiefs. She was sold several times and

---

44    SEM/E 24, 323: Imkullu, 1886.06.21.

moved from one place to another. She had been a slave for two years in Abyssinia.

There was no translator for the Kunama women and we do not know what had happened to them.

Hirphe from Jimma was taken captive together with others during the war between Menilek II and the king of Jimma. She was a slave for five years and sold several times both in Oromo land and in Abyssinia. Trungo and Asha were kidnapped while collecting firewood. Bakale was stolen as a small child during the war between two Oromo chiefs. She lived for a number of years in another Oromo province before she came to Massawa.

Bakita Ali grew up in Gallabat but she had come from elsewhere. Another Bakita from Gallabat was stolen as a small child from Sudan and then brought to Massawa.

Lansu and Ganno came from Limmu. They were taken prisoner and sold as slaves because their people refused to build a new residence for their king. Both lived in Abyssinia for two years before coming to Massawa.

Berille and others were sent by the king of Kaffa as part of his tribute to Abyssinia. She had had six masters and been a slave for two years.

Lidia continues her story:

There was a school for freed boys and one for freed girls. In the year we came, there were 36 boys and 41 girls. Gradually I lost my fear of white people. Onesimos told us that they were Christians and they wanted to stop slavery. They did not harm us. They taught us to read and write. He told us he witnessed during the third Oromo expedition (1884–1886) some 700 slaves passing near the Awash River. Almost all of them were girls between 8–16 years old. Only few were boys and they were made eunuchs, as demanded by the Arabs. He himself had passed under such severe life situation and the fact that the life of others had not improved made him very sad. He was in a depressed state when he came back to Imkullu. That was the time we arrived and he was glad to teach us in our language.

When I was 16 years old I wanted to be baptized and attended confirmation classes. As a sign of my new life I chose a new name. From then on I was called Lidia (Acts 16, 14+15). We were eight girls who were baptized: All chose their new names: Hirphe was afterwards called Feben, Ganno –

Aster, Terfe – Rebecca, Gore – Ruth, Ayantu – Haimanot, Bakale – Lea and Bottu – Elsabet. We had been homeless, but now were citizens of the kingdom of God.

Something sad had happened the same day: Halima, one of the Kunama girls, passed away after long suffering.

We had learnt to read and write, so we could refer to the biblical stories our teachers had told us, whenever we wanted to. I liked the story of Joseph, the son of Jacob. Joseph had been sold by his brothers to traders and was taken to a foreign country. He became a slave like me. After many years God rescued him. Later during a time of famine Joseph saved the lives of his brothers and their families.

Becoming a believer meant becoming literate. The Evangelical movement turned listeners into readers. The Bible helps me to understand my life, e.g. when I read about Moses. He led the people of Israel into freedom. They crossed the Red Sea. The water did not kill Moses and his people, but the waters killed the Egyptians who were after them. That is the same water that we, the slave girls, should have crossed by boat. Water is more dangerous than the dry desert. The miracle was that we did not have to cross the dangerous water. We got our freedom like the people of Israel.

Once we were free we had no one to belong to. Is that freedom? The time of slavery had taught us to mistrust everyone and to be afraid of everybody. Our souls were wounded. I can say many of us were slaves of a sad life story. We were in need of healing.

Our second freedom came with the gospel. God made us truly free. He sent missionaries from a far away country. They adopted and educated us. In the schools of the Orthodox Church, only boys and mostly the sons of the chiefs were able to learn. In our wildest dreams we would not have thought of becoming educated women. But this is what happened. From then on I wanted to serve God. My wish was to become a blessing to others.


### First jobs and the first marriage years

After my years at school I was assigned to the boarding school and I also worked for Mr. Nils Hylander and his family in their house. He wrote:

*The Galla (= Oromo) girl Lydia, who has been my servant for two years, has given me much joy. She has been a constant sunbeam on my road. She has been a great help to me in learning the language.*[46]

The missionaries learnt our language because they hoped to go one day to our country. We also spoke Swedish. Language learning is important.

Onesimos had a talent for languages: he learnt Amharic and Arabic in a short time. Then he learnt Swedish and English. He managed to learn these languages in six years. Afterwards he went all by himself to Sweden. At the Johannelund Seminary he studied theology. In addition he was trained in building, carpentry and music. When the school was closed he visited congregations. Their members were the ones contributing to the mission with prayers and donations. Onesimos stayed for five years and formed close relationships. Some of these people came as missionaries to Eritrea and some became his trustworthy co-workers.

Back in Imkullu he married Mehret, who had been brought up by Swedish missionaries. Mehret passed away in childbirth in 1888. They had three children but all of them died in infancy. In the coming years Onesimos was busy translating and teaching.

When I was 19 years old, he asked me to marry him and I did so. We moved to live in Asmara town. Onesimos served in the Evangelical Church at Asmara as city evangelist at the market place.

My husband and I had deep concern for our people. Our homeland was isolated from all sides. Many indigenous and some foreign missionaries had tried to enter, but in vain. The Abyssinian government closed the door to the Oromo and other people in every direction. If only the Bible could reach them through traders, that book would bring hope and life to our people.

Onesimos and Aster translated the Bible. It took them 17 years of hard work. The British and Foreign Bible Society took the responsibility of publishing the Bible. The SEM decided the books to be printed in Chrischona in Switzerland. It had to be printed in Sabean script, because of a decree that anything written had to be in Sabean. As the Swiss printing society was not familiar with that script, my husband, Segerberg and Olsson went and supervised the printing process.

---

[46]  SEM/E I 77.2092 Hylander to Board, Imkullu, 1893.10.03.

That time was not easy for me. One of our children got sick and finally passed away. That message reached Onesimos and he wrote to the mission in Sweden:

*"This week I have received a most discouraging letter which told of the death of our latest baby and the illness of the second one. The third one is now improving but is often asking for her dad. Lidia is afraid that this may cause a certain illness to me. Please, let me return by the ship that leaves on 12 November. Send brother Hylander urgently to assist Olsson. Otherwise I cannot leave. The journey seems to be necessary both for me and for my family. If one more letter comes with a similar blow, I cannot bear it, I believe. Of course, I cannot wake up my dead child, nor can I restore the sick one to health but in order to comfort the mourning mother in her grief. Your distressed friend, Onesimos."*[47]

When I heard about the plan of Onesimos to return and stop his printing job this is what I wrote:

*... on no account should you leave your work until you have finished it. If you do, you no doubt will regret it. When I heard that you thought of running away from your work I was greatly worried. I was afraid that your ship might be caught by a hurricane like that that struck the ship by which Jonah travelled.* [48]

During our separation we exchanged letters from time to time. It was originally planned that the transcription and printing process might take one and a half years, but it was completed after 9 months, on 10. June 1899. Two-thousand copies of the Bible and five-thousand copies of the New Testament were printed.

Finally we were reunited as family in Asmara. The following years Onesimos served as city evangelist at the market place. He won several Oromo tradesmen for Christ, trained them for evangelism within the areas from which they came. He taught Qes Gebre Ewostateos our language and Qes Gebre Ewostateos was the first to reach Oromoland.

---

[47]  SEM/EI 106.2687: Onesimos, to Kolmodin, Chrischona, 1898.10.07
[48]  Arén 1978, 385

## Returning home

We had been married for 12 years when Onesimos was entrusted to organize and lead the expedition to Oromoland. He had been twice on expeditions which both had failed. It had been our wish for a long time to go to our home country where we belonged.

I was afraid of the long and dangerous journey, which could take up to three months and we had to carry our small children 6–7 hours/day. One missionary family once had left their smallest child behind in the care of others for fear that the child might not survive the trip.

Before leaving, Onesimos wrote to Sweden on December 5th, 1903:

*The time of salvation has now come for the Oromo people. We have made a plan to go via Hararghe to Addis and from there to proceed to Leeqaa in Eastern Wollega. We will reach our destination in February 1904 provided that we don't come across any unexpected difficult situation. Friends of the gospel who would like to assist the work in Oromoland should pray that the name of the Lord shall be praised by the people who are walking in darkness.*[49]

At Addis Ababa, we got permission from King Menilek II to proceed.[50] The pass reads:

"Menilek, King of the Lion of Judah, King of Kings of Ethiopia with the Grace of God. Onesimos, the bearer of this letter, who is travelling with ten people and three guns, has been permitted to go to the country of Dajjazmach[51] Gebre-Igziabeher. Don't hinder him to do so."[52]

Eighteen days later we arrived in Naqamte. All the children survived the expedition and I was relieved from the daily worry for food and shelter, health and safety.

At Naqamte we were received with great honour, because Onesimos was known as translator of the Oromo Bible that had reached the area years

---

[49] Hirphoo, Tasgaraa: Abbaa Gammachis, (Oneesimos Nasib), 1999, translated by Margarsaa Guutaa, 2007, 67
[50] Emperor Menelik II adopted a relatively liberal religious policy compared to his predecessors' harsh policy Christians who did not belong to his own state church.
[51] High military title, Commander or General of the Gate
[52] Hirphoo, Tasgaraa, 68

before we came. The governor gave him a large tract of tax-free land in
Nedjo and Onesimos build houses and a school. After few months 60 students enrolled.

## My family

I was busy at our home, taking care of the family and the many guests that
came. My children were still small. When they were baptized in Asmara we
gave them biblical names. But after reaching our homeland we gave them
Oromo names. Barnabas our oldest was called Gammachis, so I was called
Hadhaa Gammachis (the mother of Gammachis) as is customary. Today
Onesimos is still known to many as Abba Gammachis. Dina we named
Ayyanee and Tamar was named Yadate. In Naqamte, I gave birth to Galate.
The old photo shows our family while living in Asmara.

Gammachis married and had children. Three sons and one daughter
died when an epidemic broke out in Naqamte. Ayyanee, our daughter and
her baby daughter died as well. The epidemic killed one of our students. It
took the lives of people in the countryside and in towns. Many houses were
devastated. There were so many deaths to the extent that there was no more
space in the church compound to bury the dead.

When Ayyanee passed away the priests refused to bury her body in the
Orthodox graveyard. A new rule prohibited burying members of Evangelical faith within the holy graveyard of the Ethiopian Orthodox Church. It
forbade any priest to conduct burial ceremonies for Evangelicals. Because
Ayyanee's husband was a local chief, her burial could eventually be nego-
tiated. However, the priests made sure that the law be implemented everywhere. Before Evangelical Christians had taken their children for baptism
to the Orthodox Church; the Lord's Supper and burial ceremonies were
given to them. But suddenly, the Evangelical Christians were considered as
cursed by the priests.

## Years of persecution

The years in Naqamte were not easy. After our return from Nedjo a local
church council excommunicated Onesimos as Roman Catholic. The abuna

*Lidia Dimboo and Onesimos and their three children in Asmara, courtesy of EFS Archive.*

confirmed, but the emperor annulled the verdict and permitted us to stay and support ourselves by farming and trade.

We, the Bible reading Christians, faced many challenges. The Bible had got into the hands of ordinary people. Onesimos said: *"No one can snatch the Bible from the hands of believers for whom the Bible has become so dear."* We could sell and sometimes give away Bibles and other spiritual books from our house.

Literacy makes people free and literacy makes people unafraid. Government and the official Church wanted the type of education which strengthened their own authority. Hence they did not want to see education beginning in the Oromo language or the gospel being expanding in Oromo land.

Onesimos was allowed to teach at home but forbidden to preach in public. Aster could go from home to home to visit and teach women. For many years we had five or six young people living with us and he taught them while they helped us in the field in return. And I was busy feeding them.

People filled our living room and learnt the word of God without fear. The priests remarked, *The whole town has accepted the teaching of the Evangelicals.* Another complaint was: *It is not right that the Bible should get into the hands of ordinary people; if it does it will bring a terrible disaster upon them.*

Once people read the Bible they refused to believe the teaching made up by the priests. Therefore they wanted to forbid the use of the Oromo Bible.

There were other indigenous missionaries supported by the SEM like us. In 1907 we hosted a conference of teachers and gospel ministers in Naqamte. The participants came from seven areas: Jimma, Siiban, Bodji, Aallee Anbalto, Sayyoo and Ammayaa. They gave reports and advised each other to handle the work with great care and wisdom in their respective areas.

In 1912 the king ordered Onesimos to leave the area for good. But not a single crime committed by him could be found.

Onesimos was forced to travel several times to Addis Ababa for court cases. The Orthodox priests in Naqamte accused him of heresy. They labelled him as an enemy of Saint Mary, a liar and a servant of white men. He became the target of opposition to the Evangelical movement. Addis

Ababa is more than 300 km away and he had to travel by mule. This meant he was absent for weeks and months and I had to shoulder the management of our big household alone, with Aster on my side.

It was important that whenever Onesimos was in Addis Ababa he could stay with his friend Cederqvist. Hakim Cederqvist, as he was called there, was the first Swedish missionary who was able to come to Addis at the time we reached Naqamte. It was 38 years after the first missionaries from Sweden settled in Eritrea. Everything has its own time.

In the court cases of Onesimos the king of Naqamte supported him. He had even sent his own servants to our house for literacy training. Once Onesimos returned after a long absence and people of the town were firing guns into the air to welcome him as an expression of their joy.

Once while he was not at home all his books had been burnt by his own companions who had also come from Eritrea. It was most painful to face internal opposition.

I supported my husband as much as possible. He suffered from rheumatism and repeated colds. Illness and opposition were a great strain on his mental health. He missed the close fellowship of like-minded friends who shared his spiritual concern for his people. He was lonely and often depressed. In a letter he expressed his feelings and spiritual concern:

*I long for those friends who labour for the welfare of non-Christians. When everything was quiet about me at night, I had much to do with the God of my life. For there was no one who understood my worries and my suffering ... persons who are able to grasp my intense desire and yearning which is nothing but the conversion of the Oromo people to the God of Israel.*[53]

Onesimos was given the opportunity to go to Addis Ababa and prepare spiritual materials in Oromo and Amharic and he was also invited to Sweden. He did not accept these offers, giving the following reasons: He had no one to maintain the thatched roof of his house. He had no one to entrust his family to during this time of persecution. Finally there was no mature leader who could visit the sick, encourage believers and conduct burial cer-

---

[53]   In Arén 1999, 291, referring to a letter from Onesimos to Lindgren, 1920, SEM/MT 1921, 44 – People say that Onesimos never neglects an opportunity to talk of God to persons he meets.

emonies. This shows how many responsibilities he shouldered. I was glad he did not go and leave us alone.

## Years of blessing

In 1916 Cederqvist succeeded to obtain in obtaining official permission for the Evangelical enterprise in Ethiopia. The permission given by Lij Iyassu's government finally established the liberty to proclaim the gospel that Onesimos had hoped for when he moved from Eritrea to Wollega. Aster and I opened a school for girls.

God allowed us to see the fruits of our work. Bibles had found their way to many homes. Several Bible students condemned polygamy, slavery, false witness and lying, things they had earlier practiced with an easy conscience. Many thousands were convinced of the truth of the Bible.

In 1923 the first Swedish missionaries arrived in Naqamte, Dr Söderström and his family. We felt spiritually refreshed by experiencing again *the 'communion of saints' that fellowship we tasted in Eritrea and missed so much during the lonely years at Naqamte*[54]. In the coming years a church, a hospital and a school were built. Many people contributed to the buildings.

Soon later the Nordfelds arrived, who had been assigned to Eritrea, but were refused entry by the Italian colony. Following the repeated invitation of the governor of Nedjo, the Nordfelds built up mission stations in Nedjo and Bodji. They experienced a big openness, even if the opposition that we had experienced still remained. Our son Gammachis became the director of the school that had to be closed down when we were there. We were happy to see that the beginnings were taken up again, 25 years after we had started.

## Onesimo's death

The day before Onesimos died, he inspected the fence of our compound. This evening he had Idossa Gammachis, our grandchild with him and advised him strongly to repair the fence as often as needed so that hyenas and

---

[54]   Arén 1999, 296

dogs should not enter the compound. He gave him the gun with which he could guard the house.

The next day, a Sunday, Onesimos as usual went to church. He ran instead of walking. He did not stop to greet people on his way as he used to do, but passed them in a hurry. He said to the people he met on the way, *"I am going to die today, and that is why I am in a hurry."* and passed by. When he arrived at Dr Söderström's house, his heart stopped beating. He stayed in coma the whole day and passed away in peace in the evening and went to his Lord whom he had served his whole life. His body was buried on Monday morning. Representatives of the king, priests of the Orthodox Church in Naqamte, local administrators, government employees and friends of Onesimos attended the burial ceremony.

It was the very Sunday that the SEM in Sweden celebrated their 75 years of mission anniversary. Onesimos was born in 1856, the year the mission was founded. His day of death June 21$^{st}$ is commemorated in the book of worship by the Evangelical Lutheran Church in America as a man who has done great work for the Church.

He desired to be buried at a place where every traveller in the province could see his grave, not outside one of the churches downtown. The inscription of his tomb stone reads: O Land, land, land, hear the word of the Lord, Jeremiah 22: 29.

His diary for 1928–1931 shows a man who lived in a prayerful fellowship with God, constantly aware of his frailty and his need of daily cleansing.

Notes like these are frequent: *'O, my God, forgive me all my sin for Your holy name's sake.' 'Cleanse me in Your blood, o Jesus.'*

Onesimos desired to love all men; *'God of all grace, warm and fill me with your love.' 'Raise me up and make me fervent in all spiritual work, my Lord and God.'*

During a visit to Nedjo in March 1930 he marveled at what he experienced. Day after day he wrote: *'Praise the Lord. Praise the Lord. Amen.*

*Three days prior to his death, he prayed: 'O my God, gather my thoughts so that I only think which pleases Thee'.*[55]

## 3.  Feben Hirphe: Pioneer in education

### Life and childhood in the 1860s

In those days almost everyone lived in tukuls, grass roofed mud houses and had farms with some cattle. An extended family would own several tukuls. The compounds were scattered in the fields, so that the people could protect their crops from wild animals. Farmers had a need for labour and it was common to have servants who lived with them in the same compound. The living standards of people were quite similar. Barter trade was common. No one could read or write. Selling people for money became a big business in the 19th century, driven by the need to purchase firearms from abroad.

Most of the Horn of Africa was not colonized by European empires. The country south of Abyssinia was populated by Oromos and governed by the five Gibbe kingdoms. Modern weapons had changed the power balance in favour of the Abyssinians. Firearms had facilitated the concentration of political power in the hands of a few northerners.

In 1880 King Menilek II from Shawa conquered the Oromo kingdoms and most of the territories of the pastoralists. He defeated Abba Jifar II, the king of Jimma, and invaded the town. In that way he gained access to the trade centre and demanded annual tributes in exchange for a semi independent state of the Kingdom of Jimma.

At that time of unrest Hirphe Abbaa Magaal (1860–1961) was a teenager. Nothing is known about her family. She grew up at Jiren, a village close to Jimma town. Abba Jifar had his palace with hundreds of slaves at Jiren and there was a small industrial centre with women slaves working as spinners. Jimma prospered because of its great market that attracted thousands of people. Big numbers of slaves worked on the royal plantations which produced plenty of agricultural products. Professional traders from far away visited the market. The currencies were salt blocks or Maria

---

55  Arén 1999, 323, quotations are taken from an article by Martin Nordfeldt in SEM/MTBB 1933, 632–633.

Theresa Thalers. Local products such as ivory, hides, cotton, grain, civet musk and gold made their way along caravan routes to the harbours along the Red Sea coast. In the opposite direction luxury items like jewelry and arms were traded.

The 19th century witnessed an unprecedented growth in slavery. Jimma was an important centre for slave traders with a high influx of slaves captured in the south.

### The life of female slaves

When Hirphe was a young woman of 17 she might have dreamt of getting married and starting a family of her own. But suddenly everything in her life changed. Menilek's soldiers captured and enslaved her and many other girls and boys. She would neither see her family again nor hear of them.

In the few years following her enslavement Hirphe was sold several times and had masters in Oromoland and in Abyssinia. She never told what happened to her in the hands of her masters. Female slaves had to work hard: fetching water, gathering firewood, grinding cereals, washing the feet of their masters etc. Probably her life was miserable and certainly her future was dark.

Abyssinia was the largest consumer of slaves in the region, but there was also a substantial intercontinental slave trade. One important outlet for slaves was Massawa on the Red Sea coast. Trade routes from Gondar in the highlands led via Adwa to Massawa. Slave drivers from Gondar took 100–200 slaves in a single trip. They had to walk long distances to the coast and children and those with poor health did often not survive.

Finally, slaves would be sold to Arabs who took them by boat at night to the Arabian Peninsula. Over the centuries Ethiopian slaves were sold to many places: Egypt, the Persian Gulf, India, the Far East and the Indian Ocean.

Slaves were important for their monetary value, for their labour and as sexual objects. Female teenage slaves brought the highest price because of their potential as wives and concubines. Twice as many women as men were enslaved in the Indian Ocean slave trade.

After five years of slavery Hirphe was to be taken to the Arabian world. She never mentioned the dangerous walk and difficulties on the way to

Massawa. However, her grandson reported she was transported across the Red Sea to Massawa.

Once again her future was uncertain. Once again there was an unexpected change of direction in her life.

## Free again

Italy wanted to stop the slave trade; therefore soldiers were regularly patrolling the coast. One day in 1886 they discovered a small group of female slaves and took them to the Swedish Evangelical Mission (SEM) compound in Imkullu, near Massawa. Hirphe was one of them.

Swedish missionaries had arrived in 1866, but could not travel inland. They did not give up their vision and settled near the coast.

Massawa and its surroundings were full of people: traders, soldiers and many slaves from different places and various ethnic groups, ready to be shipped away. Most of them were still children and many were Oromos, the very people the Swedish wanted to reach with the gospel.

Liberated slaves in Massawa had no place to go to. The missionaries decided to take that opportunity and established a boarding school for boys. They wanted to give the former slaves a home and an education. They were educated in the same way as Swedish children. The subjects were: languages, geography, mathematics etc. The Swedish missionaries had also a school for freed girls.

## Hirphe chose a new name

For Hirphe a new life started. She went to school and attended confirmation classes. Two years later she decided to become a Christian.

On the day of her baptism she got a new name, a biblical name of her choice: Feben. The Apostle Paul wrote that Phoebe was a friend to many people and that he had experienced her friendliness. He asked the Christians in Rome to receive her in the name of the Lord and to give her any help she might need from them (Rom 16, 1+2). Maybe Hirphe was attracted by Phoebe's personality and the mutual support network in the early church. Hirphe had lost her own family and through her baptism she became a member of the Christian family.

She stayed in Massawa for many years. In the dry and hot climate, her thoughts might have travelled often to the green rainforests and mountains of Jimma.

Hirphe was one of the girls who showed exceptional learning abilities and she was among the first girls to get a European education.

**Tafesse Kassahun**, her grandson, who grew up with Feben, remembers many things about her:[56]

Feben was trained as an evangelist. Her first assignment was to teach at places like Tsazega, Belessa, Imkullu, Massawa and Asmara. Secondly she assisted with the translation.

One of the three graduates was Ayele Yimer, who came from an Oromo clan called Wara Illu in Wollo, Borna District. Ayele worked for his father, a well known Muslim merchant, and transported goods and people to Asmara. In search of business, Ayele met Swedish missionaries and transported some people and goods between their stations in Eritrea.

It was there that he met Feben and heard her teaching. He was impressed not only by her teaching abilities but her beauty too. So he asked her hand for marriage. At first, she rejected the proposal saying she had no intention of marrying. But he kept on asking and later through the intervention of friends she agreed, making two conditions. First that Ayele continued Evangelical work with her and secondly, that he would never ask her to go to his country. To these conditions he agreed and they got married.

In 1903 politics had changed and another expedition to the Oromo people was planned. Feben and Ayele were chosen for the job based on their work experience and dedication. The team of ten people included three children. All were freed slaves, educated by the Swedish, and each of them was dedicated by the Evangelical Church in Asmara as a missionary.


## To Oromoland

Their journey began in Asmara, continuing from Massawa to Djibouti by boat and from there to Addis Ababa partly by train and partly by animals.

---

[56]  Tafesse Kasahun, " ተሐድሶአዊ የልማት ሥራ መግቢያ , 2018; translation into English in process.

Kantiba Gebru[57] (1855–1950) helped them to be presented to the Emperor, Menilek II, who gave them permission to go and teach and the group travelled safely to Naqamte.

In Naqamte, they found out that the governor had temporarily moved his seat to the town of Nedjo. The group discussed amongst themselves and decided to split: Onesimos and Lydia, decided to proceed to Nedjo; Feben and Ayele wanted to go to Jimma and Habte Mariam Kassa was to go to his birth place in Nonno, east of Naqamte. As for Aster Ganno, an unmarried woman, it was unsafe to go to her birth place alone; therefore she decided to join Onesimos and Lydia. Accordingly all bade farewell to each other started their journeys towards their different destinations.

When Feben and Ayele got to Jimma, they found out the whole area was occupied by Muslims. It was dangerous to live there let alone try to teach. Thus they went back to Wollega.

On their way back, they stayed again for some days at Sayyoo, with the governor Fitewary Yadessa and then proceeded to Nedjo, and within a few weeks they rejoined Onesimos' group. He welcomed them and they started serving together.

## Service and conflicts in Bodji

After some time Hirphe and her husband were transferred to Bodji. Six years earlier two couples, Qes Gebre Ewostateos and his wife Gumesh, Daniel Debella and his wife Tirru. They had been the first to succeed in reaching Oromoland and settled at Bodji Karkaro, an administrative centre of a populous district on the trade route to Kurmuk in Sudan. They preached the gospel in the villages and market places and opened a number of village schools. Many persons, including the youth, believed in the Lord. Even though Daniel and Qes Gebere Ewostateos soon afterwards died, their wives and some other evangelists continued the work.

At the beginning, the relationship with the Orthodox Church was good. Every Sunday they attended services at 6 am at St Mary's Orthodox Church

---

[57] Kantiba is the title of a town major; Gebru Desta became the major of Gondar. He was one of the students of Flad and his Falasha Mission. Gebru attended school in St Chrischona, spoke German and stayed connected with protestant missions.

and at 10 am the Evangelical believers heard the same message in their Oromo language in the house of Fitawari Dibaba. This went on for a long time without any problem. During this period, the priests at St. Mary's Orthodox Church conducted baptism and burial services for all Christians. As time went by the women's work and the school of the Evangelical Church gained more attention from the public which the Orthodox did not like. Differences like Fasting; Fitat and Tezkar (ceremonies after a person died); monthly observation of Saints' days; the role of St. Mary in the church etc. gradually started to widen the gap between the two groups of believers.

The conflict reached its climax on the day of Epiphany when the Arc of the Covenant was carried by a priest and the masses were following him singing and dancing in the procession. All of a sudden youth from the 'Evangelical believers' disturbed the procession by almost reaching for the Ark of Covenants on the head of the priest. A fight broke out, some local elders came in between the two groups and the situation calmed down.

The Orthodox Church had been waiting for such an occasion to bring charges against the followers of the Evangelical group. The leaders, Ayele among them, were sent to the Governor at Naqamte. He referred the matter to higher authorities in Addis Ababa. Lij Iyassu, had taken over the power after Menilek's death and the prisoners were brought to his court. The Bishop requested their execution for their heretical teachings. However, the War Minister said that the case should be reviewed because he did not see enough reason to put all these people to death. Iyassu passed the case to his advisor, Ras Tesema, for review before final action was taken. Ras Tesema judged that this was a simple conflict between two churches and there was no evidence to warrant death sentences. Instead, he advised that the problem could be solved if the non native people were not allowed to return to that locality, but returned to their own birth places. Iyassu approved this decision and all prisoners were freed and told not to return back to that locality.

Ayele, when asked from where he was, said he was from Wollega because his wife Feben was still at Bodji. So he went back to Bodji. However, they could no longer live there and moved to Sayyoo, Fiteway Yadessa's country who allowed them to settle at a place called Arere.

## A couple without children

Feben had passed child bearing age and knew that she could not have children of her own. She had fasted and prayed a lot about it. In her culture a childless wife could have a second wife for her husband, who would become like a daughter to the first wife and like a sister to the husband. She brought to the attention of Ayele this idea, which was new to him and made him so furious that he strongly rebuked her and warned her never to bring it up again. But Feben went to Fitewrari Yadessa and other dignitaries and discussed the matter with them. They said, this was an acceptable practice in society and encouraged her to go ahead as she was on the right track. Hence, through the intervention of these and other elders, Ayele was persuaded and finally agreed to the idea. So he was married to a local girl called Etinyadne Gobena.

The Evangelical church at Naqamte was so upset upon hearing this news that they held an urgent meeting and passed a resolution stating, that considering their dedicated years of service and the culture of the society, both Feben and Ayele could remain members of the church without being excommunicated, but their names were not to appear on any of their writings. Feben openly complained about this resolution.

## Eye problems

They lived at Arere for about eight years, became rich and were happily living there with the first of three children being born to the family. The last two children of Ayele were born after the family moved back to Bodji Karkaro.

Feben started to have eye problems and soon was unable to read or write. Ayele took her to the hospital at Naqamte where Dr. Söderström operated on her eyes and ordered her to wear eyeglasses. She was able to read and write again without any problem.

During this time at Naqamte, the Swedish Mission asked them if they could return to Bodji and restart the work. Feben and Ayele accepted the offer and moved back to Bodji. The penalty imposed on them earlier was not lifted, but years had passed, many people had left the area and things had cooled down at Bodji.

After the eye operation, Feben wore eyeglasses for the rest of her life. As it was unknown to wear glasses during those days, the local people called Feben *the old woman with four eyes*. Tafesse Kasahun remembers that some people asked him to take them home and show them the old woman with four eyes. He happily did so. She asked which area they came from, prayed for them and sent them on their way.

In 1925 the first elementary school in Naqamte was opened by Onesimos and his wife Lidia and Aster. They called Feben to assist them and she came and taught four girls in Christian faith, reading and writing both Oromo and Amharic and domestic skills, for a full year before the school officially opened. The school had three grades and thirty students, boys and girls, and half of them were boarders. In 1926 the school had 54 pupils divided into four grades. Every day Feben also visited inpatients in the new hospital and spoke with them.

## Death of her husband

People were exposed to many dangerous diseases. Sometimes whole families and villages were eradicated. A typhus epidemic hit in 1926 and many people died. Ayele, the husband of Hirphe, caught the disease; Dr. Söderström tried his best, but couldn't save him. Feben was 66 years old when she became a widow.

After the death of her husband she returned to Bodji as a Bible woman and took responsibility as an elder. She was almost 70 years old and she was *'not to be intimidated'*. She had become a local authority in her own right.

Feben, Etinyadne and the last child, Mulunesh Ayele, continued to live together. Many years later Etinyadne, the mother of the children, died and was buried at the Bodji Karkaro believers' cemetery. This was the start of a new cemetery at the Evangelical Church.

## Old age

Feben became unable to be on her own. Temporarily she lived at the home of her son, Asfaw Ayele, who was working as the director of the Moroda

Government School in Nedjo. He could be relocated any time, so this was not a permanent solution.

During this time, Asfaw's elder sister Wodinesh Ayele was employed as a school teacher by the Ministry of Education in Addis Ababa. She was undergoing the process of divorce from her husband. The SEM, through Kes Badima Yalew asked her to move to Nedjo and live with Ade Feben. If she accepted, they were going to hire her as a teacher with the same salary she was getting at Addis Ababa. She and her three children could live free of charge in the pension house built for Feben and her children would get free school education. Although she knew that staying in Addis Ababa offered better opportunities, she thought that this was an important family responsibility and she agreed and moved to Nedjo.

In Nedjo Tafesse Kassahun, the son of Wodinesh, grew up with Feben, living under the same roof until he went to Naqamte for high school studies in 1960. Ade Feben died in 1961 at the age of 101 and was buried at the Nedjo Evangelical Church cemetery. One of her favorite songs which she often sang was: Behold, I am coming to you.

## Tribute to Aster, Lidia and Feben

Freed from slavery living in the Diaspora and assisted in their work by Swedish missionaries the works of these cultural pioneers played a major role in the religious, linguistic and educational life of the Oromo people.[58]

Many years later they went with an expedition to the Oromo. Leaving behind the safety and fellowship of the Evangelical Christians in Eritrea, they returned to their native country. Their mission to bring the gospel to their people was supported by the prayers and finances of the Evangelical church of Asmara, a church that had grown out of an Orthodox reform movement in the highlands of Hamasen and the work of the SEM.

In Wollega they lived for many decades. Besides their family responsibilities they were dedicated to educational and evangelistic work. What they had experienced themselves they wanted to bring to other women: freedom through education and freedom through the gospel. Their lives

---

[58]   Merkuria Bulcha: *The Making of the Oromo Diaspora*, Kirk House Publisher, Minneapolis 2002

differed from those of other women in their immediate environment, who had only been exposed to one culture.

Lidia and Onesimos were married for forty years. She stood firm when her husband was persecuted and accused. Lidia and Aster Ganno lived in Naqamte on the same compound. Feben was a very dynamic woman and served in various places.

Their lives gave witness of a new time to come: education opened their minds up for new ideas; their hearts were transformed by the values of the gospel. They turned out to be strong, emancipated women, if need be resisting opposition and persecution.

# Slavery and human trafficking

Three formerly enslaved girls stand at the beginning of the evangelical movement south-west of Abyssinia. Furthermore the presence of a formerly enslaved girl in Germany and Switzerland in the 1840s and 50s is one of the two roots of Protestant Oromo missions.[59]

The slave trade at the Horn of Africa[60], like slavery itself, is of great antiquity. Ethiopia was the channel for the Oriental slave trade from Africa. However, slavery remains one of the blind spots. This is peculiar in light of the fact that the territories of the Horn of Africa left a significant imprint on the socio-cultural fabric, and the ports along the Horn of Africa coast fed the slave trade to the Arab, Ottoman, and Indian Ocean worlds for many centuries.[61] In the 19th century in particular slave export and import of firearms were connected[62].

The information below on slave children from the Horn of Africa gives the historic context, by adding some first-hand data from a recently published book by Sandra Rowoldt Shell.

A report on the life of the Evangelical women pioneers and their experience of slavery would be incomplete without connecting it to experiences of Ethiopian women today, who for economic reasons are leaving their families and country, their culture and language. Two women leaders of the EECMY did their master thesis on this topic and contributed an article each.

---

[59] Smidt, Wolbert: The role of the former Oromo slave Pauline Fathme in the foundation of the Protestant Oromo mission in Ethiopia and the Missions, LIT Verlag; 77–98.

[60] Modern Ethiopia occupies the largest portion of the territory known as the Horn of Africa

[61] Bonacci, Guilia and Meckelburg, Alexander; Revisiting Slavery and Slave Trade in Ethiopia in Northeast African Studies, Vol 17, Nr 2, 2017, 5–30

[62] Merkuria Bulcha, The Making of the Oromo Diaspora, Kirk House Publisher, Minneapolis 2002

## 1.  Slave children from the Horn of Africa

The experience of enslavement in the Horn of Africa[63] was not uncommon in the 19<sup>th</sup> century. However, first hand reports of girls and boys sold into slavery are rare.

Therefore scholars had difficulties understanding who the enslaved children were, which regions they came from, what their ethnicity was, in which types of homes they were raised, what their parents' occupations were, their relative wealth and social status and so on. Nor was it possible to write anything substantial about the moment of capture, the identity of captors, the prevalence and periods of domestic enslavement, or the length and nature of the journeys to the coast and to the external, oceanic slave trade.

In *Children of Hope*[64], Sandra Rowoldt Shell traces the lives of sixty-four Oromo children from their lands to the south of Abyssinia who were enslaved in the late nineteenth century. Aboard the dhows that would take them across the Red Sea, they were liberated by the British navy and taken to Aden in Yemen where they were looked after by missionaries of the Free Church of Scotland at Sheikh Othman. But many fell ill and many died so the children were ultimately sent to Lovedale Institution, a Free Church of Scotland mission in the Eastern Cape, South Africa, so they could be cared for in a healthier environment.

The Scottish missionaries in Yemen interviewed each of the Oromo children shortly after their liberation resulting in sixty-four structured life histories told by the children themselves.

In her analytical group biography or prosopography, Shell renders the experiences of the captives in detail and context. Comparing the children by gender, age, place of origin, method of capture, identity, and other characteristics, Shell enables new insights unlike anything in the existing literature for this region and period.

---

[63]  Modern Ethiopia occupies the largest portion of the territory known as the Horn of Africa

[64]  Shell, Sandra Rowoldt, Children of Hope: The Odyssey of the Oromo slaves from Ethiopia to South Africa, Ohio University Press, 2018

*Oromo children on arrival at Sheikh Othman/Aden, September 1888*

It has been consensus that slave trade in the Horn of Africa was largely a trade of children and Oromo children in particular.

All 64 children came from the area south and southwest of Abyssinia and 83.7 % were of Oromo ethnicity. Their average age was 14.5 years.

A new finding was that 31.4 % of the slave children were orphans according to standard UNICEF definition.[65] While 12.8% were full orphans, 17.4% were paternal orphans (leaving them particularly vulnerable without their father's protective role)[66] and only 1.2% were maternal orphans. Orphans were less motivated to escape without a family to return to.

Fifteen percent of children were sold into slavery by a family member or neighbor. Of these slightly more than half (53.8%) were orphans. The bulk of the kinship sales took place in the early days of the worst drought, famine and rinderpest ever experienced in Ethiopia[67] while thirty percent of

---

[65]  UNICEF: an orphan is a child who has lost one or both parents.

[66]  A great degree of stigma was attached to children raised without a father.

[67]  The Great Drought and Great Famine lasted from the failure of the summer rains in 1887

captors were people the children knew. The majority of the children identified their captors as Sidama (Abyssinians) or raiders from neighboring territories. Few were enslaved directly by foreign forces; those who bought,
sold and transported children were likely to be part of smaller, regional
trader networks.

African domestic slavery[68] was endemic and almost 2/3 of the children
reported enslavement in Abyssinian or Oromo areas as their primary experience. Oromo girls realized the highest prices in the external slave market[69]
and reached the ports faster than the boys. More boys entered the domestic
slave system, while 50% of girls were sold directly into the export network.
Young girls between the ages of seven and fourteen represented the largest
group of captives exported from the Red Sea ports during the 19th century.

Every slave from the southern lands had to pass through the kingdom
of Shawa ruled by Sahle Mariam who assumed the name of Menelik II
when he ascended the imperial throne. He levied a tax on every slave passing through his kingdom and exacted an additional tax on every slave sold
within his kingdom. These findings together with the identity of the captors,
point to a thriving local slave system.

The children were from every social stratum; from the lowest slave environment to local royalty. No family or group was safe. They were captured one at a time and did not know one another until they reached the
coast.

The children's eye witness accounts have allowed for a much closer
analysis of slave experience traveling on the road to the maritime slave
trade depots than has been possible using the available travel accounts, or
indeed any other sources.

---

until the drought broke in 1892. One third of the people died due to the famine. Rinderpest reached Africa in 1887 after the Italians imported cattle from India to Ethiopia. The
epidemic decimated 90% of the cattle and from there the rinderpest spread all the way
down Africa to the Cape of Good Hope.

[68]  The term in this context is defined as enslavement of Africans by Africans as opposed
to raiding of slaves by agents of the external oceanic slave trade. Among the Oromo,
slave ownership was common while child war captives were adopted (= *guddifachaa*)
rather than enslaved.

[69]  The price of a female captive in the Red Sea ports was 10–15 times more than at the
place of capture in the interior.

The average length of the first passage time was 394 days. They criss-crossed the country from one market to the next. Children changed hands 2–10 times on the way. Adding the segments of journeys the average length was 1752 km/child[70] or the equivalent to the distance from Addis Ababa to Dar es Salaam.

All children experienced being sold and bartered at some stage after their initial enslavement. Eight children were sold for money others were exchanged for food or goods at the moment of capture.[71] Many experienced ill health and ill treatment. Nine children recounted specific acts of cruelty. Two boys and one girl said they were chained; others were tied rather than chained. Attempted escapes of mostly boys (38.1%) were severely punished.

Only a handful of children reported suffering any illness during their journeys. However, the death rate was high according to Pankhurst's figures of up to 60% of the caravan were dying on the road to the coast.[72]

The photos of the former Oromo slave children show them as pitifully thin, consisting only of skin and bones. The first group of liberated Oromo slave children were landed in Yemen in September 1888; by Christmas that year, one fifth of them had died. This led the missionaries to relocate the surviving, but often sickly, children to a mission in a healthier climate on the African continent. They decided on Lovedale Institution in the Eastern Cape, South Africa.

What happened later?

The academic performance of the children at Lovedale School was above average. The Oromo had long held a reputation for easy assimilation into other ethnicities and cultures, so settling in South Africa may not have been too much of a challenge.

---

[70] For girls the average distance was 1644 km.

[71] Cash prices were transacted in the contemporary unit of currency in world trade of Maria Theresa dollars. The principal commodity for which children were exchanged was *amole*, or salt bars, then regarded across the Horn of Africa as an alternative currency.

[72] Pankhurst, Richard: "Ethiopian Slave Reminiscences of the Nineteenth Century" in *Transafrican Journal of History* 5, no 1 (1976): 102, cited in Bulcha, "Red Sea Slave Trade," 110–11.

Many learnt a profession and all found a job. By 1909, approximately one third of them had established relationships or were engaged in careers and stayed in South Africa and beyond. A further third of them returned to Ethiopia, eight independently and seventeen as a group in 1909. The final third had already died by that time.

ON MARCH TO THE COAST

*Billy King's descent from highlands to coast*[73]

Fourteen percent of those whose dates of deaths were known survived beyond the age of 50 years. The continuing high mortality even after relocation[74] reflected how persistent the trauma of slavery turned out to be.[75]

**Christel Ahrens** with input from **Sandra Rowoldt Shell**, the author of *Children of Hope*

---

[73]  A rare contemporary aquatint of the first passage has survived among a series of six drawings of 'Billy King' a liberated slave in Mahe, Seychelles.

[74]  In Lovedale South Africa the climate was mild, their nutrition was good, their treatment was benign and even in the alien disease environment they had access to adequate health facilities. However, Eastern Cape doctors were unfamiliar with tropical diseases and lacked the knowledge and remedies to treat those who suffered from recurrent malaria. The Oromo children died faster than their fellow students in Lovedale. Within ten years, ten of them had already died, mostly the younger ones.

[75]  See also Sandra Rowoldt Shell, "Trauma and Slavery: Gilo and the Soft, Subtle Shackles of Lovedale" *Bulletin of the National Library of South Africa* 72, 2 (December 2017): 149–164.

## 2. Human trafficking

On the occasion of the 500th anniversary of the Reformation in 2017, **Ebise Dibisa** presented an article on human trafficking.[76] Ebise is a woman theologian holding a Master's Degree from the Netherlands and an expert on this topic. She is lecturer at the Mekane Yesus Theological Seminary.

### Definition and scope of the problem

Human Trafficking is defined as "the recruitment, transport, transfer, harbouring or receipt of persons, by means of threat or using force ... for the purpose of exploitation." Exploitation includes all forms of sexual exploitation, forced labour or services, slavery, servitude or the removal of organs. Many countries are using the protocol of the UN high commissioner of Human Rights to prevent and combat trafficking of persons, paying particular attention to women and children.

The scope of human trafficking is widespread: 155 counties were affected in 2003–2005, showing the problem is not restricted to poor countries. 98% of trafficked humans are women and girls, most of them aged 18–24 years.

Human trafficking has reached dimensions that are comparable with other illegal businesses such as drug trafficking. Worldwide, women and children are forced into abusive labour, (for example forced labour, low wages, and heavy workload), prostitution and exploitation.

Ethiopia is a country of origin of human trafficking primarily for labour and to a lesser extent for sexual exploitation. Young women from all parts of Ethiopia are trafficked for domestic servitude especially to Lebanon, Saudi Arabia and the United Arab Emirates.

### Trafficking versus smuggling

In terms of terminology, women who are deceived and coerced into bonded labour are referred to as "trafficked" while those who migrate willingly with an agent to work in exploitative conditions are usually considered "smuggled."

---

[76] Burghardt, Anne (editor), Human Beings not for Sale, LWF publication, 2017, 15–24

Smuggled women enter the country of destination illegally. The "smuggling of migrants is a crime as it is an illegal entry of a person into a State of which that person is not a national or resident." If such women are caught by the police they will be beaten, fined and/or jailed. There are many such cases of Ethiopian domestic workers in Lebanon for instance.

## The effects of trafficking on human beings

Human trafficking has serious consequences. Common abuses experienced by trafficked persons include rape, torture, debt bondage, unlawful confinement, and threats against their family and other persons close to them besides other forms of physical, sexual and psychological violence, resulting in problems affecting the person and her self-perception.

Such women often suffer from health problems, e.g. the rates of injuries to Ethiopian women are the highest in the categories of broken bones, head trauma and bodily injuries that may finally lead to death. Women are deprived of sleep, food, and other basic necessities, leading to fatigue, weight loss and vulnerability to infection. Sexual abuse may lead to sexually transmitted diseases including HIV, unwanted pregnancy and unsafe abortion.

Trafficked migrant woman often develop self-hate, different phobias, abnormal feelings of shame, self-imposed isolation etc. They may suffer social alienation in the host and home countries. The absence of emotional and social support has an enormous effect on the women's ability to withstand and cope with the stress of their situation. They can easily develop a feeling of worthlessness in their society.

## The causes of human trafficking

The root causes of human trafficking are socio-economic realities. Women leave Ethiopia hoping for financial independence. They want to support their families, who often lack resources for food, medical care and education. Frequently it is the family themselves who force their young girls to work abroad; they may still have a 'normalized' view of slavery, which in some countries remains deep rooted.

Suffering may be viewed as selflessness and as a religious ideal to follow. There is a concept of a 'theology of suffering'. Jesus suffered for the sake of the people. Women with a Christian background may take his suffering as a model and accept their own experiences of suffering, believing that it is a good thing in order to redeem someone. 'Living for others' may result in the women giving up their own identity. Instead of being the image of God, they lose their self esteem and are dominated by others. Their identity becomes invisible and they lack self-affirmation and self-reliance. In many regions of the world, the church's misuse of moral teachings contributes to the discrimination against women.

The Christian God is a liberating God. Women are not to limit themselves or to submit in their suffering. Jesus came to heal people and restore their dignity. He often encouraged them and said "Stand up." Women should use their strength and patience to stand up and resist oppression.

## The theology of resistance as a way out

*Enlarge the site of your tent, and let the curtains of your habitations be stretched out; do not hold back; lengthen your cords and strengthen your stakes (Isa 54:2).*

The theology of resistance helps human beings to become self conscious and to fight against trafficking. No more holding back and waiting for other persons to speak up for them. It is time to 'strengthen their stakes' to resist trafficking.

The journey of resistance is threefold. The first part leads from lack of self-esteem to self-definition, through becoming aware of one's objectification and reacting against it by developing self-worthiness. The second part of this journey is from submission to developing the will to change the oppressive circumstances. And the final part of the journey leads from shame and guilt to self acceptance as a person with dignity, by developing self-pride.

The church has to re-examine her classical moral teaching of suffering and address the victorious image of the divine in the churches' teaching and counseling. Suffering is a struggle from transformation to liberation; suffering is not final for human beings.

The church needs to revisit the biblical teachings of crucifixion. This will empower women to see that death is not the final answer in the gospel.

An interpretation of the theology of the cross can motivate them to see Jesus as a model to overcome suffering.

It is the church's responsibility to ensure that young girls and boys, men and women, are educated. Education can be a powerful tool to overcome the gender stereotypes that are keeping women in a subordinate position. Awareness building in the congregation includes identifying available resources, support services and organisations that can provide support for the victims, both with regard to their physical safety (shelter, food, medication and hygiene) and psychological well-being; to advocate for the equitable treatment of men and women. This will contribute to understanding the dignity of every human being. God did not create human beings for sale.

**Ebise Dibisa**

# 3. Ethiopian female migrant workers in Saudi Arabia

**Miriam Tesfaye** is the head of *Symbols of Hope*[77]. This project addresses irregular migration issues in Ethiopia and has the objective to reduce people's interest in irregular migration by giving correct information and by providing locally alternative means of income.

Miriam obtained her Master's Degree in Human Rights from the University of Addis Ababa in 2015. For her thesis she interviewed fifteen female returnees from Saudi Arabia. Quotations from the interviews give a voice to their experiences.

## Introduction to Migration to the East

During the Ethiopian Eritrean war (1998–2000) Ethiopia's economy deteriorated and the exodus began. Young Ethiopians in increasing numbers left Ethiopia in search for work abroad.

The Arab world on the other side is in need of manual workers, hence less educated and less skilled people migrate to Arab countries. Initially most migrants came from the north and east of Ethiopia many being Muslims or Muslim converts. In 2017, however, the majority came from Arsi,

---

[77]   The project Symbols of Hope is funded by the LWF, Department of Mission.

Oromia and the Southern Peoples Nations and Nationalities (SPNN). Numbers of irregular migrants are difficult to get because they are not registered.

Irregular migrations involve dangerous journeys through desert areas to Djibouti or Somaliland and then boarding unsafe boats to Yemen and South Arabia.

Ethiopians are also migrating in large numbers to South Africa or Europe, but the biggest number of women is going to the Arabian Peninsula and Lebanon.

## Experience of Deportation

Saudi Arabia has a long history of hiring workers from abroad. In previous decades workers came from Asia, e.g. from the Philippines. These days, workers are coming from the African continent.

In 2013 the Saudi government announced they would send back any migrant without documents residing in their kingdom. From November 2013 to March 2014 irregular migrant workers were collected in detention camps and deported to their countries of origin. In this process human rights were violated. Migrants were kept confined in detention centres; parents and children were separated; many acts of physical abuse as well as lack of food and drink were reported; wages were denied and a high number of migrants lost their luggage and returned back empty-handed. Returnees reached Ethiopia physically and mentally traumatized, sick or even dead.

Ethiopia was not prepared for such a huge reception of her own nationals and asked for assistance. The EU promised to support 20,000 returnees. In the end 160,000 returnees were repatriated. Upon their arrival the Ethiopian Government Offices and Non Government Offices took part in the rehabilitation, reunification and reintegration processes and offered training to resettle the returnees in the Ethiopian labour market.

## Profile of interviewees

The following interviews give insights into the life and experiences of female migrant workers. Three of them received rehabilitative treatment as they suffered from mental problems due to the experiences they had gone through. Of the remaining twelve, six were married and three of them had children; the other six were single. The average age was 29 years, ranging from 18–41 years. All except one had completed grade eight or above. They had worked an average of six years in Saudi Arabia, ranging from nine months to fourteen years. All returned involuntarily.

## Why do women migrate?

Traditionally, girls and women in Ethiopia stay in their families, where they are protected and controlled. Women are confined to the heavy burden of household tasks and in general they are not very visible in public life. Nowadays they are going abroad all by themselves. The decision to leave is often made and financially supported by the family. Women understand their suppressed situation and know that elsewhere they can earn money with the same job. Many Ethiopian women leave the country to show their potentials and to be recognized.

*"I went to Saudi Arabia through a legal process in the year 2011. I preferred the legal way for its safety although it made me wait longer. I graduated from Admasu College and worked as a secretary in the Ministry of Defense earning 1400 ETB. My salary and the income of my husband were enough for survival until I delivered my son. I wanted to give him a better life, but I couldn't. In addition my family did not support my marriage. My mother disliked my husband's drinking habit. He did not drink much before and I didn't mind so much at first, but later he became addicted to alcohol. He also harassed me and never shared in his paternal responsibilities. My parents are with middle income. They both tried their very best to give all their children good education and see to it that we all live in better conditions. But my life was the most miserable of all my siblings. I decided to at least go to Saudi Arabia and work. I processed the whole thing to Saudi alone and told only my mother about it at the end, because I couldn't afford to pay the transportation alone. She borrowed some money from her friend and provided me the money. Thus, I went to Saudi."*

In this case one can see a woman deciding all by herself to migrate. The next interview was made with a woman waiting outside the Immigration office.

*"I am processing my passport and plan to leave for the Middle East soon... I am doing it with the help of my father who is a farmer and also by my personal*

*money from selling dairy products ... I decided to go because in my birth place (Yirgalem) there is a high rate of abduction. Not many girls can escape that even if the local District and Zonal people tried to stop it. It is really difficult to live amongst men who always wait to take advantage...*

*I have a neighbour who still lives in Saudi Arabia. She has helped and changed the life of her family. She will be waiting for me there... I have never been a domestic worker before but going to Saudi Arabia and working as a domestic worker is rewarding, they pay well... The country's weather is very hot and working is difficult there... Although my father is a rich farmer and he has enough to support me, he says it is better if I work there, because their money has more value than ours – five Ethiopian Birr equaling one Arabian Riyal... I was there for 9 months and managed to learn some cleaning. Now I am here because my madam didn't want to keep me when the mass deportation was announced. She handed me over to the police... I want to go back and work and show my respect to my dad.*

*When I came my passport was confiscated, so today I am here to get a new passport and travel in at least two weeks' time. The man I was talking to outside the immigration campus helped me the first time I went. He will help me to do it the same way again; he did it for me well then. I travelled through "Puntland? it took us over three weeks to reach ... "*

Women shoulder enormous responsibility as bread winners and childcarers. Economic reasons are the main reasons for migration. Migration has become a source of income. The family pools funds to pay for the journey and expects remittances in return. Women also migrate to escape unhappy social situations; harassment, violence and idle husbands. Migration helps them to become independent and to gain self worth.

## Work conditions and detention

*"I was very afraid when I went to Saudi because I was only a TVET graduate and had no work experience. I had never worked as a domestic maid and I didn't speak Arabic. But the people were very nice to me. They helped me learn the language and I was only the babysitter of their baby boy. Many who came from Saudi complain of hard work and sleep deprivation but my employers were good. After working for six months I complained and wanted to have a mobile phone. I was able to contact and meet an Ethiopian maid who worked in the neighborhood. One day we talked and she told me that her salary was 2000.00 Riyal, while mine was only 800.00 Riyal, because I went in a regular way. She told me to run away and*

*she could get me hired with even more than her salary and till then I could stay in the ijazza, a place for foreign workers. These are group homes that are cheap and located in shanty areas of Saudi. So I ran out and as she was looking for a job for me the shorta, the Saudi Arabian police, came to the ijazza and took us all out to the detention centre. Had I stayed at my first employer's home I wouldn't have returned."*

Another returnee:

*"The work I performed was very demanding: I only slept for two or three hours a day, I had to do the laundry and clean the whole three floor house owned by the grandfather. The total number of the household members was eight and I served as cleaner for all. They paid me 1800.00 Saudi Riyal, so it was good. My first payment was only 800 ... I escaped and with the additional money I supported my family back home. The mistress never liked me ... she is the one who handed me to the police but gave me my payments for two months. She never had a disagreement with me but she had a former Ethiopian maid whom she disliked a lot ... "*

Most returnees did not want to come back to Ethiopia. They preferred staying in Saudi Arabia, their repatriation was involuntary.

## Effects of Mass-deportation

*"All I know is there were several attempts by my mistress to attack me. She turned rude after I asked her to send my salary to my guardians who lent me 10,000 ETB for transportation. She never wanted to see me assertive ... I asked for my salary after working for 10 months. When she denied paying me I felt betrayed ... I kept asking but one day she gave me some food and it made me really sick. I think she poisoned me or intentionally gave me rotten food. She usually wakes up only at 11.00 am, but that morning she came to my room early and checked on me. All I remember is she pulled me down the stairs by my arms and the man took me to the hospital. The doctor said I was dehydrated and gave me a glucose infusion. I prayed and cried out to Allah. That happened frequently and they stopped taking me to the doctor. At last I was like paralyzed, I urinated on the bed and everything got worse. You can imagine when they found out that it was a serious disease they left me at a rehabilitation centre. After I had stayed for 10 months they took me to the Ethiopian Embassy. I didn't even have shoes on my feet and walked bare footed. For many days I was with a gown that only covered my hip. I couldn't talk and felt pain all over my body. I don't know why the embassy people never provided me clothes, I don't think they had any, but an Ethiopian who joined the Ethiopian*

*camp gave me clothes. When they transported me to Addis I had no shoes, no nothing. I couldn't even speak. I recovered in Agar shelter after getting intensive medical care... they were nice to me... they showed me love... crying... I hope to reward them someday... Allah will reward them I know ... "*

*"My employers paid me my money before the deportation. But when travelling we were told not to wear jackets or have bags and so I put my money in the baggage. I only had a little in my pocket and I lost everything there... had two bags and not one of them was found... it was all gone... thus all my hustle ended with nothing... just like that... in vain."*

## Challenges faced by female emigrants

Four of the fifteen interviewees are the living witness of the abuse and violence faced in Saudi. Many lost their lives.

Female domestic workers in Saudi very often face discrimination and are stereotyped by their employers. In general their culture considers domestic workers are of low social status; they view them as being cursed and they call them "harem", forbidden, unclean.

The consequences are maladjustment, stress, depression and mental illness and even suicide. They experience anger towards employers and become disobedient or take revenge. There are also times when they get attacked by the employers, burnt with oil or hot water, thrown from windows, partly paralyzed and, at the worst, killed. The trauma also contributes to developing criminal minds; many have run away, distributing alcohol and drugs and some have killed the mistress or children.

## Returnees under pressure after return

*"I used to send all my money to my family when I worked there. On return I had only little, my salary of four months. When I got home I found that there was nothing left, they had used it all and still they expected me to give more money. Without any support from my family I preferred to live alone and rented a house. I have no job now and when the restriction is over I hope to go back to Saudi Arabia. It is much better there. After repatriation I got trained and was given a small shop, but my earning cannot cover my house rent. I plan to stop that and get hired as a domestic maid for the time being... crying... and plan to go when it gets opened... "*

*If it were only about me it would not have been a problem in the first place. I would not have left my country... I have two children... I have to feed them... send them to school... dress them... all this I do without my husband's support! I thank God that my family owns a small Kebele house and its house rent is fair and they are willing to keep us all. But honestly speaking, I can say I only wasted the little money I brought back, actually I myself am wasted by going there. I learnt nothing except pouring out my energy in the huge cleaning there in Saudi. In Ethiopia I got several trainings, e.g. food catering and I took the COC and again I was trained in business skills, life skills... but honestly I have nothing left now... not even for myself, let alone for my children... I finished all my money... I was organized in a group of nine to run a small restaurant but it is without profit... working in groups is so difficult... some are not committed to the work some are... the organizers never look back and see that we really do not get along... I know if it was profit making we could even kill each other... it would have been better to work alone... "*

*"You people come and ask and ask. I told all of you that it is better there in Saudi, I was trafficked and had suffered 16 days and nights at the wilderness, I know the Red Sea is cold, I worked there for seven years, I was degraded... look at me now. I am here and I ate up all that I have brought from Saudi... one year passed... I do nothing or earn nothing... I do not mind even if I do the 16 days journey again. It is better there as you work hard and get money. I got trained and I tried to invest here with whatever I had but no change... it is only subsistence living, no change at all... I only wanted to please my parents. My mom raised me selling tela, local Ethiopian beer... I want my mother to laugh and die... I hate to see her suffer in poverty... I will go whichever way never mind... "*

*"On my return to Ethiopia I came with a two way ticket from my employers... I also had my Arabian papers with me... My employers were not so good but I respected my work very much and the Mistress wanted me back... they were not rich either... they paid me my salary but often borrowed it back and tend to tell me they had returned it back and thus I lost lots of money. I told them I don't need any money now, because I knew they were to finish it all up borrowing from me again and again... that increased my loyalty to them. I came back for leave but soon afterwards many Ethiopians were deported.... I hate the Arabs because they look down on Ethiopians... I brought back fifty thousand ETB and started a business without any support from any organisation... it went well, so I decided not to go... but the major problem here is the shop owners... they keep increasing the rent every six months... how can you grow like that... and people*

*when they know you were in Saudi they think you are rich ... I know how hard I earned my capital money and I have no intention to waste it ... "*

*"A few days after my return I was contacted on my brother's mobile and invited to the Kokeb Building training for three days. There I got trained about how to work and change in one's own country. Then I was transferred to Wingate for further training. There I took three months training and was provided with a shop and I was asked to have work license and tin number. I started working but you know my shop is located on the second floor of the building in Bethel area. I am only allowed to sell products of the country. I decided to sell food flour ... no market at all ... I mixed my items with shoe products of local factories ... no market again ... I almost finished my money by making partitions of the shop and purchasing the selling products ... no income at all, I do not even sell a kilo of "shiro? in one day ... you can imagine ... it costs me to get to the shop 12 birr each day ... my parents help me but I am afraid taxation is to charge me more."*

*"I took all trainings given and also the COC exam ... I was asked to prepare a license and tin number but for very long I was not allocated a place ... I kept going to the offices nonstop ... they are always at meetings – that is the answer I get from the secretaries ... I wanted to work and change my future I sometimes pleaded ... lastly I went with my brother thinking they might at least listen to him ... he was about to fight one day ... and they gave me a place at Gotera condominium ... it is the end part of the condo ... when I went to receive it there were others whom I know from the training. They asked, for what purpose I was to receive the place, production or shop? I said shop and they said we are using it for the same purpose and no transaction here, we long to see people passing by, but there are none, so no chance to sell anything ... I told the officials that it does not fit my business idea ... they ignored me ... They told me I am not here to make choices ... I did not receive it ... my license I will return it back. I cannot be bankrupt while I cannot support myself ...*

*I graduated from Tegebraed College in textiles before I left Ethiopia. I always dreamt of working but I couldn't get hired and my parents supported my brothers so I felt I was a burden to them and left for Saudi. I came back with nothing because I lost my baggage at the airport. My Kebele contacted me to get training ... I chose to train in vending and processed a license and tin number from the Ministry and was also organized in a micro income generating group of three. Our license is for fruits and vegetable vending ... they allocated us on the first floor of a condominium apartment ... we made our complaints, saying our type of business would work better on the ground floor ... no response ... we tried working*

*in the shop for the first time and filled it with fruits and vegetables... no one pur-*
*chased... we ate what we could but most of it got rotten... we still are facing*
*difficulty"*

*"We were given training and rushed to have a license and tin number, though I did*
*not want to do it... For that matter we were only given the training but never given*
*the COC exam, an exam that gives certification of competency. We went and asked*
*and asked at the sub city office so they examined us but nothing... Now again*
*I am contacted to be trained again... they plan also to organize us... is there*
*a way you can help me not be organized I'd rather work alone... laughter...*
*being organized just because you come from Saudi does not work... I know none*
*of them on training, I tried to associate myself with one and when she explained*
*her status in Saudi she said she was imprisoned for selling alcohol... who knows*
*what else... how can I get organized with her... it is not easy... I do not trust*
*anyone... "*

From these stories we can see how returnees get betrayed by family members and how house rent, subsistence and transportation use up the hard earned money. They start to live alone and isolate themselves as they feel deceived and end up in great confusion. They left with the hope to improve their lives and now they are back feeling they wasted their energy in Saudi. The trainings by different stakeholders do not answer their needs. They need to be employed and to become economically independent. Returnees make decisions based on the options they have in their country and compare those with their experiences as a migrant worker. The thought of re-emigrating comes up. Of the twelve interviewees, six decided to migrate again to Saudi Arabia, fully aware of its challenges, and two of them will even leave their children behind.

The UNHCR (1998) defines reintegration as "a process that enables former refugees and displaced persons to enjoy a progressively greater degree of physical, social, legal and material security so as on return the returnee or refugee is able to secure sustainability (in reasonable time). Their political economic and social conditions need to maintain life, livelihood and dignity."

**Miriam Tesfaye**

# Mekane Yesus – The Mother Church

# Addis Ababa in 1904 and the first Protestant missionary[78]

Addis Ababa is no ancient city. The slopes of the Entotto Mountain where Ethiopia's capital is located were for centuries inhabited by pastoral Oromo people. They called the place Finfinnee, because of the hot springs found nearby.

King Menilek II married <u>Taytu Betul</u>. He was her 5th husband. Taytu played an important role in founding Addis Ababa because she suggested building a house near the boiling water and gave the new settlement its name: New Flower or Addis Ababa in Amharic. According to Merab, Menilek permitted her to name the city as compensation for not having a child to christen.

After the victorious battle of Adua, Addis Ababa transformed itself from a predominantly military encampment into a civilian capital. Addis Ababa covered a large area intersected by numerous valleys, at the bottom of which small streams flowed.

The emperor's enclosure, generally known as the *gibbi*, occupied a low hill almost in the center of the city. Its most prominent buildings were a reception hall, which could seat up to four thousand banqueters, and the emperor's private residence, a white washed, two-storey house with balconies and exterior staircases. These buildings were surrounded by storehouses, workshops, an arsenal and the quarters of soldiers and attendants of the imperial household.

Grouped all around the gibbi were the enclosures of the principal men of state, high officers and other notables. The size of each enclosure and the number of huts clustering around it indicated the importance of the individual owner.

Most provincial governors also maintained a compound in the capital having in mind their annual visits to the emperor to pay taxes, on which occasion they might be accompanied by hundreds and thousands of retain-

---

[78] This chapter is based on: Envoys of the Gospel 1999, chapter 3 by Gustav Arén.

ers. Tents of all sizes and shapes would then dot the hillsides and give the capital the appearance of a giant camp.

When Cederqvist arrived in 1904, the inhabitants were estimated at some fifty thousand, mostly living in circular huts with thatched roofs hedged by cacti, shrubs and thorny bushes. Addis Ababa became the seat of several European diplomatic missions and the city was more international than was generally the case in other African cities at the time: Englishmen and Germans, Frenchmen and Austrians, Swiss and Russians, Greeks and Italians, Armenians, Indians, Arabs and Cederqvist, a Swede.

The large market-place extended from below St Giorgis Cathedral over the slope of a hill which eased down towards the valley below the gibbi. The Addis Ababa market attracted some ten thousand visitors regularly. Many traders came from distant parts of the country and travelled for two weeks or more to profit from the supply of commodities that they could not find elsewhere. A British diplomatic mission to Menilek stated in 1897: 'Nearly all the sellers were, we noted, Galla.'

## Rev Karl Cederqvist

The first Protestant[79] missionary to take up work in Ethiopia's new capital was Rev Karl Cederqvist of the SEM. He arrived 38 years after Swedish missionaries efforts had started in Massawa. His arrival in 1904 marks the beginning of evangelistic work in Addis Ababa. Who was this man, how did he come to Ethiopia and what was his ministry like?

## Background and first ministry in the Horn of Africa (1892–1902)

Karl Cederqvist, a skilled builder and carpenter, was born in Sweden. When he took up theological and missionary training, he became a close friend of Onesimos Nasib. After his studies Cederqvist served as sailors' chaplain in German and British ports until 1892, when he accepted a plan by Onesimos to reach out to the Borana Oromo from the Somali coast. He took a course in medicine in Great Britain to be better qualified for mission work in Africa.

---

[79]   Protestant is meant to include Lutherans, Presbyterians, Baptists, Seven Day Adventists, Anglican and Pentecostals

Then he went and led the 4th Oromo Expedition. Unfavourable political circumstances forced them to give up after two years. A new attempt was made in 1899 and again the desired goal was found to be unattainable, but his ministry led to the founding of the so-called Juba mission. The humid heat on the coast was oppressive and constant fever took its toll. In 1902 Cederqvist was forced to return to Sweden to recover.

### His ministry at Addis Ababa (1904–1919)

Two years later, when Onesimos realized that his dream to take the gospel to the country of his ancestors would come true, he doubted that he would be allowed to proclaim the gospel freely in the vernacular unless he was allied with a Western missionary duly permitted to work in Ethiopia. The man he desired to have on his side was Cederqvist.

Onesimos in Eritrea and Cederqvist in Sweden resolved to introduce evangelistic work in Wollega and Borana respectively.

This new enterprise was to cause much hardship to Cederqvist but gave rise to a fruitful pioneering ministry, which he persevered until his death.

Cederqvist's departure from Europe was delayed. He and Onesimos had agreed to meet at the port of Djibouti and proceed to Addis Ababa together and to present their respective plans to the Ethiopian government. Upon reaching Dire Dawa Onesimos and his party had left six weeks earlier. Cederqvist obtained a travel permit, but had contracted malaria and dysentery. In addition smallpox was diagnosed. Nevertheless, he was determined to reach Addis Ababa and used all his will power, even to stay in the saddle. The 25 days journey almost cost him his life. When he reached Addis Ababa he found out that Onesimos had given up waiting for him and left for Wollega the day before Cederqvist arrived.

Cederqvist swapped his Boorana dream for his Addis Ababa reality. For him the town was matchless as a commercial centre. The Oromo, the people of his immediate concern, would be found there in large numbers. The capital offered more fruitful contacts than any other place. Besides, it would not be wise to establish a mission in Borana far away from Wollega if he was to give any support to Onesimos and others. He concluded Addis Ababa was the only realistic starting-point of a fruitful missionary enterprise. Some members on the SEM Board disagreed, but finally they approved.

Many Ethiopians believe the failure of their rendezvous was God's plan so Cederqvist could kindle the light of the gospel in Addis Ababa. Readiness to endure personal discomfort and perseverance in adversities were among the characteristics of Cederqvist, who was to do the pioneering mission work single-handed for over fifteen years.

### The 'Hakim'[80]

Not long after his arrival sick and wounded people came to him for treatment. Modern medicine had been introduced to the public during Menilek's reign, and was available to people who could pay. When the Russian Red Cross withdrew its medical mission in 1906 Cederqvist's service was much appreciated. Medical care took most of his time, he became known as hakim, doctor. In 1908 Cederqvist treated 30 people per day. Medical work removed prejudice and turned public opinion in his favour.

*It grieves me deeply to be forced to turn anyone away whoever it may be, because there is hardly any doctor far and wide. A journey to Gambeela on the Sudan border takes 35 days and to the British centre in southern Borana it takes 30 days. Eastward there is no doctor at all between Addis Ababa and the coast.*[81]

Medical care was not within reach of beggars, slaves and other unfortunates. Cederqvist catered without distinction for whoever sought his help in matters of health, be they high or low, rich or poor. He was particularly concerned about the domestic slaves and the numerous attendants to officials and feudal lords who received utterly low pay or nothing at all. By inner constraint he treated these people free of charge although his superiors in Sweden blamed him for overdrawing his budget for medicine.

### A base for the SEM

Cederqvist was expected to establish a mission base in the capital. To find suitable premises turned out to be difficult. In several cases people were

---

[80]    Hakim is Arabic: wise person, philosopher, healer, physician
[81]    Arén 1999, 121SEM/EI 187.517

warned not to have anything to do with him. They were threatened with jail, if they rented a house to him, and they would be denied church burial and risk eternal damnation.

After frustrating years of repeated moves from one place to another, Cederqvist purchased a site for 4000 thalers. It was the compound near Siddist Kilo, where the Mekane Yesus congregation is located. A chapel, a school and a boarding house for boys and a private residence were built.

On this compound Cederqvist discovered a fine vein of water, deeper than any well nearby. When the labourers did not dare to dig the new well down to the depth required Cederqvist took over their work. From dawn to dusk he laboured alone down in the pit; he even took his food there until the right level was reached and the wall was properly built. After completion, he assembled all the people of the compound, praised God for giving them plenty of pure and healthy water and prayed that it might never cease to gush 'till the Lord comes back'.

A chapel, a school and a boarding house for boys and a private residence were built.

The compound was the link between the SEM in Stockholm and their Ethiopian co-workers in the countryside. Cederqvist supplied them with salaries, books and medicines. They stayed with him, when they had to come for court cases. Onesimos was his frequent guest.

## The English School

In 1907 Menilek II issued a proclamation on general education. The French community established a school for Ethiopians in Addis Ababa. The ecclesiastical authorities were not in favour of Menilek II's idea of general education arguing it would spoil established values. Cederqvist declined an offer from the emperor to become the director of the newly opened Menilek II School, citing that the job was incompatible with his life's mission of spreading the gospel.

The acquisition of the new compound allowed admitting a larger number of students into the so called English School: the number had doubled to 49 in 1914. The purpose of his school was to provide modern education to the local youth, so that they could hear the message of the gospel. In

*Rev. Karl Cederqvist, the first protestant missionary in Addis Ababa, courtesy of EFS Archive*

addition he trained evangelists from amongst the Oromo for future service in their rural areas.

Cederqvist's main concern was to distribute the Bible and other spiritual literature in the Amharic language. The British and Foreign Bible Society was in a dilemma over having books distributed, as for the archbishop and his conservative ecclesiastics, for whom the Ge-ez Bible was sacrosanct, any vernacular version was unacceptable. Cederqvist imported scriptures and publications on his own. Some critics disliked the appearance of books in Amharic and took samples to the emperor to have them prohibited. The monarch read all of them, found them quite good and useful and ordered that they should be on sale.

## Cederqvist's daily schedule

By sunrise he used to come out of his hut and prepared breakfast for his students. Having laid the table he rang the bell to wake them up. At 7 o'clock he took his morning coffee and a piece of bread together with them. He had his place between two students at the table and shared all his meals with them. He kept this practice all through the years.

After morning devotion the students went to their classes. Besides Literacy, the curriculum comprised Bible, Amharic, English, History, Geography, Natural Science, Hygiene, and Singing. At this time of the day Cederqvist received his first patients and tried to finish by noon. For several years he ran the clinic on his own without any trained assistant.

In the afternoon Cederqvist taught Bible and English and also Hygiene, Natural Science and Geography, unless he had to look after some patients in town, who were too ill or too weak to come to his clinic.

Dr Lambie wrote about him:

*He was, I think, happiest when with his boys. They all lived together, ate together, studied together, played together – the old man and the little boys. They took long walks to the mountains, for he was a sturdy old fellow, and when the little boys would get tired he would carry them or put them on his riding mule while he walked alongside. Did anyone ever see such a thing in Abyssinia – a European walking while little Abyssinian boys rode his mule?* [82]

At times he might even wash the clothes of a student who was ill and could not do his own laundry. He seldom asked any of his students for help. They despised manual and domestic work as degrading and below their worth as students but were quite ready to run errands in town to the post office or to patients in need of some medicine. Cederqvist realized that he spoilt his students by the way he treated them. He was possessed by a desire to live up to the example of his Master who made himself a servant of everyone.

In the last few hours of the daylight he might work in the garden or saw and chop firewood for cooking and heating. Burning the midnight oil, he spent his evenings writing letters, studying theology and keeping up with contemporary missionary thinking. At about 2 a.m. he went out to inspect the entire fence accompanied by the night watchman and two big watchdogs. This scrutiny was necessary. There occurred many attempts to break into the compound to steal. His schedule was grueling; he seldom allowed himself more than 3–4 hours of sleep per night.

---

[82]  Arén 1999, 145

## Concerns

Onesimos was worried and wrote to the leaders in Stockholm:

*This grey-headed man labours with material and spiritual things from early morning till far into the night and renders people in Addis, Leeqaa and Wollega great services. Our mission station in Addis Ababa is like a home where those who are persecuted in our areas find refuge and receive food and clothing. If Cederqvist perishes it will be very difficult for us to persist.*[83] *May 1914*

Despite the gravity of his concern, the letter found no response in Stockholm. When the letter reached the mission headquarters World War I had broken out. War time restrictions hit hard at the school where everything was free. Somehow Cederqvist managed to keep his school going.

There were other concerns that increasingly absorbed everybody's mind: the struggle for supremacy among the feudal lords and the growing influence of Islam in relation to the reign of Lij Iyassu, grandson of Menilek II and designated heir to the throne.

In Cederqvist's experience it had never been more alarming than it was in the early months of 1916. Loose gangs roamed the city by night. Several people were killed in the neighbourhood. Many bullets whistled nightly across the school compound. Cederqvist could not exclude the idea that an assault might be launched on his place but trusted God's protection.

Admits these turbulent events Cederqvist pursued his enterprise in Addis Ababa. The mission board in Stockholm had good relations with the Lutheran Augustana Synod in the United States and managed to provide Cederqvist with medicine and other necessities. This supply enabled him to dispatch drugs to the various evangelistic centres in Wollega and to some recipients in Shawa.

## A work permit

27. Sept. 1916 was an important date not only for future development in Ethiopia but also for the Evangelical movement. Teferi Mekonnen, aged 24, was made Ras and designated heir to the throne. He was open to new ideas and liked to meet and communicate with foreigners. Ras Teferi had no easy

---

[83]  Arén 1999, p. 147

task to put his ideas of development and modernization into practice. In an ancient country like Ethiopia with a very high rate of illiterates, traditional forces can be very strong. Churches and missions were asked to assist in the medical and the educational sectors.

A factor of great importance occurred on the eve of the change of government in 1916: the State Council granted to Cederqvist official permission to work. The permit included his Ethiopian co-workers. They were considered his employees and hence would enjoy the same legal protection in religious matters as the western legations had secured for the service of foreigners. Plans were now laid for far reaching expansion of the evangelistic work, but the wartime budget set a limit and most projects had to wait.

## Female Education

Apart from domestic skills the education of women was sorely neglected. Only princesses and girls in high-ranking families would learn to read and write. Menilek's proclamation on general education was disregarded and opposed. Even the rich hesitated to educate their daughters. Many people believed that an educated woman would be a poor housewife.

The Evangelical mission made a point of educating both girls and boys. In Eritrea this policy had borne notable fruit. The Evangelical community was distinguished by its growing numbers of female members who rose above most of their sisters not only because of their literacy but also because other qualities as spouses, mothers and housewives. The female pioneers in Wollega derived their origin from this eminent group of women and desired to give their Oromo sisters a similar training. Their school at Bodji was one of the first institutions to offer a comprehensive female education, albeit on a small scale. At Naqamte Onesimos had observed that educated young men were anxious to find literate wives.

Many projects had to wait due to the war with one exception: female education. The need for female education was urgent. The work permit allowed two schools to be opened, one in Naqamte and another at Addis Ababa.

## Slavery and Gebbar system

Like Swedish missionaries before him, Cederqvist was an outspoken opponent of slavery. He believed in the equality of all human beings. He revolted at the manner in which they were treated – *worse than cattle* – as he informed his mission about the condition of slaves in the capital. They walked almost naked, in cold weather as well as in warm. They were beaten and branded. Many of them did not receive more than a single meal per day, nothing but barley and grain roasted over the fire. Even at the age of nine the girls would be forced to satisfy regularly the sexual lusts of their owner or their fellow slaves. If a girl complained, the response could be, *'wasn't it his turn?'* Besides, venereal diseases were widespread among both high and low. The lot of female slaves was extremely sad and degrading.

Cederqvist reacted to critics in Sweden who could not grasp why the Oromos persisted in retaining old beliefs instead of attending schools to learn about Christ. He elaborated the evils of slavery and the gebbar system. In territories subjected to Menilek's rule numerous peasants had been reduced to serfs or tenant farmers (gebbar). Their inherited land had been declared state property and could be sold to any buyer who might even lay hold on the growing crops, evict the owner and his family and leave them totally destitute and homeless. *How can you expect these people to have time and mental peace to attend schools and listen to the gospel?* he queried. Only compassionate men close to them would be able to teach them about Christ and give them the spiritual care they needed.

## The Evangelical Association

An estimated 100 Evangelicals lived in Addis Ababa by 1910. Cederqvist did not found any Evangelical congregation.

Among the Orthodox clergy there were six priests and one debtera[84] who shared his interest in Bible study and these men were eager to foster spiritual maturity within their congregations through teaching the biblical message of salvation. They became Cederqvist's friends. When parents brought children to Cederqvist and asked him to baptize them or people

---

[84]  Debtera or singer of zema, is an unordained member of the clergy who is well versed in the Ethiopian church rituals, in aspects of the liturgy, and in the scriptures,

desired Holy Communion, he sent them to these priests to avoid attention and spare them the risk of persecution.

Cederqvist did not know until 1912 that his friends belonged the so called 'Evangelical Association', a spiritual affiliation for mutual encouragement and support. Cederqvist stated that they

*... stand unwaveringly in their faith and are determined to hold whatever may happen. Their chairman is my close friend and he suggests that we join hands. I have, of course, no right to disclose their names and their number but, surely, here we have those men of God who deserve our co-operation.*[85]

He asked the mission leaders in Stockholm for permission to join them and enlist their assistance.

'The Evangelical Association' was a brotherhood of devout Orthodox churchmen who followed Peter Heyling, a learned German missionary of Lutheran conviction who had lived in the 17th century at Gondar as advisor to Emperor Fasil. Heyling translated the New Testament into Amharic to promote scriptural knowledge among ordinary people.[86]

The mission leaders readily granted Cederqvist the permission he desired, as his request was in accord with their policy to stimulate more Evangelical concern within the ancient Ethiopian Church instead of forming a church of its own.

Besides this, Cederqvist pursued his ordinary ministry. Germans and Armenians mostly turned to him for pastoral services. This included weddings and burials.

---

[85]   Arén 1999, 135

[86]   Peter Heyling left Abyssinia in 1652. He taught his friends nothing but the unadulterated Gospel in the vernacular and formed a brotherhood of devout churchmen. Each at his own place strove to inspire true faith by translating the Holy Scripture both in church and at public gatherings. Their influence gradually extended from Gondar via Begemder into Gojjam and Shawa and even into Wollega. During the reigns of the Emperors Tewodros, Yohannes and Menilek, however, they fell into evil times. Several of Heyling's followers were put in prison, tortured and even executed. Abuna Mateos, in particular, was ruthless in his efforts to quench this movement. Yet some of these Bible scholars managed to escape detection. They tried to keep their individual involvement secret. One of these was Hiruy, a close friend to Cederqvist.

## The 'November Illness'

A virulent form of influenza, also called 'Spanish Flu' affected the whole world. In the Horn of Africa the disease started in November 1918 and has lived in public memory as the 'November Illness'. It swept across the country like a whirlwind and carried away both high and low, rich and poor, in thousands and further thousands. When the illness raged at its worst, proper burial ceremonies could rarely be held, since the clergy also fell ill and died as others did.

In Addis Ababa people *died like flies* according to a British diplomat. Many of them were buried in mass graves. The eleven doctors were totally inadequate for the need but *'worked day and night fighting the disease.'* One physician was so afraid of contracting the disease that he refused to let the patients come into his clinic. The authorities cabled abroad for replacements of doctors who passed away.

Though no medical man by profession, Cederqvist was now much sought after as a hakim. In the opinion of Onesimos – be it fair or not – *'no one had the people at heart except Cederqvist. He went from house to house and looked after high and low, men, women and children, and did whatever he could for them. He feared God and put his trust in Him and was never put to shame.'*

Zewde Kidane-Wold (1901–1991), who was a boy then and used to accompany Cederqvist in his sick-calls, could not but marvel at the aging missionary's untiring care for his patients irrespective of their standing in society. This example set marks in the mind of his young assistant, who closed a brief account of his reminiscence in an interview by asserting: *'I loved him more than I loved my own father.'*

At the compound of the SEM everybody fell ill, fortunately not all at the same time. Some had recovered and assisted in nursing the others when as many as two thirds of the students were in bed. Cederqvist concluded his report on the disease with a remark of gratitude: *'By the mercy of God all our students were restored to life and health. God also blessed our work and our medicine out in the city. As far as I know, everyone of those who sent for us and for whom we did everything that we were enabled to do recovered'.*

## Cederqvist's death

His care of the diseased affected his health. Food became very expensive, support from Sweden was overdue. He feared that he would have to close the school and send the boys back. Yet, he was not someone to give up. His determination to persist also came to the fore in the intervention on behalf of Teferra Bellihu whom he had commissioned to Sayyoo in 1915. A messenger arrived from Wollega and informed him that Teferra had been kept in jail for over two months. The following day was a Sunday; that gave him *'a little more time to talk to God about the matter'*, as he noted in his diary, before he began to pull every string conceivable to have Teferra released.

Cederqvist's last diary entry was dated October 30th, 1919, two days after his sixty-fifth birthday. This entry recorded his treatment of that day's ten patients and his dispatch of some medicines to his co-worker in the west.

His shoulder had been injured and caused him such pain that he could barely use his hand and hold the pen to write. He felt tired and worn out. A couple of days later he was unable to leave his bed. It was evident that his days were numbered. All through the evening of November 11th, 1919 Captain Charles Bentinck of the English Legation sat at his bedside and read passages from the Holy Scripture to which Cederqvist listened with gratitude till he fell into a slumber never to wake up again.

The news of his death caused exceptional wail and lament, according to Onesimos, since many had benefited from his medical service. Captain Bentinck took upon himself to conduct the funeral service. The deceased was laid to rest at a cemetery for foreigners established by Menilek II close to Petros and Paulos church, west of the city.

# From the Evangelical congregation to the Addis Ababa Mekane Yesus Church

Rev Karl Cederqvist was the first Protestant missionary in Addis Ababa. From the day of his arrival in 1904 until the day he died in 1919 he gave his life to the people of Addis Ababa. He was buried among Ethiopians.

Cederqvist bought the compound near Siddist Kilo, but he did not establish a congregation. In 1921 under his successor, Rev Eriksson, a man distinguished for his literary works, an Evangelical congregation was established and the first church hymn book *Sibhat LeAmlak* with 135 hymns was printed. Rev Gebre Selassie Tesfa Gaber became their first indigenous pastor.

The young congregation saw an influx of Evangelical Christians from Eritrea, because of restrictions in the Italian colony. The newcomers found a place where they could speak their language, find friends, and experience spiritual fellowship in a new country. Over two hundred former members of the Evangelical church in Eritrea were soon well established in their new homeland.[87] Evangelical Christians from Wollega came for work to Addis Ababa and joined the new congregation.

On May 5th, 1936 Italian forces entered Addis Ababa. The missionaries had left and Rev Badima Yalew and Dr Emmanuel Gebre Selassie were selected to assume responsibility at this distressing time. However, they were not allowed to discharge their duty.

After the Italian occupation (1936–41) the Ethiopian people wanted to be free and national feelings ran very high. The Evangelical congregation at Siddist Kilo was re-established and a governing council of elders was elected; Emmanuel Gebre Selassie became the first president. Rev Badima

---

[87]  Arén 1999, 242, referring to a Jonas Iwarson: Vision and experiences from Ethiopia and Galla, 1937, 42

Yalew,[88] the first pastor served until 1966. Rev Badima named the congregation Mekane Yesus, a Geez name meaning *dwelling place of Jesus*.[89]

Enabled by considerable contributions from the members and a generous donation from Emperor Haile Selassie I, a new church could be built a few hundred meters from the patriarchate of the Ethiopian Orthodox Church. The emperor renewed his support in his speech:

*I am as glad as you are today at the completion of this church building. I am especially gratified that the church was built on my father's estate. The members are among those who served our country honourably during the enemy's occupation and they are serving in different capacities in the government today. My happiness is greater today because the construction was done by my countrymen. We are not responsible for the division of churches in denominations. Nonetheless prayer chapels are necessary to all Christians regardless of denominations; the human heart is God's abode. I am hopeful that your lives will be above reproach. When you assemble in this place, we request you to remember us and our beloved people in your prayers.*[90]

In 1957, when a nationwide Church had not yet been constituted, the Addis Ababa Mekane Yesus Church (AAMY church) applied for membership in the Lutheran World Federation (LWF) and was accepted.

For many years this congregation was the only known and registered church of the EECMY in Addis Ababa. Emmanuel Abraham succeeded Emmanuel Gebre Selassie as president of the congregation and vice versa; this went on for 26 years. In 1973 the congregation was reported to have had 2.500–3.000 believers.

The AAMYC has been given the endearing name of *Enaat Mekane Yesus*, literally Mother of Mekane Yesus for her distinguished service of love. The congregation gathered the persecuted under her wings and stood up for them as their advocate. Like a mother she has always provided a safe

---

[88] Qes Badima had been employed as a teacher and later was in charge of the boy's school at Entotto. He stayed on the compound throughout the time of the occupation and served his family and the neighbourhood.

[89] As of 1959 Mekane Yesus is used for the nationwide Lutheran Church

[90] Fekadu Gurmessa, Evangelical Faith Movement in Ethiopia, Origins and Establishment of the EECMY, Lutheran University Press, Minnesoata 2009, 213+214 (translated from Amharic by Ezekiel Gebissa)

*Addis Ababa Mekane Yesus Church*

haven to Evangelical churches in the country when they faced difficult times to gather and worship. The AAMYC has helped troubled congregations to overcome their difficulties and encouraged the various churches in different parts of Ethiopia to work together. Its church is still a centre where foreign missionaries and local Evangelicals congregate.

## 1.  Fifty years of women's ministry (1925–1975)

In 1975 the women at AAMY church celebrated the golden anniversary of their group and published a jubilee booklet with the history of their fellowship. This is how it began:

In 1925 Mrs. Thekla Nelson had started the women's work at the then Evangelical church at Siddist Kilo. She might have thought of the women's mission support groups in her home country, Sweden. Some of the founding members lived until the golden anniversary.

During the Italian invasion the weekly meetings stopped, as did all other church activities, but were revitalized after five years.

When the congregation resolved to construct a new church building in 1948, the construction could not start because they lacked start-up capital. A lot of efforts were made to raise funds such as music concerts. Members of the congregation teamed up in twos and went out into the city to raise the funds. The women went door to door to business firms, government offices and other organisations and raised substantial amount of money.[91]

From 1948 to 1963 annual girl's youth camps were held at Debre Zeit.

Every year at Christmas the women of the congregation would bring food and celebrate together with their families at the church, bed and clothes waiting for those who came from far and had to stay overnight. There was a strong spiritual unity in the group.

Women met for handicraft work such as spinning cotton, knitting and embroidering. Women missionaries brought the yarn from abroad. With the income from the sales they supported the congregation, gospel work and needy people like drought affected people in the 1970s.

Their aim was to see the growth of the church in spirit, love and gospel light. When some of them became weak, others came to encourage them.

---

[91]   Enaat Mekane Yesus, Evangelistic Work 1904–2004, AA EMYC, 2004

Young women were included and supported the older women. They gladly looked back on 50 years: *Our association continued and was strengthened by the power of God and the love of God in us.*
The jubilee booklet[92] included contributions of Aster, Abeba and Tihun.

## Aster Woldemariam

*Paul said: Imitate me, so we, the women in the group, also imitate Christ. I hope the new generation will take over our example and will serve the Lord. If they support each other without losing hope, then they get life from God. Our vision is to build a guest house for the needy and poor and elderly people... if God gives us the capacity. Our prayer is that God comes down to his tent and spends the night with us, his people.*

1975 happened to be the International Year of Women, an issue that had started to gain world-wide attention. Mama Aster when asked what she thought about the proclamation of their equality responded:

*The thing from the past has passed, continuing that is useless. Now people talk about equality. If we say she is inferior, then why did God not create her from the foot of Adam? She was not created from his head either. God created her from the side of Adam to show that Adam and Eve are equal.*

*Equality means that men stop saying: You are under me and step or kick her. Women should not say: I am equal to you and feel proud. They should search for equality in terms of spirituality, humbleness and kindness; that is the equality they should look for like Paul wrote in Phil 2.*

## Abeba Kiflegzy

*I have been a member of the women's group for 25 years. When we come together we greet each other and praise God. If someone is late, we ask: Why did you come late? What happened? Sometimes we say: We got a guest. I am quoting a time conscious woman of our group: No guests on Wednesdays! Her saying turned into a prayer: May God forbid a guest on Wednesday. We don't want anyone to steal this time from being with him. These days transport has improved. In the old days we used a mule and came in time, but the children of these days ...*

---

[92]  translated into English by Ebise Ashana

*We talk about our childhood and say: They, the present generation, are doing what we did in the past, when we were children. Now we appreciate the elderly mothers; their speech is important, it does not fall on the ground, and their advice is not mistaken. We can learn many things, which is amazing.*

*When we first met we took turns in preparing coffee on a charcoal stove. We celebrate with a traditional coffee ceremony. We comment on how she does it. Later we made a rule of serving tea and bread, no cake, only tea and bread. The one who prepares chooses a verse from the Bible and reads it to us. We sing a song, we pray, she serves tea and bread. Tea from our home is not as tasty as the one we drink together. What is special about this tea? What makes this tea so sweet is our good relationship with one another, our warm hearts, our unity and love. After two hours of staying and working together we wish each other peace until the next Wednesday and we go home.*

## Tihun Tola

*The blessing and the commandments were given to both men and women – to rule the creation and work together.*

*Because of our culture we have many tensions between men and women. The women could not play their role. Society says women are weak and have to fulfill what men say. This authority given to men created the feeling of inferiority in women. God's commandment is clear; he gave authority to men and women.*

*It is human beings who created culture. Our culture took away the authority of women. The violence on women came from culture not from God; this violation is outside of God's commandment.*

*The Bible says: As Christ is the head of the church so man is the head of the woman. It continues by saying:* Men love your wives as you love yourself. *But what did Christ do for his church? Did he suppress or exploit her? Did he take away the rights from the church? No! Out of his love he humbled himself and gave his life for her. This is what the husband has to do for his wife. If there is love, where does the cruelty come from? There is one thing we cannot deny: Love and violence do not go together.*

*What perception do we have about our sisters? Some women rather than sharing their problems with women choose to share them with men. They do this because they think men keep secrets and believe good advice comes from them.*

*Women and men have different behaviour. It is true that women have weaknesses. The reason we do not trust each other is, the lack of true love among us. Don't you think so? If there is love there is trust; then we consider the problem of our sister as our own. Then our conscience does not allow us to expose the secret of our sister. Love prevents going public.*

*We have heard the phrase women's rights several times. Women say: we lost our rights based on the word of God and we lost the authority given to us. Let us examine why women's rights are violated. We should tackle the problem of culture, manmade situations which created gender differences. It is better we discuss with our brothers under the guidance of the Holy Spirit; saying that our brothers suppress us, does not help. Women's rights may be violated either out of ignorance, which is lack of knowledge or out of wickedness. Once we find a solution to this there would not be any question of women's rights any more.*

## Women's ministry during early Christianity

Like the AAMY church, most EECMY congregations have groups of women who meet regularly, raise income for their congregations and support each other on their spiritual journeys throughout life.

In New Testament times Luke in his gospel gave much credit to women. A group of them accompanied Jesus and Luke acknowledged that they *used their own resources to support Jesus and his disciples* (Luke 8, 2–3). Martha and Mary hosted Jesus and his group (Luke 10, 38–42) and gave a special meal for Jesus after the resurrection of Lazarus (John 12, 2). A small group of women followed Jesus up to the cross and his burial place (Luke 23, 55–56). They prepared spices and perfumes and very early in the morning they went to the tomb (Luke 24, 1 ff). They followed their Jewish traditions and did this out of love for Jesus. Their solidarity made them unafraid.

Jewish culture and religion was restrictive and excluded women from education and worship. Jesus, a Jew, acted differently: he used chances to talk to them. He praised one of them for her great faith. He spoke publicly about the generosity of a widow. He taught the Samaritan woman and she went to tell her people. Martha recognized the identity of Jesus and witnessed: *I do believe that you are the Messiah, the son of God, who was to come into the world* (John 11, 27). Mary Magdalene, known to have had seven demons was chosen by God to be the first to see the resurrected Lord. Jesus told her to bring this news to the disciples.

Paul sent greetings to the church in Rome and mentioned specifically twenty-eight people (Roman 16, 1–16). Their mostly Greek names are unfamiliar to the contemporary reader: twelve names were those given to slaves or freeman and ten names were names of women. Who were they and what made them memorable?

Top on the list of greetings Paul recommends Phoebe, who had been a friend to many people and served the church at Cenchreae, near Corinth. He greeted Priscilla and her husband Aquila, his fellow workers who had risked their lives for him. They were bold and kept their house open for church meetings. Paul remembered Mary, who had worked so hard for the Christians at Rome. Junias had been in prison with Paul, and he wrote she was outstanding among the apostles and had been a Christian before him. Tryphena and Tryphosa, perhaps sisters, even twins, were appreciated for their hard work in the Lord as well as Paul's dear friend Persis, meaning Persian woman. The mother of Rufus had treated Paul always like a son. Greetings go to Julia and the sister of Nereus.

Though Paul had not been at Rome when he wrote the letter he knew what was going on and appreciated women and their contributions.

## 2.  Gumesh Wolde-Mikael: Wife of Qes Gebre Ewostateos and Bible woman

Gumesh Wolde-Mikael[93] (1875–1962) was born in Hamasen, Eritrea, in the years of Derbush, which was the time of war between Mahdist Sudanese and Ethiopian forces. Her father was 'Basha'[94] Wolde Mika'el. Her mother, Gide'om reared the three children alone and used to hide them in a small hut. One day when the soldiers reached the hut, her mother spread the shawl on the ground before them and was pleading to save them. The soldiers heard her plea and said, *"Leave this woman alone"*. Thus her children were saved.

Later Gide'om took the children to the Swedish mission station in Imkullu where they received spiritual and physical support. When

---

[93]  Arén 1978, 386, 391–2, 400–1, 408
[94]  Basha = title

*Gumesh Wolde-Mikael, courtesy of Tsega'ab*

Gumesh's brother was given the title of 'Basha' after his father he was taken from the mission station and separated from his two sisters. After some time, the sisters were called to visit their mother who was reported to be ill. The missionaries feared the girls would be given in marriage and did not allow Gumesh to go. As suspected, her sister did not come back, while Gumesh was able to stay and continue her education.

Gumesh became engaged to Qes Gebre Ewostateos, an Orthodox priest from the same area. He asked her, whether she was willing to go with him to where God would send him. He declared that he was fully determined to obey God's call and offered to break their engagement if she hesitated to accompany him. She made a commitment, saying, *"Wherever you go and wherever you stay, I will be at your side and share your lot"* and she kept her vow.

Before they got married Gebre Ewostateos had made the acquaintance of Onesimos which gave his life a new direction. From that time on his heart was set on the Oromo people for the rest of his life. He secretly learnt their language in order to be prepared and qualify for the task, which lay ahead.

In the first years the couple became engaged in translation work with SEM missionaries. Their contributions to the Tigrinya translation of parts of the Bible were much appreciated.

In 1897 two couples, both with a small child began their long journey to Oromoland: Gebre Ewostateos and Gumesh and Daniel and Tirru. Gumesh was pregnant. After reaching Jiren near Jimma, Gumesh gave birth to her second girl *under the shade of a big tree* and she herself cut the umbilical cord. They named their daughter Wolete Hiywet.

When the girl was to be baptized, the wife of Niguse, a fellow missionary who had settled at Jiren, pleaded with Gumesh to the godmother. She asked because she was without child and believed God would be kind and would give her a child. Gumesh agreed. The wife of Niguse gave birth to two children in the coming years.

In 1898 Gumesh and her family reached Bodji. Her husband became the priest of Mariam Church. In the liturgical service he introduced scriptural readings and sermons in Amharic and Oromo. When church service was over he invited everybody to his home for a cup of coffee to break the fast. The guests listened to yet another sermon and sang Evangelical hymns. Such gatherings were nothing new, but traditionally the fellowship was exclusively for men. Gebre Ewostateos adopted the tradition and reformed it by filling it with a new meaning: Widening the fellowship to include all, irrespective of sex, age and social standing.

Gumesh and Tirru started teaching at a newly founded school in Bodji.

Gebre Ewostateos was unique at his time in that he also shared household chores, such as preparing the traditional food: *injera* and *wat*. When people asked him why he did that he responded, *Gumesh is a messenger for the gospel and that is why she came with me; her foremost work is to teach the gospel. Therefore, whenever she teaches at school or feels tired I must help her; I do what is expected of me.*

In 1905 Gumesh's husband passed away in a tragic accident, while rescuing Tirru, the widow of Daniel and their five children from their house that had caught fire.

Gumesh remarried and asked permission for her daughters to be educated in Eritrea at the expense of the mission. The SEM Board approved,
but nothing happened. Onesimos enquired and found out that her request
had been a precaution in case her new husband would not like their presence in their home, but he did, and the girls stayed.

Years later, in 1911 two daughters were sent for schooling to Eritrea.
Six men from Bodji accompanied them on the long trip and attended confirmation classes in Eritrea.

In 1921 Gumesh moved to Addis Ababa and was employed by the SEM
as Bible woman. She went around teaching women and children in their
homes. Even those who did not belong to the congregation benefited from
her service. She served the congregation as an evangelist, supported the
sick, visited women after a delivery and disciplined children with unacceptable behaviour.

Mrs. Thekla Nilsson (1889–1984) invited her to start a women's ministry in the Evangelical congregation at Siddist Kilo. With 39 women
the Mothers' Association was established and they have been meeting on
Wednesdays ever since. Spinning cotton for weaving big warm blankets
was one of their tasks. Every month one cotton blanket was produced for
the congregation.

Gumesh also worked as a matron in the Empress Menen Girl's boarding
school[95]. The royal family appreciated and respected Gumesh and assigned
her to look after the girls because of her high ethical standards.

At the boarding school Gumesh taught spiritual and national songs. Every evening before going to bed the girls sang. Afterwards Gumesh and her
grandson knelt beside their beds, read the Word of God, prayed and said
the Lord's Prayer.

**Isayas Tsega'ab, her grandson**

---

[95]   Itege Menen Asfaw (1891–1962), the wife of Haile Selassie and became Empress of
Ethiopia in 1930. The year after her coronation encouraged by the Emperor she endowed
the Empress Menen School for Girls.

## 3.  Aster Woldemariam: Mama Aster

The Swedish missionary <u>Sigrid Berggren</u> (1874–1967) had been active for twenty years among the women in Eritrea. When she was refused re-entry visa by the Italian Colonial Government she was sent to Addis Ababa, to organize a new girls' school with boarding. For that reason she urged that her co-worker at Tseazega, Woizero Aster Wolde-Mariam (1900–2000) should be sent to assist her as a teacher. Thus Aster moved from Eritrea to Addis Ababa.

*The Girls' boarding school was opened in 1927 on the compound of the congregation. The school commenced its work with an enrolment of twenty-two boarders and six day-girls. In addition to the normal subjects of formal education the pupils were given instruction in the Bible and learnt female skills like spinning, sewing, embroidery and basket work. The third year the school had forty pupils, half of them were boarders.*[96]

Despite the preparations for war that were going on in 1935 the School for Girls could continue, since the classrooms had not been deemed fit for treating wounded soldiers. Most of the boarders, however, were sent home for safety.

Miss Sigrid Berggren and Aster Wolde Mariam and others in those months were confronted with a new challenge. The great majority of the women in town had seen their husbands or sons go forth to fight the enemy. They feared that the men may be killed or crippled. The wives of the soldiers needed counselling. Evangelical women visited many of them in their homes and strengthened them with the word of God.

After the Ethiopian resistance against the invaders was broken the remainder of the Ethiopian forces fled towards Addis Ababa. Rev Nilsson wrote to Sweden that *they arrived hungry and fatigued. Some of them are deprived of their clothes. Yesterday we fed hundred and fifty and distributed clothing to some. Today the flow continues, just like yesterday.*[97]

The Swedish missionaries left and the Ethiopian personnel were all allowed to stay in the church compound. Other members of the Evangeli-

---

[96]  Arén 1978, 230
[97]  Launhardt, 73

cal congregation, who had sought refuge and found shelter in the vacated School for Girls, were allowed to stay. They formed a small congregation, coming together for Bible study, singing hymns and worship. Ato Gebre Medhin Habte Egzi and Aster Woizero Aster Wolde Mariam gathered the various families and encouraged daily prayers at home.[98]

*Aster turned out to be a well accepted teacher among the pupils and their parents. But her positive influence reached further. She became a leading figure among the women of the Evangelical Congregation. Her biblical insight, her prayerful care, and her spiritual leadership were outstanding. She was regarded as one of the 'mothers' of the congregation.*[99]

## My Mother – Aster Woldemariam

She loved her mentor, the Swedish missionary Sigrid Berggren. From her she learned and eagerly adopted the Swedish lifestyle. One of her surviving students, 95 year old Marta Abraham, told me that Mama Aster's room smelt of Swedish ginger cookies, not the typical onions and *"berbere"* scent of Ethiopian cooking.

Three Swedish Missionaries signed her wedding invitation card: Nils Nilsson, Thekla Nilsson and Olof Eriksson. Literally they were her *'loco parentis'* giving her away to her husband to do as good parents do. In the note they wrote:

*"Our daughter Aster is marrying. May we ask you to come to the Church compound on (date) and celebrate this day with us?*

She learned how to make real Swedish meatballs. In and of itself that achievement may not be earthshaking but what surprises me is her use of the Swedish word – *"Köttbullar"*. As a toddler, *"Köttbullar"* became my favorite food. I could not pronounce the Swedish word *"köttbullar"*. So my word for it became *"Wachilat"*. Imagine an African toddler in the mid-1930's pestering his mother for more *"Wachilat"*.

In 1935, as Mussolini's fascist army marched southward destroying everything on its way, the Emperor Haile-Sellasie called on his people to mo-

---

[98]   Arén 1999, 476
[99]   Launhardt, 37

bilize. My father who was working in the Ministry of Public Works at that time joined the fighting unit composed of workers from the ministry. When he left for the front at Maichew, I was five months old and my brother Ezra was in mother's womb. All Swedish missionaries had left the country earlier. Mother had to cope alone under difficult circumstances. My father was away for more than a year and my brother Ezra was born during his absence.

In 1941, the allies led by Great Britain helped a triumphant Emperor Haile Sellasie return to his throne in Addis Ababa. I remember the day – 5 May 1941 – he returned. I was almost seven years old. Mother took out dozens of dismembered Ethiopian flags that she had kept hidden in a secret place for five long years. What do I mean by "dismembered Ethiopian flags"? She had separated the red stripe from the green and yellow stripes and kept them apart in a hidden location. Apparently during the Italian occupation anyone caught with an Ethiopian flag would be severely punished.

On 4 May 1941, the night before the parade, mother took out the parts: the green and yellow and the red and sewed them together to form a proper Ethiopian flag.

The next day she gave each one of us a flag and told us to wave them as we stood on the street where the Mekane Yesus Youth Hostel now stands. I remember the Emperor riding in an open car waving. I waved back, just like my mother said I should.

During the difficult years of the Derg[100] (socialist) regime in Ethiopia, mother and father came to spend time with me in Kenya. They returned to Ethiopia in 1980 when my father passed away in August of that year.

Mother returned to Nairobi for an extended stay, 1982–1990, and I learned a great many amazing things about her.

She was not a blind respecter of the status quo. She accepted change as inevitable. She did not condemn those far from her own worldview. Compassion seemed to come naturally to her. She would give everyone –even the hardened criminal – a second chance. Her favorite reaction to a merci-

---

[100] The Derg (Ge'ez: ???, "committee" or "council"), officially the Provisional Military Government of Socialist Ethiopia, was a Communist Marxist-Leninist military junta that ruled Ethiopia from 1974 to 1987, thereafter the formed the People's Democratic Republic of Ethiopia led by the Workers' Party of Ethiopia,

*Aster Woldemariam, courtesy of N. Gebremedhin*

less act: *"Poor fellow, he acts that way because there must be something bothering him."*

Do I understand my mother perfectly? No. I could not understand why she never read anything other than the Bible. But that she read over and over again. Perhaps it is a good indication: all one needs is the Bible.

The congregation in the old Mekane Yesus Church, Addis Ababa, must have felt the same way. They must have said: Mama Aster knows her Bible; let us select her for the Board of elders. She was the first woman to hold that office.

I have an unusual photograph of her sitting on our sundrenched lawn in Nairobi wearing dark designer sunglasses. That picture says so much about my mother.

Aster Woldemariam died in 2000, a few days short of her 100th birthday. She is buried at the Eritrean Evangelical Church cemetery in Asmara.

**Naigzy Gebremedhin, her son**

## 4.  Abeba Kiflegzy: Leader – woman, and music affairs

Abeba Kiflegzy Yedigo (1929–2011) was born in Addis Ababa on 20 January 1929 on St. Michael's Day, the day after Epiphany in the Ethiopian Orthodox calendar. She was the sixth of ten children of Kiflegzy Yihdego and Amete-Tsion Kaleb, who moved from Eritrea to Addis Ababa a few years before Abeba was born. 'Blatta', later 'Dajjazmach'[101] Kiflezgy served as a prominent judge in Addis Ababa and later was appointed to the Higher House in Parliament. The family was an early member of the Lutheran Church and later of the Ethiopian Evangelical Church Mekane Yesus (EECMY).

Upon reaching school age, Abeba was enrolled at the American Mission School for girls in the Gulale area of Addis Ababa. Later, she entered Empress Menen School for Girls and the private Sandford English School until she reached Grade 12.

She taught at the American Mission School for a year before she married Emmanuel Gebre Sellasie[102], an upcoming leader of the Evangelical congregation in Addis Ababa, who later became the first President of the EECMY.

Abeba was an active member of the Mekane Yesus church and increasingly played a leading role among the women, serving as President of the Women's Service from 1955–57, 1960–62, 1967–69 and 1975–77. Her support role continued at various levels throughout the following two decades. From the early days, church women met on a weekly basis producing handicrafts and selling the products as a revenue earning service for their congregation. Organized into solidarity and prayer groups, they visited sick and bereaved members as well as those who drifted from the church.

Abeba's service was not limited to the women's group alone. She served on a number of committees such as the Spiritual Growth Committee and the Family Committee. In the mid-1970s she was elected as Vice President of the Women's World Day of Prayer Committee as well.

In later life, Abeba tailored her contribution to the musical development of the church. In charge of the Music Committee, she led the senior choir

---

[101]  Blatta and Dajjazmach were among a number of titles in pre-revolutionary Ethiopia.
[102]  Pronounced Amanuel

*Abeba Kiflegzy, courtesy of H. Amanuel*

in her congregation for years, conducting young and old alike. Her sterling contribution is believed to be her editing and translating of 501 hymns, and authoring others now included in the church hymn book 'Sebhat LeAb'.

A motivated musician, Abeba spent countless days over a period of years painstakingly reviewing and revising the hymnbook with the support of members inspired by her determination to complete the formidable task. Her name appears below the words of many hymns in the book, which also includes the name of her older sister Yemissrach, and in at least one case, the name of their father. She was a familiar figure on many a Sunday, directing the choir, playing the organ, and ensuring that all practised adequately the day before performing in front of the congregation.

In the course of time, Abeba joined the elders of her congregation (known as the mother congregation) of the Mekane Yesus Church. She may have had strong opinions, but these were tempered by her basic sense of fairness and a soft heart for the less fortunate. She learnt the lesson that while frank and even blunt talk was necessary, there were better ways to get one's point across and convince people. In later years, her sons recognized this facility and on occasion remarked, to her amusement, that her forte was, simply put, diplomacy. In the mid-1990s during particularly stressful years for the leadership of the fast-growing church, Abeba was among the few who sought for counsel from Ethiopia's President Dr. Negasso Gidada who wished to support mediation efforts to safeguard the unity of the EECMY. Recognition came from abroad as well. In February 1993, Abeba found herself at an international prayer breakfast in Washington DC attended by US President Bill Clinton.

The thirst for learning and the desire to achieve drove Abeba's ambition throughout her life. Married and at the age of 30, she enrolled in a three-year evening course in the French language at the University College, Addis Ababa and began to communicate in the language, picking up shorthand along the way. Thirty-five years later in 1994, Abeba, now a grandmother, received a Theology Certificate after completing a course of study at the EECMY Seminary in Mekanissa, Addis Ababa.

Abeba's curiosity to see the lands of the Bible, coupled with a life-long love of travel, took her to the Holy Land on at least two occasions through her membership of the Orthodox Church-led Jerusalem Association of Believers. Committed to ecumenism, she was in addition a life-long member of the Bible Society of Ethiopia.

Travelling contributed to bringing out another talent that delighted people around her – the art of poetry. Abeba began writing poems whenever she found the peace of mind to collect her thoughts and channel them into verse. This could be in her garden, on a park bench while visiting Paris or in a hotel room in Bethlehem. Her readings of poems dedicated to a special occasion, like the wedding of her second son and that of her niece, were warmly acclaimed; poems that were never published but stashed at home and waiting in boxes for someone to discover them.

A slender, attractive woman with an endearing personality, Abeba Kiflegzy lived a full life – for her family, church and community. She passed away after a short illness on 3rd November 2011 and was laid to rest beside her husband at the Petros and Paulos cemetery.[103]

At the farewell service held on the day of her funeral, Rev. Markos took to the lectern to give his heartfelt testimony to a life well lived in the service of the church. He paid tribute to Abeba's attributes which he described thus: *"she was exemplary, productive, faithful, strong and steadfast, skilled and capable, and endowed with charisma and beauty"*.

**Hiruy Amanuel, her son**

Abeba Kiflegzy had many gifts, one of which was a musical talent, which she put to the service of the congregation. She composed, translated and wrote many songs for the hymn book. She played the organ and taught many choir members how to play the organ. We did not worry about the music of the congregation because she was always there.

**Rev. Markos Hadero**

## A tribute to women's contribution as singers and song writers

Abeba Kiflegzy stands in the tradition of Miriam, Hannah, Judith and Mary, who all sang their songs of praise.

Miriam, after crossing the Red Sea on dry ground, took a tambourine and all the women following her were dancing and shouting, *Sing to the Lord, for he is highly exalted.* (Exodus 15, 21)

Hannah prayed in distress for she was without child. Her prayers were heard and she thanked God by responding, *My heart rejoices in the Lord ... there is no-one holy like the Lord...* (1. Samuel 2, 2–10).

Judith had won victory for Israel and was praised the heroine of Israel. She sang a song of thanksgiving with all Israel present and the people joined in this song of praise, *The Lord is a warrior who ends war.* (Judith 16, 2–17)

Mary was pregnant and visited Elisabeth. At the end of their fellowship she sang, *My soul glorifies the Lord and my spirit rejoices in God my Saviour.* (Luke 1, 46–55)

Likewise women throughout church history have not been silent, but they had to pray, preach and praise Jesus for what he did for them.

---

[103] Abeba Kiflegzy is survived by two sons, Hiruy and Tsega, and six grandchildren; Endrias, Alysha, Mahlet, Lauren, Senay and Marsala.

The hymns sung in Mekane Yesus congregations during the 1940s and 1950s were mostly translations of European hymns with tunes from Sweden or Germany. That changed in the 1960s when new hymns and choruses were composed by Ethiopians, written and copied by hand into exercise books. Indigenous tunes found their way into the churches. The congregational choirs, mainly composed of young people, made the new choruses known. The texts and rhythms were very much liked by the singers and audience alike.

Choir members were expected to believe in Christ; singing in front of a gathering was a Christian witness. They stayed together for Bible study and prayers. Thus the choirs became the spearhead of the Evangelical churches. They did not only sing at their own church, but travelled, when possible, at their own expense to other congregations or places to witness to the love and power of Christ.

It should not surprise us to read that the Evangelical choirs were a special target of attack during the communist time. Choir members often were the first ones to be repressed and detained.[104]

A song written by Almaz Balihu became known in Christian circles beyond Ethiopia. The song was written in the 1980s, a time of persecution for youths and young Christians in Ethiopia.

**What kind of love is this?**
You showed this love, Jesus, there to me on Calvary.
1. When I behold Jesus, Lord and God who died for me,
   I wonder much at His love as He hung on the tree.
2. For me you gave all your love, for me you suffered pain.
   I find no words, nothing can my tongue at all explain.
3. Your hands and feet, all were nailed to that old rugged cross.
   You died my death, took the curse, and carried all my loss.
4. You had no sin, Holy Lord, but you were tortured, tried;
   on Golgatha there for all my sins you bled and died.
5. Incarnate love, Saviour you of sinners and mankind;
   help me adore, worship now, your love so great I find.

---
[104] Launhardt, 296

## 5.  Elleni Alemayehu: Besides every great man, there is a great woman

In the AAMY church there were and are members with leading responsibilities in church and society. The most prominent one was the late His Excellency Ato Emmanuel Abraham, who played a key role as EECMY president for 22 years, serviced 27 years on behalf of the EECMY at the LWF and his more than 40 years of service in the government. His daughter Ruth E. Abraham wrote about her mother.

This is the story (in brief) about my mother, Woizero Elleni Alemayehu Fantahun (1926–2002). Everyone knows about my father – Ato Emmanuel Abraham (1913–2016). Much has been written about him in his dual role – in public service during the Emperor Haile Sellasse's time (1935–1974), and as the 2nd President of EECMY (1963–1985). But about his life partner, who was by his side for over half a century (55 years to be exact), little is known by others than her family and friends.

However, in his autobiography *Reminiscences of My Life* (2011), my father wrote this moving tribute to her, addressing her as "My Life Companion"

*"I have no words with which to thank my God for giving me Elleni Alemayehu for a life partner and helper ... Woizero Elleni has cared for me as wife, mother and helper from the day we were united in holy matrimony. For this I offer her heartfelt thanks."*

Woizero Elleni Alemayehu, my late mother, was a woman of faith, beauty, with a strong personality in her own right. I am blessed to be requested to write this tribute in her memory and in her honour, in which I will focus on her role and contributions as my father's life partner – as a wife, mother and friend to the friendless.

My Mother was born in 1926. Her father, Lij Alemayehu Fantahun was from Gondar, and her mother, Woizero Fantaye Ambaw from Gojjam. She lived in Naqamte before she moved to Addis Ababa for schooling, and became fluent in Afaan Oromo. She seemed to have a knack for languages, as I recall she also learnt to communicate in Italian in later life, when we were living in Rome. She had a very hard life growing up – due to various circumstances, she never knew or even saw her father and grew up separately from her mother. She was well trained in traditional cuisine.

It was while she was at the Empress Menen School for Girls in Addis Ababa, that she was introduced to my father, and agreed to marry him. She was just twenty years old when she married him on 12<sup>th</sup> January 1947 at AAMYC.

Two years later, at 22 years of age, she was suddenly thrust into a completely new world and into the limelight, accompanying my father, as the wife of the first Ambassador of Ethiopia to India, following its independence from Britain. This was the first of several foreign assignments for my father. Away from her homeland for the first time in her life, she managed to the best of her abilities, to adjust to a completely new life, supporting my father in his ambassadorial duties. In India due to shortage of housing at the time, she and my father spent almost two years living in a hotel. For the next ten years she accompanied him wherever he was appointed to different diplomatic posts, as well as caring for four small children – two girls and two boys.

Far from friends and family, she made the best of her new situation and environment. She ran the domestic side of the embassy, also managing the embassy staff. She had a friendly disposition; she mixed easily and made people feel comfortable.

Thus began her sojourn abroad from 1949–1959 – going from New Delhi to Rome, again as the Ambassador's wife, and finally to London. Photos of her during this period show her as being beautiful, serene and poised, standing erect by my father's side, greeting dignitaries invited to various functions at the embassy – with a smile and a friendly word. She was the perfect hostess, besides my father's sometimes austere look!

She gained a wonderful reputation for the delicious Ethiopian cuisine she prepared herself. I recall, when I returned from the UK to Ethiopia years later as an adult, several people came up to me and asked if I was the daughter of Woizero Elleni Alemayehu, as they remembered her wonderful Ethiopian dishes which they enjoyed at Christmas parties at the Embassy in London when they were students. She was a real asset to life in the Embassy, and in the lives of all those students who longed for authentic

*Elleni Alemayehu and Ato Emmanuel Abraham receiving guests in London, courtesy of R. Abraham*

home cooking . . . and of course in her husband's and children's lives! They remembered her long after they had completed their studies and returned home.

From the time I was eleven years old until I was twenty one, I was abroad at a boarding school and university in the UK, and so I didn't have the opportunity to live with her day by day and get to know her intimately. But after I returned home, I lived with my parents until I got married, so I had a good number of years together with her.

I recall that until my father returned from the office at lunch time – however late – she refused to eat until he came home. She would wait for him whatever the hour, so that they could eat together. She managed her household responsibilities brilliantly, so that there was never a shortage of anything and made sure that my father in particular, and the rest of the family, were fed with delicious foods, and that his rest times were respected.

She conversed easily with my father about the news of the day, as she kept up with what was happening around her and in the country, by listening regularly to the local radio station. If she had a strong opinion about something, she would share it with him, and she didn't hesitate to give him advice when needed. She was strong minded and I dare say may have disagreed with my father on certain things, but I do not recall any breakdown in communication.

When the Derg government took power and rumours were rife that empty land and property might be confiscated, my mother decided to move from their rented house, into the house that my father had just started to build before he was incarcerated by the DERG in April 1974. It was located near *Alem Bekagne* – the main prison complex in Addis Ababa. The construction of the house was completed by her and there was great joy when he walked into his new house upon his release nine months later. They lived together in this house for twenty-seven years before her death.

During the nine months my father was incarcerated, my mother decided to give up the luxury of sleeping in her bed. She chose instead to sleep on the floor. In her mind, whilst her husband was so inconvenienced in a prison cell, she could not imagine doing anything other than that, showing her solidarity with him. From that time on she stopped wearing jewellery. Further, every day three times a day for the first four months, and once a day later on, she would take food for my father, which she was careful to prepare and supervise herself. I offered to relieve her by taking the food myself to the prison, but she refused. She wanted to do it herself. My mother's deep faith throughout her life, served her well during this time of stress. She was a woman of prayer and believed fervently that her husband would be released, in accordance with God's will and timing.

In his autobiography my father expressed his thoughts this way about my mother:

*"I would be remiss if I did not acquaint the readers of these reminiscences the great debt of gratitude I owe to my wife and life partner, Elleni Alemayehu, for the*

*service she rendered to me with deep love and patience during the nine months I was kept in custody with my colleagues, the Imperial Ministers... ".*

One final point I would like to add about my mother, is that her life of service was not only limited to her husband. Her life complemented that of my father's in a significantly different way. Whereas his service was to the Church and in the public fora, hers was right at home and close by where she lived in her own neighbourhood.

Though not learned in the discipline of theology, hers I dare say was a 'practical theology', which focused on the everyday implications of her Christian belief. She applied what she believed about the truth of the gospel in very practical ways – she fed the hungry and the thirsty, she befriended the stranger and the lonely, she clothed those who needed it, and she visited the sick. She didn't have to go far to do this – they came to her from her neighbourhood, where she lived. Everybody called her *Immaye* – an endearing term meaning My Mother.

Three times a year – at Easter, New Year, and on Holy Trinity Day – she would invite the vulnerable and the poor to our house to share a meal. Hundreds would show up and she was at her happiest when she saw them eating together. All the food was cooked in the house and chairs were borrowed from neighbours. This tradition, which she instituted, went on for many years.

It would be unrealistic to write everything my mother did in her life time as partner and supporter of her husband in good times and bad. I hope however, this brief account will give the reader a glimpse of what a wonderfully supportive partner she was, as well as being a loving and caring mother to four offspring – Sarah, Amenti, Dawit and myself – and a grandmother to three grandchildren – Naomi, Thomas and Daniel.

There is absolutely no doubt in my mind, that my father would not have had the successful life he had as a leader, both in the public arena and in the Church, without the warm and comforting presence, contributions and constant prayers of my mother throughout her life.

My mother passed to eternity on 8 August 2002 in Addis Ababa, at seventy-five years of age – fourteen years before the passing of my father at 103 years. My father had the following verse written on her tombstone: "*A good wife is the crown of her husband"* (Proverbs 12:4). The family added another verse from Proverbs 19:17 – *"Whoever is kind to the poor lends to the Lord, and will be repaid in full"*. How apt both these verses are!

My mother and father are now in eternity – together – just as they were during their lives on earth, their grave at Petros and Paulos Cemetery, Addis Ababa

**Ruth E. Abraham, her daughter**

## 6.  Tihun Tola: In the steps of Hakim Cederqvist

From a conversation at her home on September 12th, 2018:

Christel Ahrens and I, Ebise Ashana, made an appointment with Sister Tihun Tola. Her husband, Mr. Kebede Bogale was waiting for us by the side of the road. He greeted us, opened the gate and let us into a compound with a beautiful garden. He informed Sr. Tihun: *'Your guests are here!'* with his soft voice and accompanied by a smiling face.

Sr. Tihun stood up from her sofa and greeted us warmly, kissing us on our cheeks according to our culture. She politely told us to have a seat, and when we sat down she expressed her worries for us concerning the transport. We apologized that we were delayed by over an hour.

Sister Tihun Tola is a professional nurse and worked for over 40 years. Her husband was trained as photographer in France. They have now been married for 43 years and have three children.

Here she tells her story:

*I was born in a small village called Nedjo, Wollega province in 1948. My father was the housekeeper of Rev Manfred Lundgren. My father could read and write and my mother was illiterate. I studied from grade 1–8 in the Swedish Mission school in a class with few learners, seven boys and three girls only. The other girls were Balaaynesh Danuu and Warqinesh Nagaasaa.*

*After completing grade eight in 1956, I was sent on scholarship, to the Ethiopian Evangelical Church (EEC) Debre Zeit College owned by EECMY, where I completed junior high school, which means grade ten. I was one of the first students and we were very few. Some of the girls I re-member were Elizabeth, Aynalem, Alasebu, Kidist and Fikir. They had come* *from Harar, Gondar and other places. The EEC Debre Zeit College was the best at that time. We had a matron, <u>Mama Tiberih</u>, the mother of Peter and Paul Mario, whom we liked very much. She was a special mother for us, who were without our families. When I was a student, I begged my father to send me ten birr, since every time I was in need of money. Then money had value and I could buy many things with ten birr, but my father did not send me the money.*

*I decided to become a nurse; because I was attracted by the white uniforms, with head shawl, and red-cross badges. In Addis Ababa I joined the Red Cross nursing school located at the then Haile Sellasie Hospital, now Yekatit 12 Hospital, and studied for three years and eight months. The curriculum was very tight and one had to take the study seriously. <u>Karin Holmer</u> was our nurse teacher, herself born in Eritrea where her father was an evangelist. The nursing school at Asmara was also known to be very good in those days. On the request of Haile Sellasie nurses had come from Asmara to work at the new hospital in Addis Ababa.*

*After graduation some of us including myself were assigned to Gondar but we refused and stayed in our boarding school in Addis Ababa for another three months. We regularly went to the Ministry of Health and asked for reassignment. Finally we got employed in the old St. Paul's hospital located near the bus terminal in Mercato.*

Sr. Tihun told us that she worked as teacher and head teacher at the Menilek Hospital Nursing School and after training in psychiatry she served as a counselor. There were times in her professional life she was challenged because of her being a Protestant. She travelled to America for further studies (Wayne State University, 1966–1968) and earned a Degree in Administration and Education. In this capacity she served in the Ministry of Health until she retired.

Sr. Tihun Tola travelled widely (Canada, Fiji Islands, Denmark, Sweden and Uganda) either representing the women of EECMY or attending meetings of the International Nurses Christian Fellowship.

After retirement she volunteered for 'My Sisters' for fifteen years, by teaching their health promoters. *"Working with Aster Haile Michael, the administrator of the organisation is lovely, for she is a very good advisor."*

*Sr. Tihun Tola, courtesy of T. Tola*

Sr. Tihun is attending Sunday services of the AAMY congregation and catching up with new developments such as the charismatic movement.

Christel read for her the English translation of an article Sr. Tihun had written for the 50th anniversary of Women's Work in AAMY Congregation. After hearing the article sentence by sentence, she confirmed it was her article.

When she was asked to compare the situation of women 50 years ago with today, she commented the status of women has improved and in general it is better in Christian families, but still there is male dominance in the society.

After we had finished our interview we were invited to a delicious dinner. We left with thanks in our hearts for her life in the steps of Hakim Cederqvist, who dedicated himself to the sick of Addis Ababa.

**Ebise Ashana**

## 7. Urgue Gambaa: Ethiopia's first woman graduate in Economy

### Family and Schooling

Urgue Gambaa was born in 1946. Her father was from Bodji Dermaji and her mother from Gimbi. Her family belonged to the landlords. Urgue spent most of her childhood in Gimbi town.

Due to her excellence in English she was sent to Naqamte, where she lived on the compound of the Swedish Evangelical Mission until she completed grade eight. Thereafter Urgue completed grade twelve with the last batch of *Empress Menen Girls' school* in Addis Ababa and then studied public administration. She gained some years of work experience and earned money to support herself and her siblings until she joined Haile Sellasie I University. Urgue graduated as the first female student in Ethiopia with a degree in Economics. On the day of her graduation Emperor Haile Selassie I talked to her and said: *"You worked in time, do not allow time to work on you!"*

### Employment

Urgue was employed by the Commercial Bank of Ethiopia (CBE). She spent two years in Pakistan to study computer science and to lecture banking economics. On the occasion of the South East Africa Economic Conference she presented on mixed economy and '*made my country well known and proud*'.

Back in Addis Ababa Urgue introduced computer networking in big organisations like the Ethiopian Airlines, the Ministry of Defense and at the CBE. For thirty-five years she worked at various departments of CBE and hold positions as Vice Director and as Executive Manager.

### Voluntary work

While at Empress Menen Girls' school, Urgue joined AAMYC and formed the student fellowship. She was a member of the charitable association within the women's ministry known as '*Reddiet*'[105] and also of the Young Women Christian Association. She taught at the AAMYC School English, Amharic and Bible for grade 1–8 and volunteered for social life at the local community.

Despite her physical ill health at this time she is still energetic and psychologically fit. Urgue volunteers for the Ethiopian Bible society, which is currently her main concern.

## Her encounter with pioneer women

Urgue knew Gumesh, who was the matron at the boarding of Empress Menen Girls' school.

Urgue got acquainted with Elizabeth Karorsa and for a short time she lived with her family. She remembers Elizabeth had worked at the CBE as a very strong and enthusiastic administrator and as an example for Urgue to live up to.

Naasisee Liiban had spent a night at Urgue's mother's house in Gimbi while on her way to Addis Ababa. Naasisee and her four children lived at the SEM compound in Entotto and she was a member of Mother's Association at AAMYC. Naasisee and Asfaw Ayele proclaimed the gospel in town. She could speak Amharic but used to teach in Oromoo. Naasisee died in Addis Ababa.

## Her support to colleagues

Urgue encouraged women colleagues to make education their top priority. At that time secretarial work was assigned to women in the commonly held belief that women cannot learn other subjects. She encouraged the secretaries at CBE to go for other subjects, such as accounting. A number of female bank professionals were the outcome of that encouragement.

She gave financial, psychological and spiritual support to her female relatives so they continued their education. Some became teachers and medical professionals; others got engaged in other professions.

---

[105] Pursuing the church's motto of "Serving the Whole Person" Reddiet was responsible of financially supporting families of the deceased, comforting the bereaved with God's word, and visiting the sick.

*Urgue Gambaa in 1973, courtesy of U. Gambaa*

Urgue is convinced that women's education is crucial for the society in order to reach gender equality.

## Her perception of singleness of women

In the Ethiopian society marriage is the norm. Urgue said marriage foremost takes place according to the will of God; He chooses for you.

The reasons for her to remain single were: Her older sisters married early and did not get adequate education; but Urgue herself preferred to be educated. During the time of the socialist regime she decided to support her sisters' children in school.

Urgue stated, in Ethiopia singleness is difficult and no one shares their burdens.

## Challenges

When Urgue first arrived in Addis Ababa to attend Empress Menen Girls' school, she was taken to the EECMY hostel; but there was no room for her. The problem was solved by arranging a place with Swedish missionaries. Later a room was found for her at the boarding of Empress Menen Girls' school.

The second challenge at high school was a teacher, who was interested in her friend. However, that friend refused to become his girlfriend. He was frustrated and harassed both of them. Years later Urgue joined the Economics department of the university. That teacher was then a lecturer and insisted that she, though she had finished all courses, also had to take Economics Geography, thus forcing her to study one year longer than all the other students.

The third big challenge was life in Pakistan. She did not know that women had to wear a veil. One Iraqi man said to her *"your King is a killer"*. Her response was *"my king is not a killer but the shelter and a savior of a Muslim"*. She could not cope with the weather in Pakistan. The biggest challenge was when she lost her passport and other documents at the airport. It was a tragedy because there was no Ethiopian Embassy in Pakistan and she had to report the loss in Jakarta. In the end she managed to get a temporary passport from India and travelled back home.

After Pakistan she was re-assigned to CBE. Due to conspiracy her documents 'disappeared' and she could not trace them; thus she lost her job. She worked for thirty-seven years, but the CBE considered thirty-one years for her pension. For long time she had a court case with the organisation to claim her pension.

For more than 50 years Urgue lives in a house built by Swedish missionaries and given to her sister on the AAMYC compound. Urgue had been taken to court and forced to leave the compound. Recently that house was demolished in connection with major reconstruction work. She has been given a room next to the finance office of the congregation, where she lives with her nephew.

**Ebise Ashana**

## On being a single

Jesus did not marry. He was a single. We know that some of his disciples were married, whereas his friend Lazarus and his sisters seem to not have been married at his time.

Jesus taught about marriage, divorce and singleness (Mt 19, 1–12). He also raised the issue of adulterous men in his Sermon on the Mount (Mt 4, 27–32). Once people confronted him with a woman caught in adultery (John 8, 1–12).

Paul chose not to marry, in order to be free for the work of the gospel. The Christians at Corinth had asked him in a letter about several matters, one was about marriage and singleness. Elsewhere Paul spoke in favour of marriage (Eph 5, 22–33 and Col 3: 18–19), but in his answer to the Corinthians he wrote: *A man does well not to marry and it is good for a man not to marry* (Cor 7, 2 +7), *but because of immorality this is impossible therefore each man should have his own wife and each woman her own husband.* Paul wished all were like him, in other words marriage is not mandatory. *But if you do marry, you haven't committed a sin; and if an unmarried woman marries she doesn't commit a sin. But I would rather spare you the everyday trouble that married people have* (Cor 7, 28). To marry or to remain single throughout life is not a question of right and wrong.

Throughout the 2000 years of church history men and women have opted for different reasons to remain single to dedicate themselves whole-heartedly to serve God. Some of them became missionaries like Cederqvist, Hilma, Lydia, Annemarie and Jorunn, whose stories are in this book and some indigenous women followed in their steps like Aster Ganno, Urgue and Sophie.

# Envoys of the Gospel

The witness of women pioneers in this part is connected to the coming of mission organisations to the west and south of Ethiopia.

Missionaries from America (1919)[106], Sweden (1923)[107], Germany (1928)[108] and Norway (1949) went to the remote rural areas of Ethiopia and spread the gospel in word and deed.

During the Italian invasion in 1936 indigenous people had to take over responsibility. The determination of gifted leaders stands at the beginning of the formation of a national church, the EECMY.

All missions started schools and medical services, responding to the urgent needs of the people.

Moreover, the gospel came in a book and language people could understand which preserved their culture and heritage.

---

[106] For details see chapter 7 in Arén, 1999
[107] For details see chapter 6 in Arén, 1999
[108] For details see chapter 8 in Arén, 1999

# American Mission: Sayyoo (1919), Addis Ababa (1923) and South Ethiopia (1929)

## A new era begins

The First World War was also a turning point for Ethiopia. Zawditu, the daughter of Emperor Menilek II, became Nigiste Negestatt (Queen of Kings) or Empress of Ethiopia (reigned 1916–1930), while Teferi Mekonnen was made Ras[109] and designated heir to the throne in 1916. The two persons elevated to the highest positions were very different with regards to what the future of the country should look like.

Teferi Mekonnen, a devout member of the Orthodox Church, had been educated by catholic priests in Harar. During a tour through Europe (1924) he visited the SEM headquarters in Sweden and asked them to expand their activities in Ethiopia. After his return, he was determined to modernize his country and he believed that foreign missions had a great deal to contribute to this goal, especially in the areas of education and health.

In a country like Ethiopia with a very high rate of illiterates, traditional forces can be very strong. The nobility and the Orthodox Church cast him in the image of someone who was out to sell the country. He was accused of having become a catholic with all the connotation of betrayal. Through wise diplomacy he managed to overcome their opposition.

Following the death of Empress Zawditu in 1930 Ras Teferi Mekonnen was crowned King of Kings Haile Selassie I, Emperor of Ethiopia. He prevailed over the traditionalists and gave full freedom to the foreign missions in Ethiopia. Thus ten Protestant mission societies with altogether about 150 people operated in the country by 1935/36.

---

[109] Literally 'head' (in Amharic) was the second highest rank and title after negus in the feudal-military hierarchy of the Ethiopian empire

## Towards Sayyoo

Sayyoo is a district 650 km to the west of Addis Ababa and close to the Ethiopian-Sudanese border. This region, like the country as a whole, had undergone major changes.

For hundreds of years the Oromos had been pastoralists and led a life that is always on the move. In previous centuries they had settled as farmers, a development that was followed by a change in governance, from the Gada system[110] to monarchy with one leader that controlled land, markets and trade routes.

Jootee Tulluu, the king of Gidaamii ruled over a large area which he called Qellem. He became Dajjazmach[111] and obtained 2000 rifles for the purpose of conquering the adjoining territories. Semi independence had its price: He had to pay large tributes to the regional king, a burden he passed on to the people. He also had to accept Orthodox Christianity and to allow its expansion in his territory. It became clear that being Orthodox offered higher social status with the new government.

Jootee was notorious for cruelty, a big slave trader and despot. His own countrymen appealed several times to the government in Shawa. Jootee's relationship with the new government was disrupted and he was removed from power in 1908 and imprisoned in Ankober.

Birru Wolde Gabriel, Menilek's foster son, became the new governor of that principality. He arrived with thousands of soldiers and other government officers, who took over the administration of the large area.

These newcomers did not get a salary but had to depend on the people for their livelihoods. Five to ten families were assigned to support one rifleman[112] or one government official, which meant that people had to work for them four days a week. It was a time of harsh economic exploitation, disruption of social life and destruction of cultural values also known as the serf system[113]. People were poor because the time they spent on their

---

[110] The successive rule of age-groups for a period of eight years

[111] High military title

[112] Naftannya, soldier settler associated with invading imperial army in southern parts of Ethiopia, in the late 19th and much of the 20th century.

[113] Peasants were reduced to serfs or tenant farmers (gabbar). Their inherited land had been declared state property and could be sold to any buyer. The misery of the dispossessed

own fields was so limited. The Orthodox Church also participated in these practices.

## A call for a medical doctor

The American United Presbyterian Mission (AUPM, hereafter American Mission) started in Assiut, Egypt (1854) and extended to Nasser, Sudan (1901). Back in 1869 it had already been resolved to start mission work among the Oromo on the basis of a letter by Krapf, but the resolution was not implemented. Again in 1893 an application for permission to begin work in the country had been turned down by Emperor Menilek II.

Fifty years after the first resolution (1919) the American Mission received a Macedonian call from Birru Wolde Gabriel, *"Come over and help us!"*

It was the 4th call from Ethiopia since 1912 and this one was stronger and to the point. Birru asked for a doctor to come to Sayyoo: An intense outbreak of influenza evoked much terror. The political, economic and social life of the capital with tens of thousands of people dead, indeed of the country as a whole, virtually came to a halt. Birru feared for the lives of his soldiers and his position as governor. He asked for medical help from Addis Ababa, but they could not spare any of their few doctors. Instead he was directed to Sudan, Nasser just 150 km from Gambeela, where an American doctor was serving. That doctor happened to be Dr Thomas A. Lambie (1885–1954). The contact was made through a British inspector, Major James McEnry, stationed at Gambeela. Thus, Lambie was urged to come to Sayyoo at this critical time.

---

went hand in hand with the ease and the new wealth of the new masters. Some of the best land had been allotted to government officials or to retired soldiers. Tenant farmers were obliged to till, weed, and harvest both government land and land in private possessions in addition to any scanty plot assigned for their own subsistence. One tenth of their produce should be delivered to the church, irrespective of their own religion. Numerous people were at the mercy of greedy officials and distant land owners. Most of the ruling classes in the south were made Balabates (gult holders) until Emperor Haile Selassie I abolished the control institution of feudalism by 1966 after growing domestic pressure for land reform.

In 1919 the first American missionaries entered Ethiopia. When they entered Ethiopia, there was only one foreign missionary, Rev Karl Cederqvist, a Swede, who operated a school in Addis Ababa.

The influenza epidemic subsided before Lambie arrived, but Birru gave him a warm welcome and pleaded with him to stay. He offered to employ Lambie and pay him a salary. Lambie recalls their conversation:

*I said to him, "I am here to preach Christ and if you in any way prevent this, I cannot stay. I intend in the hospital you promise to build me to teach the patients the Bible and pray with them. Do you agree?" Birru responded, "You are the chief in your own house and if you wish to do so, no one will prevent you."*[114]

When the Lambie family arrived they found temporary residence in the house of a Greek family. A colony of 20–30 Greeks was living in Dembi Dollo, most of whom had native wives. They monopolized every imaginable activity and trade across the border to Sudan except the slave trade.

The Greeks introduced coffee as cash crop. Many men found employment and carried coffee loads down to the port in Gambeela and came up with salt and cloth, the major import products. But the porters had to pay a high price: they often developed malaria. Gambeela's port, the last stopping point for the steamer on the Baro River, played a major role in the rise of Sayyoo to commercial prominence. Dembi Dollo developed into a modern town.

Birru gave land for a clinic, residences and other houses to be built on. Since Lambie considered evangelism as important as public health, he made a habit of speaking about Christ to every patient who sought his help. But he could not do much preaching for lack of translators. Lambie, like Cederqvist, revolted at slavery, the oppression of poor and other social evils that he witnessed. In one of his first reports from Sayyoo he wrote, *The more one sees of slavery the worse one hates it.*

---

[114] Lambie, T., 'Abyssinia and the Abyssinians', in RM/UP, 1919–12–03, quoted by Arén 1999, 353

## Arrival of the gospel

As more and more American missionaries settled in Dembi Dollo, they started constructing their own houses. An Afro-American blacksmith named D.R. Alexander from Chicago, who had lived in Addis Ababa since 1907, helped with building the clinic and the residences.

In their effort to reach people with the gospel the American missionaries concentrated on four groups of people: patients, students, maintenance workers and beggars: 160 beggars came to the mission compound every week. One of them, Gidada Solen[115] was blinded by smallpox when he was only five years old and became the key person in the spread of the gospel far beyond Dembi Dollo town.

The good news of salvation came in a difficult time, when the spiritual life of many people had come under the control of evil practices leading to economic exploitation through qaalluus.

In this condition people heard about Jesus in their own language. Moreover the message of salvation was accompanied by medical services and education, meeting both physical and intellectual needs. Because of this many accepted the message of salvation; 132 believers confessed their faith in Jesus Christ in 1924. They attended the worship of the Ethiopian Orthodox Church in the morning and met afterwards for Bible studies in their mother tongue, Afaan Oromoo.

From 1919–1937 there was no opposition to the preaching of the gospel in an open and official way only an individual basis there were minor resistance and opposition.

For eight years Gidada had an evangelistic outreach ministry at Burqa Badesa, a place where caravans to and from Gambeela would stop, stay overnight and pay their toll tax. As many as 50–100 porters came every day and Gidada was engaging them in conversation and told them of Christ.

When the rains stopped the shipping on the Baro came to an end. Gidada would return to Sayyoo and the porters to their various villages. Back

---

[115] Gidada Soolen, see his biography: The Other Side of Darkness, 1972. His two sons made significant contributions to Ethiopia: Dr Solomon Gidada as Development Director of the EECMY and Ambassador of Ethiopia in London (1992–1998) and Dr Negus Gidada became the first President of the FDR of Ethiopia (1995–2001).

home they narrated to their family, relatives and friends what they had heard
about Christ. Later some men and women found a spiritual home in the
Evangelical Bethel Church. During the time at Burqa Badesa Gidada learnt
to read Braille and his brother taught the Amharic alphabet to whoever was
interested. Gidada could speak Afaan Oromoo, Amharic and English.

The gospel expanded further, as described in a letter of an American
missionary:

*In 1926 a number of indigenous people engaged in Gospel teamwork. They came
stating a matter was on their hearts, they wanted to do more to show others the
way: Christ. They thought that the plan Christ had used, that of having his disciples
go out in pairs, might be worthwhile. Encouragement was given and a group began
to carry out the good tidings quietly into our whole vicinity.*[116]

The outreach village evangelization became a routine undertaking of the
members of the 'nucleus', as the strong group of first fruits was called by
the Americans. The nucleus paid another blind evangelist (Shoro Embelle)
and his guide. They replaced Gidada at Burqaa Baddeessaa after Gidada
became evangelist and went from one place to another to preach the good
news of Jesus.

The work intensified when the evangelists went to villages farther away
from Sayyoo, as far as tow-days-journeys. They stayed for more than two
months at a time without returning while their wives managed the household and farm all by themselves. In 1933, twenty-five such trips were made
and 17,834 people heard the gospel.

The first generation of believers created an association (Wal-argee ha-
fuuraa) six years after the arrival of the missionaries. The members would
spend one night per month in prayer and Bible study. The objective of the
association was to strengthen prayer fellowship among themselves and to
contribute money for evangelistic work. They hired a 'mailman' to keep the
line of communication between the evangelists on village ministry and their
relatives and Christians at home. They took the task to reconcile members
if something went wrong between them.

---

[116] Bulletin for 80 years of American Mission in Dembidollo, 1999

Women were the backbone of these associations. Among the early converts Henne Maracho also known as Hadhaa Nassi, the mother of Nasiissee, was preaching the liberating gospel.

The spread of the gospel was supported by the cure provided by the Mission hospital. In 1931 the first person, a seventy-year-old man from Begi, was baptized. He had come with his two sons for treatment of leprosy. Back in Begi he shared the message of Christ with his neighbors. In the following year missionary Buchanan and Gidada went to visit him.

The healing undermined the reputation of the qallus or witchdoctors to cure diseases, as did the survival of those, who denied the qallu, despite them predicting their death. Then their power to cure was nullified by the preaching of the gospel and dispensing of medicine. The people were set free from their fears under which they had lived for many years.

## Schools

A visiting woman missionary by the name of Mrs. Ashenhurst started educational work in 1919. Whereas the medical work was appreciated by all, the teaching at the mission school at Sayyoo was not at that initial stage. The school had a modest beginning. Before the end of the first school year forty pupils were enrolled. But opinions vary regarding the teaching, especially to teach Christian faith in the local language. This, notwithstanding, several 'big men in other provinces' often sent word and asked, 'Please, may we send our boys to your school?' However, the school was closed by the order of Abune Mateos, Patriarch of the Ethiopian Orthodox Church, because the teaching was done in Afaan Oromo and included religious education.

Some years later (1923) during a conversation with Ras Teferi Mekonnen, Lambie called his attention to the closure of the mission school in Sayyoo. The regent issued an order that the school should be re-opened instantly.

Mr. and Mrs. Fred Russell took full responsibility for evangelistic work, building and running of the school in 1921. Mr. and Mrs. Henry and Ms. Mary Isabel Blair followed in 1922 to help with evangelistic work and the school and they had on their side one female teacher: Henne Maracho and several male teachers. After worship service Henne Maracho used to take a roll of pictures along to illustrate the Bible stories she narrated for women and children. In 1936, when the Evangelical believers were deprived of their church building, she together with Gidada Solan (later Rev.) and Mamo Chorqa (later Rev.) mobilized the members to pool their resources together to build their own new place of worship.

## The Women's Association[117]

When the Mission School was closed in 1922, women missionaries thought that the order did not include women's training and decided to start a women's sewing circle. They met every Thursday for prayer fellowship, for Bible study, sewing, knitting, and handicrafts as well as enjoying the time together. Haadha Nassi, Haadha Gamuu and Silge were among the prominent women evangelists. It is said that Haadha Nassi and Gidada kept the courage of the group during the first hard days after their place of worship was taken by the Italians. Women remained a source of encouragement to the community of believers as a whole. When the new church building was erected, the women labored alongside the men.

Miss Hazel McGeary was assigned to Sayyoo in 1947 and started the School for the Blind[118]. She also strengthened the Women's Fellowship. In 1948 there were sixty-eight women workers conducting prayer meetings and doing evangelism work among the women. This trend continued through the years and women took full responsibility to get organized under the name of "Women's Association" in 1956. Women groups were established in every congregation, meetings were held once a month and financial contributions were made. Their aim was to contribute to the advancement of the gospel. The Association employed two women evangelists to travel from Presbytery to Presbytery to encourage and strengthen women in their faith and participation in the ministry of the Church. Secondly, they

---

[117] Debela Birri, Divine Plan Unfolding, Lutheran University Press, 2014, 200–202
[118] Four of the early evangelists were blind and two were taught by Gidada to read the Braille. IN 1947 a school for the Blind was opened with four students enrolled and 3 more joined later. By the 1948/49 school year, the enrollment had reached eighteen, including both male and female. Among the female was Adde Waancaa. Some of the students later became evangelists, preachers and teachers.

opened two schools with grades one and two at Leeqaa Golbo and Gar-jeda Abbaa Gimbi, covering all the running costs including the salaries of the teachers. Thirdly they contributed 2000 ETB to help flood victims in India in 1966. Among the prominent leaders of the Association were: Chawake Alabe, Galate Nonno, Zenebech Mamo, Hambise Gorbaa, Qusii Baatii, Xayitu Rebu, Dinbe Gobano, Damme Suyo, Yaanne Fayisa, Awetu Disasa, Warqitu Hinseenee.

### Towards the capital

On his way to the US for furlough in 1922, Dr. Lambie was introduced to Ras Teferi Mekonnen which paved the way for the AUPM to start work in Addis Ababa.

### Teferi Mekonnen Hospital

Dr. Lambie was granted an audience with Ras Teferi Mekonnen, on which occasion the regent expressed his desire to have a hospital in town, built and administrated by the American Mission. The doctor was open to the idea. They met several times, worked out the terms of cooperation and signed an agreement. The land for the hospital was given by the regent. In the United States Lambie found an individual who donated the total amount needed to cover the expenses of building the hospital.

In 1925 the first Mission hospital in Gulale, then outside the city, be-gan its work. During the inauguration speech Ras Teferi took up Lambie's assurance that the poor would get as good treatment as everybody else. He also shared Lambie's hope that one day in the hospital Ethiopian doctors and nurses would be trained. The Italians expropriated this hospital. After liberation the Ethiopian government took over and named it *Pasteur Institute* and later *Central Laboratory*. Today it is the *Ethiopian Public Health Institute*.

### A school for girls in Gulale

Next to the new hospital the American Mission constructed a building for their staff. Today those buildings are the location of the Bethel Synods' Coordination Office.

*The Girls' School in Gulale, courtesy Debela Birri*

Before 1923 the Protestant Missions ran schools for boys in town. The question of female education came up later. It was a new and strange idea to offer modern and higher education for girls, an issue that was debated back and forth in missionary circles.

The first girls' school was opened in Sayyoo due to the pressing needs to have Christian women for the young converts of the early missionaries, *otherwise their life would be threatened and the whole missionary effort would be endangered.*

Crown Princess Menen Asfaw heard of it and encouraged the American Mission to open a school for girls in the capital and so they did in Gulale. This school challenged the prevailing notion of keeping girls at home. Another school for girls named after Itege Menen was opened in 1931 at the request of Princess Menen.

The Women's Board of the United Presbyterian Church stepped in and assisted with funds to cover construction and running costs of the Mission school. The first name of the school was Annie Campbell George Memorial school, named after the wife of a generous benefactor who substantially contributed to the construction of the hospital. Gradually, as this was an institution where Americans worked, the community around the school, as well as the Ministry of Education's records on exams identified it as the American Mission Girl' school. As American personnel began to leave the positions to their Ethiopian counterparts, the name changed to one that represented the alteration of the setting. The School was renamed Yehiwot Birhan, which literally means the *Light of Life*. When a new Church known as 'Yehiwot Birhan' emerged, the name was changed to Bethel Mekane Yesus school to indicate its ownership and continued to function as a *Girls' School* although there is no hint in the name to this important fact.

In the meantime Ras Teferi was building a modern school for boys and the Teferi Mekonnen School was inaugurated in April 1925. Two months later the American School for Girls was ready to receive its first learners. It attracted young girls from well-to-do families. Less affluent parents might pay a reduced fee for the tuition and boarding of their daughters. The standard was kept high and it was soon considered a privilege to attend the school. During the first five years of the 1930s there was such a constant influx of girls that even verandas had to be used for classes. It was impossible to admit all applicants for lack of space.

Dorothy Rankins was the school's longtime directress followed by Elizabeth Karorsa who upgraded the school to high school level. Throughout history the school stood among the noted schools.

### Bethel Gulale Church[119]

On Easter day 1939, a group of 34 believers, most of whom came from Dembi Dollo and were working at the Teferi Mekonnen Hospital, and the missionaries, formed a congregation and elected elders. These elders and Rev Dr Chester Henry ordained Mamo Chorqa as the first Bethel pastor and that was the cause for the birth of the Gulale Bethel Church in Addis Ababa.

On the first communion service by the new pastor 146 people were added to the church and forty-eight were baptized of which seventeen were adults.

---

[119] Debela Birri, Divine Plan unfolding, 143, footnote 542

*Girls attending the school, courtesy Debela Birri*

Gidada was ordained a few months later. Both pastors took care of the young congregations during the time Ethiopia was occupied by the Italians.

The growth of the Gulale Bethel Church was slow, mainly due to internal problems. After 1970 the congregation grew rapidly, because the spiritual revival strengthened the social and evangelistic activities of the congregation and because of systematic training and commissioning of lay people.

The two synods of Bethel (Qellem synod) and Eastern Synod (Shawa, Illubabor, Kaffa synod) merged with the EECMY in 1974, their historical name Bethel being included in their new names.[120]


## 'The missionaries left but Christ remains'

Before the Italian forces occupied Sayyoo in 1936 the American missionaries left. They had lived for seventeen years in Sayyoo and went with a sense of failure because they had not managed to establish a native church.

Gidada Solen in his biography:

---

[120] Debela Birri, Divine Plan unfolding, 236

*In September 1936, Mr. West, the last missionary, left. We walked with him on the road to Gambeela; many followed as far as Gutey. Obbo Fida said to <u>Silge</u>, one of the Christian women, "This is the end of the missionaries. All of our friends are gone." She said, "May I ask you something? Has Christ also gone away from us?" Obbo Fida answered, "No, Christ will never go away from us." When he came to the church he told us what Silge had said. This saying went out to all the groups. It was true: Christ was not going away, he was always with us.*

Throughout the time of persecution Silge's message was an encouraging motto: the missionaries went; Christ remained.

## Times of persecution

The Ethiopian empire came under the rule of Fascist Italy from 1936–41. In Dembi Dollo the Italians took over the entire Mission compound: the residences of the missionaries, the chapel, the school and the clinic.

Initially the Orthodox Church had not opposed the work of the missionaries, but in collusion with the Italians they now moved against the followers of the new faith by refusing the right to bury their dead in the graveyards of the Orthodox Church.

When they were denied the right to worship in their own church, the believers started Sunday services under a tree. Prayer groups in the homes strengthened individual believers. The Italians persecuted them for two reasons: they were Protestants whereas the Italians were Catholics and they feared the influence of the American Mission on the people of the area.

The Protestant leaders and ordained pastors, Qes Gidada and Qes Mamo, were imprisoned at Jimma and were sentenced to death. However, they were eventually freed by the British forces in 1941 at the last moment.

The second round of persecution lasted from 1951–54. The Orthodox Church was not happy about the growth of the Bethel Evangelical Church. The fact that the gospel was declared in the language the people could understand made their opponents angry and fearful. In its move against the Bethel Evangelical Church the Orthodox Church had the full backing of the local government. The case took four years to resolve before churches were opened again.

The Bethel Evangelical Church experienced a third round of persecution under the Socialist regime (1974–1991).

One may ask again: Why was this church persecuted? They preached the gospel and the gospel is about truth. The truth shall set people free. When the mind and soul are liberated people begin to demand their human rights. It would be difficult to oppress and exploit people who know what is right and what is wrong.

## Towards the South of Ethiopia, 1929

Dr Lambie organized the building of the Teferi Mekonnen Hospital and the Girl's school in Gulale. But he was unhappy that the mission used a lot of the resources in the capital city for medical and educational work as presumed by the government.

In spite of the obvious success Lambie could not forget what he had seen as physician and evangelist during his caravan journeys and visits to Jimma. He realized there were many smaller ethnic groups in South Ethiopia who practiced traditional religions and never heard about Christ. He felt that his mission society should do more to take the gospel to those people in the South of the country. He proposed the idea to the mission board, who felt not in a position to undertake yet another activity in the country at that time.

## "Dr Lambie's Mission"

After twenty years of service Lambie left the American Presbyterian Mission and started a new mission with the goal to christianize the borderlands of Ethiopia. Initially this mission was called the Abyssinian Frontiers Mission, locally known as Dr Lambie's Mission. The same year his mission merged with the new work of the Sudan Interior Mission (SIM)[121].

Lambie returned to Ethiopia with eleven missionaries from various countries and different denominations. On March 1928 these pioneers set

---

[121] Sudan in this context was a geographical term describing the belt south of the Sahara and north of the equator. The SIM was founded 1893 in Toronto. For some time it was called the Society of International Missions, now it is re-named to Serving in Mission.

off from Addis Ababa towards Jimma, but missed the way and found themselves in Hossaina and continued further to Kambata, Soddo, Wallamo, Garbitcho and Sidamo.

Emperor Haile Selassie I appointed Dr. Lambie secretary-general of the new Ethiopian Red Cross to oversee the efforts of Ethiopian and foreign medical teams.

Dr Bingham, the director of the SIM, proposed a base and headquarters in Addis Ababa, since by 1937 the number of SIM missionaries had grown to about one hundred. However, the city was not considered to be a 'mission field'. Only a bookshop with printing press was started.

The number of newly baptized believers was no larger than fifty and baptism was mostly taking place in Wolayta.

Lambie's wife Charlotte while in the USA had been in close

5.000 US Dollars every year for five years to run a leprosarium. In the outskirts of Addis Ababa a leprosarium called Princess Zenebe Werq Memorial Hospital, later ALERT (African Leprosy Research Training) was constructed and has been serving ever since.

## 1. One family: Three generations of women missionaries

Rachel Weller tells her family story and its link to Ethiopia:

It all started with the determination of my great grandmother, Alice Porter McDougal. She insisted that her daughter, my grandmother, Mary Frances McDougal, should go to college and study. Not many women did that in the early 1900s. At American colleges a movement called 'The Student Volunteer Movement' was interested in spreading the gospel in far away countries. My grandmother became a missionary and here our family link to mission begins.

Her father had passed away leaving her mother behind with two girls. My great grandmother remarried and the couple decided to sell the land she had inherited from her first husband. What to do with the money? Her husband wanted to buy horses for farming and my great grandmother wanted education for her two daughters.

My grandmother earned a degree in mathematics. Thereafter she went as a volunteer, meaning she must have raised the funds herself somehow,

with the United Presbyterian Church in North America (AUPM) to Assiut
in Egypt, where she taught the children of missionaries. In Assiut she met
her future husband Joseph Maxwell, who was also a volunteer and later
would become a medical doctor. They married and got assigned to Nasser
in Anglo-Egyptian Sudan, where also Dr Lambie was working. We do not
know much about her life. She became a mother; her first child was still-
born. Feeling responsible for the loss of the first child, a boy, my grandfather, himself a doctor, made sure the next child was born in Tanta, Egypt
where there was a mission hospital and doctor. In 1925 my mother was born
as the second surviving child out of four living children.

Then the family was called to Ethiopia. They went by boat up the Sobat
and Baro rivers and by mule up the mountains to Dembi Dollo. My grandmother taught her own children. My mother about four years old learnt
the local language quickly and translated for her mother, especially when
they visited the girl's dormitory, where they made friends with Qanatu and
Elizabeth Karorsa. When my mother was eight years old they went back to
the US, where they served as missionaries in a very poor area.

My mother, Martha Maxwell (1925–2016) completed school and college,
became a nurse and returned to Ethiopia in 1946, when she was twenty-one
years old. Her sister worked as a nurse in Nasser on the other side of the
border. Mother worked in the hospital for ten years before she got married.
There were times she was the only foreign staff and had to take courageous
procedures like once an amputation.

In 1951 my father, Malcolm S. Vandevort, an ordained pastor arrived
in Ethiopia, learnt the language and replaced the director of Berhane Yesus
School for one year. After that he took over the Sayyoo Training Institute,
which eventually became the Gidada Bible School.

My parents married in Addis Ababa, lived for twenty years in Dembi
Dollo and had five children. Then they were transferred to Mizan Teferi.
My mother conducted prenatal clinics and was often out to visit women
at their homes. At that time we children were in Addis Ababa at boarding
school, as was common for mission families serving in the country side.
We only knew Mizan Teferi as a vacation place.

I remember a dispute between my parents about the care of a woman with an obstructed delivery, the head of the baby was too big to pass through the woman's pelvis. My mother wanted to call the Missionary Aviation Fellowship (MAF) to take the woman to a hospital to have an operation and at least save her life, since the baby had already died.

My father argued against doing that, possibly because of the cost and he probably did not want to start a precedent that they would not be able to carry on. I remember my mother crying knowing that the only result would be the death of the woman. And it was.

Since that time, I have asked repeatedly, what is the value of a human life?" I believe my mother would have found a way to help the woman, if she could have.

My mother had a gift of languages and taught both in Afaan Oromo and in Amharic at the women's meetings on Wednesday afternoon. She attended to different neighborhood meetings at different times.

Mom told me that she liked living in Dembi Dollo; she felt this was her home, where she had friendly relationships, especially to Qanatu, Elizabeth and Chawake. This was the place she had spent her childhood. Mizan Teferi was a new area with a new language and new people and the gap was larger between them and her though she was out with the women just as often in Mizan Teferi as she was in Dembi Dollo! She never put down roots because the mission was always talking about sending them somewhere else.

During our stay in Dembi Dollo I remember seeing Rev Gidada Solen, one of the first pastors of the Bethel church, which started in Dembi Dollo sitting beside my mother speaking in Oromiffa and her typing in English! Through his autobiography (The Other Side of Darkness) his life and Ethiopia became known by many people in the US and beyond.

I, Rachel was born in 1959 and had four siblings. We grew up together with 30–50 missionary kids. From grade four – I was nine years old – I attended boarding school at Addis Ababa (Makanissa). Every child responds differently. Though my sisters each spent much of their first year at boarding school crying to be home, I did not. I felt a bit of a sense of guilt for not being as sad as they were for the separation. All of us have many good memories of the school, but the separation put its mark on many boarding

*Martha Vandevort, courtesy of Rachel Weller*

students. I was in the last graduating batch at Good Shepherd School, before the school was taken by the qebele. This was in 1977, just before the Red Terror[122].

In the last year of my schooling I became interested in mission work myself, in the confidence that God had a plan for my life. I became a nurse and worked for a couple of years in the US and like my grandmother went as a volunteer in mission to Egypt and like my grandmother I met my future husband there: Michel Weller.

Later in 1994, after our four children were born, Michel was assigned to teach at the Bible school in Dembi Dollo, while I was a so called 'missionary to the home'. At that time we each had our salary and social security, whereas my mother as a single missionary started with full benefits, then married and became a dependent on her husband. The mission realized that married women were serving without any benefits and their husbands usually died first, so they changed that policy.

When we arrived in Dembi Dollo, we were introduced to the church as Michael Weller and "our daughter, Rachel Vandevort"! The people remembered that my father was a teacher and many men appreciated his wisdom. All the people remembered my mother as one who entered the community, spoke their language, and participated in their life events, such as birth, death, weddings as well as simply being with them in their homes. She was also a good Bible teacher, which she did among the women in their weekly women's "prayer meetings" at each other's homes.

Our oldest child was in grade 4 when we came to Ethiopia. I home schooled our children and was often concerned if they would be able to compete with those who attended school. Like women in the US I wanted to do the household work and to teach our children household responsibilities, but I discovered I had to compromise by hiring a woman to wash our clothes and another one to do the cooking while I taught the children's school. I

---

[122] Red Terror, (Amharic ?? ??? *?äy š?bb?r*) was a violent political repression campaign of the Derg against competing Marxist-Leninist groups. The Qey Shibir most visibly took place after Mengistu Haile Mariam became Chairman of the Derg. It is estimated that 30,000 to 750,000 people were killed over the course of the Qey Shibir. In December 2006, Mengistu was convicted *in absentia* by Ethiopia for his role in the Qey Shibir while leader of the Derg. (Source Wikipedia)

wanted to teach my children also other skills, so they could share in the work at home, e.g. to teach my boys to cook. This did not work out, as they went out in the afternoons and played with their peers. My daughters, however, did not find anyone to play with in the afternoons, as the local girls had to help at their homes after they came home from school. Thus our girls were not able to have friends and they were not to go out because of the trouble they would have got.

It took some years to get to know some local women, which is not different from my experience in the US. Trust builds up slowly. In the first years no one invited me. Our first term was 3 year and then there were 6 months at the end of each term that we were in the US for "Home Assignment". After our second term of 3 years – we were assigned to Dembi Dollo from 1994 to 2001 – we returned to Addis because of the education of our children.

**Question 1:** *What do you think about gender issues?*
I think it is equally a men's as it is a women's issue, women keeping themselves down being as much an issue as men keeping women down. It comes down to the question of respecting people and giving them value.

**Question 2:** *What are you now doing in Ethiopia?*
I am involved in doing Community Health Evangelism in Gambeela. I work together with Ariet Philip, a single mother of one daughter. Ariet is a strong community motivator and a good example among the Anywaa people. The Community Health Evangelism program combines the teaching of ways to improve and maintain good health with the message of the Gospel. In the program both men and women are trained as trainers and workers. One of the lesson-series is about women's health from puberty to old age. Men also appreciate the knowledge saying that they want to understand how to keep their wives healthy for the good of the family and community. Their attitude towards women changes when they learn the facts of biology. Since the lessons to be taught are written, it is necessary for men to be trained because more men than women learn to read.

**Christel Ahrens**

## 2. Chawake Alabe: A woman of great faith

Chawake was also known as Hadhaa Terfa, meaning Terfa's mother, Terfa being the name of her eldest son. She was born in 1923 to Alabe Baroda, who was the son of Ababa Saaba, meaning the father of the multitude. Her grandfather, Ababa Saaba, was a well known qallu, rather a man of knowledge and wisdom than a witchdoctor.

She was raised in Sayyoo district around Dembi Dollo town in a large clan family with a huge amount of land and livestock. Nevertheless the riches and property that her father and grandfather had never went to her head.

When she was a child, there were over forty witchdoctors claiming to be specialized in healing various diseases. People were frequently referred to different witch doctors, who were worshipped, as it was believed that they possessed a special spirit locally known as *Ayyanna*. Each witchdoctor had his own *Ayyanna* which he or she claimed was transferred to him or her from generation to generation.

### Chawake accepted Jesus as her saviour

The village in which Chawake grew up was close to a Presbyterian Mission Station established in Sayyoo district around 1919. She knew about Jesus Christ and the Bible from her childhood.

At the age of eight, just like any other child in her village, she knew about the witch doctors perched on every hill in the area. She observed people roaming around in search of different witchdoctors who took payment for their services in kind.

After she heard about the one God from the first Bible students, she thought it was better to worship one God than to pay tribute to a constellation of forty witchdoctors who were exploiting the communities around Sayyoo.

### Chawake knew the Bible by heart

Chawake had never obtained any formal education; she was practically illiterate and had no idea of numeracy. However, when she was a child her father, who had learnt to read and to write in Amharic and who also spoke some Amharic, had helped her to identify some letters which helped her to read some verses of the Bible written in Oromiffa with Amharic script. She received a Bible on the day of her baptism.

In her house there was a tradition of reading the Bible at the presence of the entire family before supper. Chawake used to assign one of her children to read the Bible out loud. Since supper would only be ready late in the evening the children sometimes omitted some section of the daily reading in order to eat supper quickly. But she knew the entire chapter and would scold the reader and ask him or her to start reading again right from the first verse of the chapter. She always used to say that one is not supposed to use a single Bible verse but to refer to the whole chapter.

## Her church activities

During her life, Chawake paid visits to many churches that were built by community members without any support from the missionaries. She physically supervised and supported the construction of many of the churches.[123] She organized fund raising programmes by women's groups in the church. She travelled by mule into inaccessible areas and strengthened local churches with particular focus on women's associations in each parish church.

Chawake believed in the self reliance of local churches and supported church elders by providing them with refreshments and meals while they were meeting to discuss church affairs. She gave her resources by hosting church elders in her house whenever they came to Dembi Dollo for annual meetings and week long annual spiritual revival conferences.

Being unable to write her sermons, she delivered the gospel to women in newly formed churches straight from her own memory without having to prepare notes. Although she could not read properly, she always carried her Bible with her, which must have been the oldest copy around.

Chawake was always busy building the capacity of local church women, helping them to generate income by providing them with skills in pottery and vegetable gardening on her own plot of land. It is also interesting to

---

[123] More than 85 parish charges were built in this manner.

*Chawake Alabe, courtesy of Arfaasee Gammadaa*

note that she worked on resolving disputes among family members in the neighbourhood of her residence. No husband and wife dared to get into an argument when she was around or in case she was notified of any dispute, whatever the issue might be.

Apart from her service in the church, she served as the chairperson of Sayyoo District Women's Association and worked hard to empower women in her district. She died at the age of 97.

## Personality and family life

Chawake's husband, Dibaabaa Lataa, was a victim of land grabbing during the Italian occupation and Haile Silasee's time and fought for his rights in the courts for over 30 years. He was constantly travelling between Dambii Doolloo, Gimbi, Naqamte and Finfinnee, which cost him a lot of energy, money and time. His struggle and traumatic experiences resulted in him losing his normal and healthy way of life. He became estranged from his wife and children. Finally he won the court case and recovered his land shortly before the Derg came to power in 1974.

Chawake experienced a painful divorce from her husband after her last child, Solomon Dibaba was born. She became a single parent and fought for the survival of her five children: Terfa, Dr. Mamo, Bafikadu, Aster and Solomon. She worked for the American Mission in the kitchen of the blind school[124] in order to ensure the education of her children. When her oldest son decided, against the wish of the school principal, to enrol at secondary school in Gore, Chawake decided to sell her ox so he could go.

As a person, Chawake was very strict in everything she did and required perfect performance from her children, even when they were old enough to handle their personal and family affairs. Whoever lived at home was supposed to get up at 5:30 a.m. and get prepared for the day. She demanded good performance at school and checked the children's notebooks every day. If the teacher put an X on the notebook of any of the boys, she used to say, *"X means wrong and shows the crucifixion of Jesus on the cross and why do you crucify the Lord in your notebook!"* At this point I would like to mention that during that time single mothers were afraid that their children would be insulted as *being raised by a woman*. Therefore, most single mothers were particularly hard on their children.

Aster, her daughter, who had contracted polio – a disease not understood in those days – recalls that the year she failed grade six, her mother pulled her ear and dragged her along the road until they reached a beggar. Then she told her, *"This is what will happen to you, if you don't learn properly."* Aster became a musician and later taught at schools in the United States, an outcome of her mother's determination.

Her oldest son became a teacher at Aira Secondary School and she came to visit him. At that time it was very unusual for a mother to undertake such a long journey just to visit her son.

Her house was always full of young boys and girls who took refuge at her home and went to school through her assistance. The young students in return worked in her house and on her fields. She supported the education

---

[124] Miss Hazel Mc Geary was assigned to Sayyoo in 1947 and started the School for the Blind, the first of its kind in Ethiopia, see Divine Plan unfolding

of girls in particular. She was almost a surrogate mother to girls like Dr Chaltu Deressa in those days.

**Solomon Dibaabaa, her son**

I got to know her as a confident, very active and independent woman. She had a good sense of humour and showed an authority which was rare for women of her age. She was a very religious person. Whenever we would talk on the phone with her, she told us she was praying for us every day and that she would mention each of our names to God. These words are still with us today and therefore she is always with us. When our children had big decisions to make they would always say, 'Our names are with God. Akko, grandmother, said our names to God.'

**Arfaasee Gammadaa, her daughter in law**

## A 'Canaanite woman' in Ethiopia

Chawake became a single mother to her five children. She had the perseverance and faith of the Canaanite woman (Mt 15, 21–28), who argued with Jesus and struggled for the healing of her daughter.

Aster, Chawake's daughter, contracted polio at an early age. It was evident that she would have problems to walk. That was seen by the society as a curse. A disabled person should not go out, as *he or she would fall in front of everyone*. Therefore such people were hidden in their homes, sometimes even neigbours might not know of their existence.

Against the opposition of society and her own family Chawake did not hide her child. On the contrary she was determined to have her daughter educated. She used to quote Empress Menen: *If you educate a boy and not a girl, then it's like looking with one eye*. She had faith that her daughter might become somebody in life.

The school was some distance from their home and Chawake's sons had to carry Aster there and afterwards they had to carry her home again. To do this job in front of others takes a lot of courage from a boy. Aster fell down often and, being gifted with a wonderful sense of humour, she used to laugh whenever that happened. Her intellect and physical skills developed. She was good at playing volleyball.

God is good and equipped her with a musical talent. After her 12th grade she attended Yared Music School and became the first Ethiopian women ever to get a degree in music. She taught music at the American Mission Girls' School and helped organise the first choir group for the church at Gulale.

Later, in the United States she taught music in schools. After many years she and her husband returned to Ethiopia. She is now retired, but never gets tired of cheering up young people with disabilities and encouraging them to go for education. Currently she is teaching basic literacy and numeracy to children from very poor families in Holetta.

Aster recalls her strict upbringing at home and at the church in Dembi Dollo, where Holy Communion was regarded very special and serious. Before receiving Holy Communion people would confess if they had stolen anything and husbands, who had beaten their wives, would confess. *"Sin was sin, there was no mixing. They put the fear of God in us. Lying was impossible."*

Looking back on her life, Aster sees the hand of God in everything. Yes, she is in a wheelchair, but her mind and heart are free. She said she would rather have that than healthy legs and a burdened heart.

**Christel Ahrens**

## 3. Elizabeth Karorsa: Aunt of many

### Childhood in Dembi Dollo

Elizabeth Karorsa (1931–1997) was born as the third child in her family, shortly after the coronation of Emperor Haile Selassie I, whom she would come to know later in life. When she was three months old both parents suddenly passed away in an epidemic.

Elizabeth, her sister Qanatu and her brother Faji were brought up by American missionaries. There were two dormitories at the mission: one with thirty-four girls, half of whom were orphans and the other with fifty boys. As a child she contracted lung tuberculosis. Qanatu said her sister was an outstanding student, strong minded and confident. Elizabeth was offered her first teaching job when twelve years old. With the little money she earned she helped her family and friends.

Dorothy née Russell remembers how she flew with Elizabeth, who was seven years older than herself and whom she considers as her older sister, from Gambeela to Addis Ababa. Elizabeth went to complete her junior high school at the American Mission Girls' School in Gulale. In the plane the passengers were seated along the side of the windows. In the middle of the big gangway cargo for the capital was transported: hides, butter and honey, with bees and sheep; the combined odor made them sick.

## Studies in Addis Ababa and abroad

After finishing high school Elizabeth's first job was that of a teacher at the American Mission Girls' School. In 1954 she got married from the Gulale house of the Russell's, who took the place of parents to Elizabeth. She married Captain Tessama Erenna, who was in the Imperial Body Guard under Haile Selassie and had fought in the Korean War. Their house was open to all young girls and boys to further their education. They believed education was the only way to beat the odds that come one's way.

Elizabeth earned a diploma in education from the University in Addis Ababa and worked for some time for the Commercial Bank of Ethiopia until she was awarded a scholarship in the United States. While pursuing studies in the States, she was disturbed to hear of the imprisonment of her husband, who was suspected of being involved in the coup d'état against Haile Selassie's regime. Because of his imprisonment she returned, stayed in Jimma, where he was kept detained, supported him and took all the necessary steps that later led to his release.

She stayed in Addis and returned to her former job as teacher at the American Mission Girls' School. After some time she was granted another scholarship to the American University in Beirut and obtained a Bachelor's Degree in History.

## Directress at the Bethel MY Girls' School (1960–1977)

After returning from Beirut she became the directress of the Bethel Mekane Yesus Girls' school at Gulale. She improved the school situation by putting

*Elizabeth Karorsa and another teacher at the Girls' School in Gulale*

new buildings and increasing staff and thus prepared the ground to upgrade the school from grade nine to grade twelve.

Jo Ann Griffiths, an American missionary shared her memories of Elizabeth:

*I did consider her as a dear friend.*

*What I remember best was that she was a very competent Directress of the American Mission Girls' School from back in the 1960's. She was the first Ethiopian to serve in that position. I was mainly her 'chauffeur', having a driver's license, and having learned to drive a car when I was a young girl.*

*One hundred girls lived as boarders on the school compound, the fifty younger girls, grades one through four sleeping in one large dorm room on the second floor, where fifty metal framed single beds were placed side by side; the fifty older boarding girls, grades five through eight, were sleeping on the third floor in their fifty metal framed beds. The dining room, where these one hundred girls ate their three daily meals, was on the ground floor.*

*There were very few discipline problems. The emphasis was on studying hard to pass the 8th Grade National Exam which permitted a student to complete her el-*

*ementary education. There were very few failures on this national exam. Those students who wanted to continue their education had very few choices as to where they might attend high school. Many married after they finished the 8th Grade. But some continued into their High School education.*

**Jo Ann Griffiths**

Elizabeth gave helpful orientation and advice to young students, those who came from the rural areas to study in the capital, Terfa Dibaba being one of them. After he finished his 12<sup>th</sup> grade he was planning to join the Imperial Ethiopian Naval Base at Massawa for further education so that he could earn money and support his family. Elizabeth advised him to go and teach at the Secondary School at Aira instead of going to Massawa.

## Contributions to the EECMY

In 1976 Elizabeth was appointed as the first female Church Officer of the EECMY and was a strong promoter of women's issues. She represented the church at national and international meetings, e.g. at the founding meeting of the All Africa Conference of Churches in Ibadan/Nigeria (1958) and meetings in Northern Rhodesia (1962) and Enugu/Nigeria (1965). The meeting in Nigeria was on the cooperation of men and women in church, family and society. Her focus on training women for church responsibilities in Africa received many comments and questions from the group.

Elizabeth as a longtime elder of the Bethel congregation at Addis Ababa organized modernizing and opening the congregation, so that the membership increased. Her role in the process of merging Bethel Presbyterian Church and EECMY in 1974 was important[125].

The Ethiopian Revolution and the military rule changed the life of many people. Many young people were dying, being put in prison or fleeing the country. The government wanted the people to organize themselves in their local communities. They could assign any job, which could not be turned down or else the person would have to pay the price of being put in prison

---

[125] Bethel Qellem Synod and Eastern Synod (Shawa, Illubabor and Kaffa) agreed to seek membership in the EECMY. They retained their historical name Bethel in their name as Synod.

or being killed. Elizabeth was elected in absentia to be the chair person of Gulale Higher 08 Kebele 14. Her life was turned upside down from that time. She received life threatening letters.

## Commitment to justice and equality

During the 1960s and 1970s, Ethiopian people became more involved in the political and social development of their country and started challenging the government. In the early 1970s, many young intellectuals, business people, university lecturers and leaders of the Macha and Tulema Self-Help Cultural Association were arrested by Emperor Haile Sellasie's government. The Macha and Tulema Self-Help Cultural Association was an organisation that attempted to promote Oromo culture, empower poor and marginalized farmers in rural areas, requested land reform and promoted social development but was banned by Haile Sellasie in the late 1960s. The government considered such an organisation as a threat. Elizabeth was chairing this organisation when two of the leading members were detained by the 3$^{rd}$ police station. Haile Faisa, a relative, accompanied her to request their releases:

*We were outside and suddenly saw the car of Haile Selassie passing by towards Gojjam. We decided to wait until the car would come back, as there was no other way to the town. When the car finally came, we signalled from the side of the road to stop. Elizabeth went straight onto the road, but the car passed and stopped after hundred meters. We were allowed to present our request and told to come with a letter to the palace.*

*Elizabeth was well known to the emperor and his cabinet ministers. She went and pleaded with him to release of the young intellectuals. As a result these people were released. Her action made her one of the most respected Christian woman in town.*

## Elizabeth left Ethiopia

When the Derg government came to power, Elizabeth was one of many Christians who were considered to be dangerous to the government. She encountered difficulties with the Derg and politically motivated leaders in the government. Living in Ethiopia was not an option for her any longer.

In 1977 Elizabeth was nominated to represent the EECMY at the LWF Assembly held in Tanzania. After the Assembly she left for good to the United States.

Elizabeth pursued her education and received a Master's degree in education with higher honour from Wichita State University, Kansas in 1980. Two years later she moved to Minneapolis, Minnesota. At that time Dorothy Hanson nee Russell remembers a telephone conversation. Elizabeth mentioned incidentally not having a warm winter coat, a must in that cold and snowy climate of Minneapolis. Dorothy explains: *This reveals her selflessness; others' needs always ahead of her own, never complaining and thus sometimes becoming ill due to her 'weak lung'*.

Elizabeth was employed by the Lutheran Immigration and Refugee Services, an affiliated social service organisation of the Lutheran Churches in America.

## Her witness in the USA

Elizabeth was one of the first Derg-refugees in the US. Many young people came after her also the children of her sister, whom she took care of like a mother and was dearly loved by them. She was one of the driving forces to create a scholarship fund called RESPOND programme that gave a full four years scholarship to sixteen students from Ethiopia.

Elizabeth helped many refugees from Ethiopia, Djibouti and Somalia in the 1980s and 1990s and assisted in their re-settling process in Minneapolis, provided counselling to the new arrivals and orientation to the US system and helped them to adjust to the new places. She was almost a second mother to many refugees in the Minneapolis area.

As a member of Bethany Lutheran Church and an elder she asked her congregation to allow Oromo speaking refugees, who were without a congregation, to worship in the basement of the church. As a result the first Oromo-Speaking Lutheran congregation in the US was established, and many were to follow. The congregations are members of the Evangelical Lutheran Church in America.

Elizabeth was known as Adada (aunt) to people in the United States and was a role model for younger generations of women. She was energetic,

*Painting of Elizabeth Karorsa by her nephew Samuel Daffa*

hard-working, and dedicated to justice and human rights for all people. Her home was a place for refugees and a home for many young immigrants. She was an advisor, a mentor, a marriage counselor, a devoted Christian and an intellectual.

She never came back to Ethiopia, as she had many people to care for in the US. Her husband came for some time to the US, but preferred to live in Ethiopia.

On February 9th, 1997 Elizabeth died surrounded at her hospital bed by her nieces, nephews and friends. She was buried with great honour and dignity in Minneapolis, a place she called her home. Hundreds attended her funeral and burial services. Her loss was felt by many people. Elizabeth was a faithful servant of God to the end.

On February 22, 1997 Rev Itefa Gobena conducted a memorial service for her at the Mekane Yesus Church at Amist Kilo. Pastor Belina gave the sermon, Ato Amanuel Abraham and W/o Tsehaynesh Keneaa the testimonies. In her life Elizabeth had opened the door of opportunity for many in education, women's leadership, and work.

## Memories of relatives and friends

After more than twenty years memories of Elizabeth Karorsa are alive with many people.

Deribe Daffa, her adopted daughter writes about her:
*God was the center of my Mom's life which was shaped and led by God from the very beginning. John 14; 18 was fulfilled in her life: "I will not leave you an orphan, I will come to you." She started life as an orphan and ended up having uncountable friends and families around the world. Even though she did not have a child of her own, she was loved and respected by nieces and nephews who she helped raise.*

*She loved her people and was against any mistreatment. That's why she worked hard to organize and assist her community. At last I want to quote a verse from Proverbs 14:31 "Whoever oppressed a poor man insults His maker. But he who is generous to the needy honors Him." Mom Elizabeth gave her time, experience, love to all that she encountered. She gave it all without any set back. She lived a full life according to God's will without any regret.*

*As a woman, she fought the male dominated society, and showed her country people that women can work side by side with their fellow men without any problem. As a Christian woman her work for her family, community and society around the world reminds me of Esther's life in the Bible. My Mom's mind was as strong as Esther's; her heart was full of love and compassion like Mother Teresa's.*

**Deribe Daffa**


*One of the most faithful, caring, loving, compassionate, astute Christian women, I got to know and admire was the late Elizabeth Karorsa.*

**Dr. Belletech Deressa**


*When I was young, we were eager to meet Elizabeth Karorsa whenever she came to our area. We admired her, because for that time, the 1960s, she was a very self-confident, educated and independent woman.*

**Arfaasee Gammadaa**

*Elizabeth was a strong and courageous woman who fought against injustice and the oppressing system in our country. She was a bold and outspoken person. She did not have the feeling of fear. Because of dirty politics she left and passed away abroad.*

**Rev. Dr Shiferraw Sadi**

*Growing up with her helped me assume that justice is for EVERYONE!*

**Dorothy Hanson, née Russell**

*My own life was blessed by knowing her!*

**Jo Ann Griffiths**

## 4. Negasso Gidada: My heroines

Not many men have written about the role of women in their lives. Dr Negasso Gidada, the son of Rev Gidada Solen and former President of the FDR of Ethiopia (1995–2001), is an exception. In his autobiography he dedicated a chapter to women who had great influence on his life[126]

He begins with his grandmother. My grandmother Awori Areda has shaped my political outlook and my understanding. She made me know the Naftanya's system as she was a victim of the rule. She served the local governor by cutting grass, collecting fire wood, grinding grains and cooking food. The residence of the local governor was at Fincho, about 6 hours on foot from where she lived. She grinded about 50 kg of grain and carried it on her back to the residence of the governor and stayed there for several days cooking and cleaning. After such a hard labor, one day she returned to her children without getting permission. This was discovered by the governor's guards and she was brought back. Then her feet were tied to a pole and she was forced to grind grains in this condition. When I was a boy I heard her complaining that her back was broken and *this feudal system was going to kill her.*

The second woman who influenced me was my mother Dhinsee Shoolii. She reared us alone as our father travelled from place to place for evangelism work. My love for her has never been quenched.

---

[126] Daniel Tefera Jembere, Daandii: Ye Negaso Menged, Commercial Printing Press, Addis Ababa, 2011

*Dhinsee Shoolii and Gidada Solen, the parents of Negasso Gidada*

The third woman is <u>my older sister Rahel</u>. She was very kind to us. Without having enough food for herself she provided for us, her siblings and her own children.

The fourth woman with much space in my life is the mother of my children, Ibsaa and Jaalallee. Her name is <u>Dasituu Qajeelaa</u>. We loved each other and got married. Sadly our marriage did not last long. Nevertheless, she reared our children all alone. It is a very big responsibility. Even if we have separated, I would like to acknowledge her. I always told my children that their mother is a strong woman and they should not irritate and disappoint her. Our communication as friends continued. When she comes to Ethiopia, she visits me. I also visit her when I go to Germany. We forgot the past and now we are very good friends. When my older sister Rahel passed away, she called me from Germany and comforted me and the rest of the family. I appreciate her so much.

Another important woman in my life is my wife Regina. From 1984 onwards my wife Regina and I have been living together. She is my heroine for several reasons.

We began our acquaintance while we were in the struggle, in the Third World House. We were supporting the Oromo movements and each other, too. She was a cashier for the Third World House. She gives full support for human rights and freedom struggles.

In her political outlook, she does not support the idea of political struggle while living abroad. She advised me, the struggle for Oromo people excluding others cannot be successful. Therefore, she said, *It is better if all the people of Ethiopia stand together.*

She strongly advised me to return to Ethiopia. In May 1990 I told her that I am returning to Ethiopia. She agreed without hesitation, and she decided to stay in Germany, work and support our daughter Taliile.

Nevertheless, her decision to come to Ethiopia to live with me was her greatest heroic decision. This decision made me realize the extent to which women live for the one they truly love, and the extent to which they sacrifice for whom they live.

Regina studied medicine in Frankfurt. She wanted to do her internship in Addis Ababa University and to earn her doctorate. Unfortunately, because I was a member of OPDO/EPRDF the Dean, the late Professor Asrat Woldeyes, was not willing to allow her to do so. Thus, she lost one year and could not become a medical doctor. Her dream was cut short. She waited for a year but her request was never accepted and she could not succeed. We were very sorry for such a negative encounter only because of political differences.

Though her educational desire had not been met, she had the idea to continue with midwifery in which she specialized. At that time I was a minister in the Ministry of Information. The surprising thing was all wives of the ministers got the opportunity to choose what they liked and were offered jobs, while Regina was denied to work in her field of study.

Later on, she got a job at Bekilo Bet, Woreda 18, Health Station and was employed at the same level as Ethiopians. However, I did not allow her to use government's vehicle and she had to push and pull with the public to get the taxi to her work place. Nevertheless, she never complained.

When we moved to the palace, she did not want to become First Lady. She did not like such things as protocol of the First Lady. What she wanted was just to work. In my position as a President, I tried to get her a decent job but I could not succeed.

She had interest to work on women and street children issues. Thus, she contacted UNICEF through Ministry of Labor and Social Affairs in Addis Ababa, and started to support the needy on voluntary basis.

The difference between me and her is I spend my time on politics while she devoted most of her time on tangible and specific issues. She has the opinion that changing the life of an individual contributes to the betterment of the life of other people and also that of the country. She focused on such issues immensely.

After we left the palace, the harsh measures taken against me had negative impact on her and our daughter, Taliile. It irritated me so much. She was irritated as well. Specially, when the authorities told us to leave the house; their disrespect and harassment had bad psychological impact on both of us.

After 2004, until she got employment with one private health institution we were in a very big financial problem, but she stood firm. My beloved wife, Regina, who stood by my side at the time of happiness and sorrow is one of those unsung heroine women.

Some people question how the *Faranji* (white woman) could bear this situation. Her culture and socialization is different from ours. However, she sees Ethiopia like her country and we are living together here. She does not like to be called *Faranji*. She cares for all my relatives and their children who live with us, considering them as her family.

She supported me immensely to have a strong political stand. She supported me by giving ideas and encouragement. When I faced financial problems, she provided for me. She lives with me in my hard situation without complaint. She shares my life and makes life simpler for me.

Currently, she drives me to Andinet party office. Every morning she drives me up to Kabana, drops me on the new asphalt road and goes to her work. The road to my office is gravel and stony, difficult to walk or drive on. She was of great help to me in this regard.

As far as dispute between us is concerned, I do not remember if we had any between us. We discuss issues and we accommodate each other, when we face problems. If I make a mistake, she tells me calmly, corrects and advises me. When it seems necessary she harshly tells me because she does not want to see me failing. The life we passed through in the 1990s was full of temptations. If she was not strong enough, I could have faced many problems. Bearing all these problems is her great strength. Great Heroine!!!

# Swedish Mission: Naqamte (1923) and Nedjo (1927)

Bodji was the place where the gospel brought by Christians from Eritrea first took roots (1898). The commitment and support of Fit'awrari[127] Dibaba Bakare was invaluable. Wuba Zenneb was the first person to introduce basic modern health care at Bodji.

*Wuba Zenneb, the wife of Gebre-Yesus Tesfai had been raised in the home of Dr and Mrs. Winqvist and had assisted them in giving relief to the sick in the refugee camps around Imkullu. Wuba practiced at Bodji what she learnt from the Winqvists. She dressed all kinds of wounds, dispensed quinine to combat malaria, daubed sore eyes with ointments and soothed pain by means of sedatives. She was fortunate to have her supply of drugs and medicines replenished from time to time by Cederqvist's store in Addis Ababa. All medical service was free of charge. Moreover, it was given with loving hands. Persons who knew Wuba and Gebre-Yesus praised their generosity and their concern. No wonder that they won the hearts of people.[128]*

## Start at Naqamte[129]

The first Swedish missionaries to reach Wollega were the Söderströms: Dr Erik with his wife Gusti and his sister Karin Söderström, both experienced nurses. They replaced Dr. Lambie in Dembi Dollo hospital for some months and afterwards established a mission station in Naqamte (1923). The clinic they opened was inadequate in relation to the massive demand for various health problems, a hospital needed to be constructed.

## Friendship replaces enmity at Nedjo

Some years later, in 1927, a large caravan left from Naqamte to Nedjo. The local chief had repeatedly invited the SEM to build a mission station at Nedjo. The caravan company consisted of Rev Martin Nordfeldt,

---

[127] Military title, Commander of the Vanguard
[128] Arén 1999, 96–97
[129] Arén 1999, 292—295, 305—311, 316 ff

his wife Ingeborg Nordtfeld with their daughter, a nurse named Hilma Olsson, Feben Hirphe and Bushan Siba. They had sixty-five mules loaded with equipment for the new mission station and thirty porters were carrying luggage.

Their arrival at Nedjo revived an old enmity. The establishment of a mission station nearby was in itself enough to cause alarm, but the employment of Gammachis Onesimos, the *heretic's son*, as teacher, was too much. Aleka[130] Qeleme-Work in his advanced age went to Naqamte to complain and chase them away. However, time and government had changed and the governor advised him to return home and end his days in peace. The old man took the advice to heart.

The morning after his return to Nedjo he sent a letter to the three Swedes with an invitation for dinner at his house the same day. These could not help but wonder how to interpret such an invitation. Smiling pleasantly, Aleka Qeleme-Work received the missionaries at the gate of his courtyard, sent for carpets and chairs from the church and seated his guests besides himself and his wife around the same table. All five took the food which the hostess had prepared in great haste. After the meal he solemnly announced that he wished all of them to be friends. The missionaries could hardly believe their ears but agreed heartily.

Small gifts of milk, coffee, grain, or bananas were now and then sent to the mission station in promotion of this fellowship. The new friendly relations at Nedjo also positively affected the situation at Bodji, where the recently completed church was converted into a school on weekdays.

The Nordfeldts pursued their work of preaching and teaching and Sister Hilma took care of the sick in a tent which served as dispensary and clinic. There was no lack of patients. From the very first day a large crowd came to seek help for their various ailments. Within a few months they built facilities for proper treatment. Medical care constituted an important part of the work at Nedjo.

At the same time they erected one building after another. Within a few years mission stations with residence, church, school and clinic were built

---

[130]  Alaqa is the title of the head of the Orthodox priests

at Nedjo and Bodji and eucalyptus trees were planted to surround the future mission compound in Mendi.

In 1930 the chapel in Nedjo was inaugurated although the interior was not yet completed. Three months later a 100 kilo church bell began to summon the people to gather for worship. Everybody marvelled at its sound.

Onesimos visited Nedjo in 1930 and praised God from the depth of his heart for the joy he experienced when he saw what was going on at the place that he had been forced to leave twenty-five years earlier and where his son Gammachis was now a teacher.

# 1. Hilma Olsson: She risked her life to rescue many

The Norwegian adventurer and 'gold-digger' William Avenstrup happened to write in his book: Gjennom Ethiopia's jungle (Through Ethiopia's Jungle), published in 1935, about an encounter with Hilma Olsson. Avenstrup had travelled with his European colleague from Addis Ababa to the area of Assosa, a walking distance of 700 km. Their caravan consisted of 47 well loaded mules plus a large number of porters and helpers.

They were close to Addis Alem, when they met two women: Hilma Olsson was *just going to Nedjo* ... with 440 km of distance still ahead, including the difficult road through the Didessa Valley. The adventurer wrote about their trip and arrival at Nedjo:

## Leading a caravan with drugs and church windows

*A small handsome fair-haired lady in a riding suit came towards me, smiling all over her face. She was a young Swedish woman, going the same way as we. Her name was Hilma Olsson. She told us that she was working for the Swedish Mission as a nurse for the people in the area. She was accompanied by a young Danish woman who was going to serve as a teacher for the little children at the station in Naqamte.*

*With great pleasure we could offer to be the ladies companions and guards during the journey through the jungle. The nurse had twenty mules packed with drugs and windows for the new Swedish chapel at Nedjo. Hilma managed the drivers and mules like a man. The teacher, however, was unfamiliar with the hardships and sometimes was crying over them. She found the world too heavy and suffered even because of that.*

*Sr Hilma Olsson, courtesy of EFS Archive*

Twenty days later William Avenstrup wrote:

*We could now see Nedjo at a distance. I saw a crowd of people gathered at the city's entrance. They were so beautifully dressed in pure white robes and each of them with a little book in their hands. 'They are my friends,' the nurse said, 'they are here to receive me!' We were two days late, her 'friends' probably slept there in order to show their love and joy of having her back again. I rode beside her towards the group of about thirty people who reverently stood and sang from their hymnbooks. I took off my helmet and was deeply moved during the hymn singing. I saw from that day, that she was more than only a human nurse. I thought essentially that she just lacked wings to fly right to heaven.*

*After she had greeted everybody, they went in a procession in front of us through the town and over to the Swedish church where we were received by Rev Nordfeldt and his wife. Getting to them was for us to come home. Their eyes were shining with goodness, and they did not know all the good they would do for us.*

*We were there for two days and arranged our camp next to the residence of the Nordfeldts. During these days I came to know the pastor as a person whom the fine Swedish nation can be proud of. He is the station manager; he is counselor, physician, builder and everything else – all to perfection. His wife helps him to teach the little children and has daily fifty of them to teach in their own language. Pastor Nordfeldt himself built both the church and its rectory, and prettier constructions can no trained professional person make at home.'* [131]

## The first clinic and the service of Sr. Hilma

In his book[132] Rev Gammachuu Danuu gives insights into the history of the first clinic in Nedjo:

*It was a time of darkness and ignorance when the Swedish missionaries arrived. People were suffering from various kinds of communicable diseases such as typhus, syphilis, small pox and gonorrhea. The typhus cases were kept separately in small huts; any direct contact was forbidden, to avoid transmission. Sometimes typhus killed all the villagers and the village became desolate. Since the people were so fearful of contracting the disease they did not dare bury their dead themselves, but paid people to do so for them.*

*When the lives of the people were at stake, Sr. Hilma was sent by the SEM to treat them. She started treating the patients at their camp (in a tent) and under a big tree and in the shadow of the houses until a clinic was built.*

*Sr. Hilma, a professional nurse and midwife, was not only working at Nedjo clinic. She trained people and employed women and men who could assist her to treat the patients at the clinic. Out of the two employees, one would stay at the clinic to work, while the second one was going out with her to treat people in different stations in Nedjo town. Out of Nedjo town, she had different sites and contact persons where she was regularly going to give health services.*

*Sr. Hilma was a very kind person who cared for the patients. She was speaking the Oromoo language fluently. For this she was loved by the people. The people were calling her 'Giiftii Hilma' which means 'Madam Hilma'. The people communicated with her like they do with their own mother.*

---

[131] Austgulen, Johannes: Ethiopia, Experiences and Challenges, BOD, 14–15

[132] Gammachuu Danuu: How did we get the Gospel of Christ? YDCS PMD, Addis Ababa, 2012

Due to the Italian occupation of Ethiopia, the SEM was forced to stop its mission engagement for ten years. Sr. Hilma had trained Jootee Gammachuu and Waqwayyaa Dhinsaa for the health service in the clinic. These two men treated the patients with love and care during her absence.

In 1946 Sr Hilma returned to Nedjo and resumed the health work. While she was treating the patients at Nedjo clinic, she gained a full knowledge of the local health problems. She approached the patients with love and friendly manner, like a mother treating her children. Sr Hilma finished her service in 1956 and returned to her home country. In 1970 she visited Nedjo and died soon after she had returned back to Sweden.

When the death of Sr Hilma was heard in Nedjo, the congregation conducted a memorial service in remembrance of her devoted service. When there was no road and telecommunication, she took the risk of treating and rescuing the lives of many people.[133]

Medical care constituted an important part of the Evangelical mission at Nedjo and other places in the west of Ethiopia. Sr Hilma stands for dozens of nurses, midwives and doctors and other health professionals who came after her from Sweden, America, Germany and Norway to serve and heal the sick.

### A new spirit in Naqamte: Ecumenical Easter Celebrations

Naqamte, the town where Onesimos, Lidia and Aster served for many decades, also received Swedish missionaries. Since Ras Teferi came to power, Western type education and medical care were welcomed by the new government and considered essential for the modernization and development of Ethiopia.

In Wollega the two mission stations at Nedjo and Naqamte provided medical and educational work. That helped remove previous obstacles, befriended leading clergy and paved the way for the continued proclamation of the gospel.

At Naqamte the Söderstöms and other missionaries were anxious to be on good terms with the Orthodox clergy in town. When Qeddest Mariam church celebrated her annual festival, they took their students along and

---

[133] Ibid p 78–79; 96–97

witnessed the celebrations. Shortly afterwards the Evangelical Congregation resolved to follow the Ethiopian calendar in respect of church festivals. On Easter Eve the two Swedes appeared at Qeddest Mariam at 9 p.m. and remained until the jubilant finale at 1.30 am on Easter morning. Their attendance was much appreciated. Dajjazmach Habte-Mariam offered his own chair with velvet tapestry and seated himself on the floor.

The Italian invasion interrupted the service of the Swedish missionaries and Evangelical Christians went underground, hiding their precious Bibles.

After World War II ended, missionaries returned. The hospital work continued, school restarted and orphans were taken care of. One of them was Tsehay Tolassa, who became known beyond Ethiopia because of her imprisonment. Thousands of supporters of Amnesty International pleaded for her release

## 2. Tsehay Tolassa: God in the midst of suffering

*To meet Tsehay was to encounter a tall, upright and attractive woman, even after her more-than-ten-year detainment in prison. When asked about it, she gladly told that God is a living God who keeps his promises and who was present during the whole time of her need.* (Aud Saeveras).

Tsehay told her story to Aud Saeveras after her release from prison. Her books were printed In Norway and Germany in 1992 and 1993.[134]

An English version was published in 2017 with revision and updating by Leensa Gudina: In the Fiery Furnace.[135]

### Childhood in Naqamte

Tsehay Tolassa was born 1931 near Naqamte into a well-to-do family that employed many servants. Everyone lived together in a big hut. The father was a farmer and had cattle and mules to transport goods. Tsehay's world was the market place. For her the future looked full of promise.

---

[134] Saeveras, Aud: Der lange Schatten der Macht, Augenzeugenberichte, Tsehay Tolassa and Gudina Tumsa, Giessen/Basel, 1993

[135] Samuel Yonas Deressa, ed.: The Life, Works, and Witness of Tsehay Tolassa and Gudina Tumsa, Lutheran Quarterly Books, 15 Jun 2017, Part II Tsehay Tolassa's Story, In the fiery furnace, p 133–230

In Naqamte, many people felt oppressed and discriminated against, since their land was ruled by the Amhara and people were not allowed to use their own languages in written form. When Tsehay was five years old the Italians conquered Naqamte. The Ethiopians put up fierce resistance and the Italians responded with brutal violence. They took what they wanted and the belongings of the Ethiopian population disappeared.

Tsehay's father was forced to transport goods for the occupying forces. Upon discovering that he had unknowingly transported grenades for them he refused to work for the Italians any longer. Soon afterwards he died.

A very hard time began. Tsehay's mother had to be mother and father for their children. Her oldest sister was given in marriage at just 14 years old. When the Italians had to pull out of Ethiopia they set huge areas on fire and the hut of Tsehay's mother was burnt down. Tsehay recalls:

*Sometimes I dream of that day. I see the terrible flames and the poor people who still were in their huts, who didn't have the chance to get out. We had to hide in the wilderness and then lived for three years in a simple hut. My mother took in two children who had lost their family. We always lived in fear of being captured by slave hunters[136].*

Then the children were abducted and robbers stole everything. Tsehay and her younger brother were left behind, because they were too small to keep up with the tempo. That was their salvation. Then a typhus epidemic struck. In every house there was death. The village was in despair.

*We children also got sick. Mother, who had no strength at all died very quickly. In the end we were brought to the mission hospital in Naqamte. We got a place in the school dormitory.*

*The Swedish missionary women cared with exceptional affection like a mother. They sang Christian songs with me about Jesus. In their home I got to know God.*

*When I look back to it now, how God has led me through life, I recognize how much good he has done.[137]*

Tsehay went to school for six years. She learnt easily and loved school. After finishing she got work in a home for orphaned children from the hos-

---

136  Samuel Yonas Deressa, 146
137  Samuel Yonas Deressa, 149–150

pital. Tsehay gave them all the care that she had experienced from her own mother and later from the missionaries in Naqamte.

## Married to Gudina Tumsa

The tall beautiful young woman met an even taller young man, exactly two meters tall: Gudina Tumsa. He was trained as a surgeon's assistant at Naqamte Hospital. It was love at first sight. They got married. A year went by and their first child was born. The birth was difficult and took three days. Her husband was not at home. He was on the road, evangelizing, as he did every free moment. Their son developed well, but one day he inhaled a dry grain of corn and it got stuck in his throat. The parents rushed to Addis Ababa hospital with him. The operation went well but on the fifth day he suffocated and died.

*The trip back lasted a day and a night. Our neighbours and friends came to meet us. They came to mourn with us. It was hard to lose sweet little Emmanuel. The path from the greatest happiness to the greatest grief was so short. ... When things are going well and we don't have any pressing need to seek for God's presence, we think about him only now and then. But in this situation Gudina and I experienced God near to us and accompanying us*[138].

Like Hannah in the Old Testament, Tsehay had made a promise to God: She had wanted her son to become a pastor. Now he was dead and would not become a pastor – therefore Gudina had to become a pastor in his place, even if people in Ethiopia said a pastor was as worthless as a woman.

*"You have to" I said, "You must become a pastor. I have made a promise already three years ago." We began to pray to find out whether there was a call from God for Gudina. Ten months later I had another child, a little girl we named Kulani. And then Gudina received a call. The church asked him to become a pastor. It was the answer to our prayers, the confirmation of a calling, which God had first laid upon me. Yes – it was, after all, God's will.*[139]

The theological training was at Nedjo, where they lived for two and a half years. She remembers:

---

[138] Samuel Yonas Deressa, 158
[139] Samuel Yonas Deressa, 158

*We had sixty Birr each month to live on. That had to cover everything – and it was hard. But God's goodness is great – and we had it good together. Gudina always showed love and concern and whenever he did get angry it never lasted more than five minutes before he came and apologized.*

*In Ethiopian families, it is quite common for a husband to hit his wife and even drive her out of the house whenever he is dissatisfied with her. It was never like that between us – our house was always a house of peace. We made it cosy for ourselves, told nice stories, and laughed a lot together. We read a lot in God's word and often prayed together. Yes, we had a really happy marriage.*[140]

For three years Gudina served the church in Naqamte. He wanted a young member of the congregation to be elected as a representative. It was unthinkable that a young person should be elected to that position. That caused trouble. Gudina shook the whole system. The church arranged that he should leave and go to work as an evangelist in Kambata. Someone else was appointed to Naqamte, and Gudina said: "Good, if they can get peace this way, it will be alright with me".

## Serving together at Kambata

Kambata is in the south of Ethiopia. Gudina preached and taught in Amharic and a Kambata man accompanied him as translator. The family was separated as Tsehay stayed with their children in Naqamte. However, for six months Tsehay accompanied her husband. She did not see her children during that time, travelling being too expensive.

*But it was good for us to be together... We went around on foot and sometimes on mules. When evening came, we stopped in a hut, where the neighbors began to gather to receive their guests... We experienced once again how people accepted the message. The joy that we had there was so great, that it made all troubles worthwhile.*

*In that area there are two big ethnic groups, the Hadiya and the Kambata. They were always in conflict with each other. Gudina took a lot of time to mediate between the two groups. In this way also he was able to preach the gospel and reconcile them.*[141]

---

[140] Samuel Yonas Deressa, 160
[141] Samuel Yonas Deressa, 165

## Derg time

The time of the Red Terror was a time of great fear. The regime struck like lightning out of the clear sky. Almost every family was affected; everyone lived in constant fear for their loved ones. If someone's homecoming from work was delayed, the family was terribly worried.

People used the new system to get rid of people they hated. You could just denounce someone as an enemy of the revolution. Countless people, young and old alike, disappeared and were never found again. Others were discovered to have been executed in beastly ways – they were trying to save on gun powder, since it was expensive. And you were not allowed to mourn the dead! In that way, they would have proven that you supported an enemy of the revolution and thus were yourself against the revolution.

The situation was especially bad for young Christians. They couldn't consent to the motto of the revolution: to honour Ethiopia as their reason for living, to deny the existence of God. Many Christian youth did not want to put anything in the place of God, including Ethiopia. In an attempt to force them to reject their faith they were detained in camps. Terrible things happened in many of the camps. The persecutions were pitiless and cruel.

*But God carried us through all these trials. He never promised us an easy life. Quite on the contrary, he said that we must reckon with persecutions and problems. They are constant companions for God's people. But it is unbelievable how much power God gives us so we can bear it. We can only thank him and praise his name.*
*...*

*Sometimes I think: Why did Gudina have to go through all that? Why did all that have to happen? But those are not good thoughts. When we lost our house, this thought came to me also. Weren't you able to help us, God? I ask God forgiveness for these thoughts. For I know better now: everything that happens is in accord with his good will, is of value for his kingdom.*[142]

## Arrested and Tortured

On 28th July 1979 Rev Gudina Tumsa, president of the Mekane Yesus Addis Ababa Synod and General Secretary of the EECMY was arrested in the

---

[142] Samuel Yonas Deressa, 187–188

evening when he and his wife were on their way home from church. It was the third arrest.

One month earlier he was offered the chance to leave Ethiopia with the help of President Nyerere. Gudina replied that he had always advised his pastors not to leave their work, and therefore he could not leave the country. His church and his congregation were in Ethiopia. He never would escape. He quoted 2. Cor. 5, 15: *Christ died for all men so that those who live should no longer live for themselves, but only for him who died and was raised to life.* Gudina pointed to Tsehay saying if anything should happen to him, Rev. Christian Krause[143] should consider her as his wife and Gudina's children as his children.

It took years to find out that he was killed the night of his arrest, one night after Patriarch Tewoflos of the Ethiopian Orthodox church and others had been killed by order of the Derg.

On February 2nd, 1980 – half a year after Gudina disappeared – Tsehay was arrested. On the following day she was tortured. It is too painful to write down or even read the details of the torture. After three months she started to improve. Her wounds were never tended to; there was no medicine and no relief.

They drove her to the Third Police Station, a place known for torturing prisoners. The torturers were incredible cruel. Nobody who was brought there could realistically expect to come out alive. Death hovered over everything.

*They brought me into a small room. There were 62 of us crammed in there. We could only stand, there was nowhere to sit, no room for sleeping. And all that with my battered bones! We lived day and night in the dark; without air and in extremely primitive conditions. If a family brought a mattress, the guards soon took it away again. The strongest prisoners stole from the weakest ones. Only much later did I got a mattress to lie on.*

*I believe it was May when they took me and tortured me for the second time . . . This time it was even worse than before. The skin that had healed split open again. The nightmare began anew . . . I got nothing to clean myself with. My body burned*

---

[143] Rev. Christian Krause then from the Lutheran Church in Hannover, Germany was much concerned to get Gudina out of Ethiopia and later played important role for the EECMY under the difficult time of Derg.

*Tsehay Tolassa three days before her detention in 1980*

*as if I had a fever. Again the others cried when they saw me. For a long, long time I was afraid to drink anything in case I had to go to the toilet, because I never would have made it. Once again I couldn't walk.*

*After this I never recovered. Since the torture, my kidneys have never worked again properly.*

*I would always remember the word of God, the Scripture which I had listened to so many times before. One verse especially gave me strength: Behold, the Lamb of God who takes away the sin of the world. And the song that I knew came into my mind: What a Friend We Have in Jesus. He accompanied me while I lived under the shadow of power.*[144]

From time to time Tsehay was interrogated, but she never got a sentence. At first she was asked for the whereabouts of Gudina and about the work of the synods. They asked for the money they got for selling their house. She told them they had sold it to pay back a loan to the church, as Gudina wanted to have all their affairs in order. Before her second torture they shouted: 'Tsehay, go ahead and pray to your Jesus!' and 'Won't he come and help you, your little Jesus?'

*They accused me not only because of my Christian faith. I was also accused of having worked to undermine the government. They could call it what they wanted. Before I came to jail, I didn't know what politics was. But I had tried to live as a Christian. And as a Christian I had to try to help everyone. As Christians we believe that all people are equal, whether they were Amhara or Oromo. If everyone is equal before God, then our duty is to help people, no matter which ethnic group they belonged to. Actually that should have fit perfectly well with the ideals of the revolution, but in practice it wasn't so.*

*To be a Christian has consequences in everyday life. And they can use the name of 'Christian' to label you as a criminal. My sin against the government was basically only that I was a Christian accountable to God alone, not to human beings*[145].

For a year and a half Tsehay lived in the 3$^{rd}$ Police Station. Despite everything she had luck. Almost no one got out from there alive and her survival was a miracle. In March 1981, Tsehay was transferred to the central prison near the OAU headquarters, where conditions were better. Martha Kumsa,

---

[144] Samuel Yonas Deressa, 195–196
[145] Samuel Yonas Deressa, 198

the age of her daughter and a dear friend, was there too. Her father was among the Evangelical pioneers in Wollega. The sixty other prisoners were mostly thieves and murderers.

Tsehay was able to greet visitors over the fence which were one and a half meter apart, and could exchange words with them. Female guards, constantly moving in the space between the two fences, handed over the articles brought, and listened to the conversations between the imprisoned and the visitors. Under such conditions she lived more than eight years.

Near the end of her imprisonment Tsehay was permitted to go to hospital in town for medical reasons accompanied by one or more police women. Even visits in homes of expatriate missionaries were arranged on short notice.

During a longer stay at the ALERT Hospital, direct contacts were possible and short devotions and prayers were held. Tsehay later stated that for her the time at ALERT was a *recreation for her soul*, and noted that friends from far away countries had visited her, while Addis Ababa residents did not come. They were afraid, since such visits were not without risk[146].

## The gospel in the prison

Tsehay said that God sent her friends from many countries to care for her and keep her alive.

*You came with food to the prison, so that I wouldn't have to go hungry. You brought yarn so that I had something to do. You came with clothing so I wouldn't be cold. You were the hand of God for me; did you know that? Oh, God's hand is longer than the long shadow of power. It reaches as far as God wants it to. What would I have had to eat if you had not brought me food?[147]*

Tsehay was regularly visited especially by expatriate friends and received baskets filled with food and handicraft materials. Tsehay used the materials to motivate despairing prisoners to work. In this way many women learnt to do handicraft and so fill up their endless days and they earned some money. The handicrafts were sold at the women's parish bazaar. What Tsehay sent out of the prison made an impression on the Mekane Yesus churches.

---

[146] Launhardt, p 252–254
[147] Samuel Yonas Deressa, 213

In the baskets that came with visitors during visiting time on Sundays, Bibles were hidden between the foodstuff and yarns so that they could be smuggled into the prison. Tsehay always needed new Bibles. Many prisoners wanted to read the Word of God. To distribute Bibles was forbidden in all of Ethiopia. Each time the baskets were searched thoroughly. It was dangerous and risky for Tsehay's friends to bring Bibles. Other Christians prayed during the visiting hours and the remarkable thing was that despite the most careful searches, no Bibles were ever discovered.

*Once the guards came and searched through everything. There lay a heap of Bibles next to me. I prayed to God that he would make the guards blind so the guards would overlook the Bibles. And they found nothing.*

*Is God not a God of miracles? He is the one who carries us through. He led the people of Israel through the Red Sea. He made its water into walls. They passed through. Exactly the same happened with my Bibles. God held his hand before their eyes. Everyone else's stuff, every bit of it, was all messed up. My things were not once touched. God never tires.*[148]

*Despite this we were afraid. When someone dies, you are afraid.*

*I saw people around me could not sleep. They were doubled up with fear. God's people, even when they cannot sleep, perceive that God stands by them and gives them his peace in the midst of all the fear.*

*That is the unbelievable difference between those who believe in God and those who don't. We live differently. They simply don't believe that someone wants to do them a good turn, that we want to do them good because we believe in God. They refuse to accept it from us.*

*But I have seen how they observe us and that, by and by, they realize that it really is so. Finally they listen to our words. After a certain time they ask for a Bible to read. They want to become Christians . . . .*

*I proclaimed the gospel the whole time I was in prison. That was forbidden, but they saw that I prayed anyway. Then the other prisoners came who said: Pray for us . . .*

*On Sundays I had contact with the emperor's family, who were imprisoned in a room of their own. Before they were thrown into the prison they had not cared*

---

[148] Samuel Yonas Deressa, 210–211

*much for the gospel. They still belonged to the Orthodox Church, but they wanted to pray with an Evangelical Christian.*[149]

## Finally free: 'I will give you a spacious compound, where you will reside!'

Leensa, Tsehay's youngest daughter, reports:

*The worst of it all – mother said – was that no sleep came to her eyes for the first 21 days after the first beating. On the 21st night she couldn't stop crying and murmured to herself that she was going to die there and that no one would ever find out what had happened. As she uttered those words she fell asleep and saw Jesus coming towards her saying: 'Do not be afraid, you shall not die here.' He took her by the hand to show her how he was going to bring her out of prison in due time. He said: 'You should pass through four gates to get out of prison, and afterwards I will give you a spacious compound, where you will reside.' After that encounter she had no more sleepless nights. Her hopes were renewed.*[150]

Ten years passed before the promise came true. On the day of her release from prison[151] she thought of the dark and gloomy dungeon where she saw the extraordinary figure of Christ. As she walked out to freedom and new life, she began to count the gates. When she stepped out of the fourth, she knew: *Now I am finally free.*

The fulfillment of the second half of Christ's words, spoken to mother in the prison cell, took another fourteen years. When she entered the 'promised compound', she vowed to set up a church right there to serve and honour him who answered her in the days of her distress, who never forsook her as she walked through the valleys of the shadows of death.

Biftu Bole Mekane Yesus congregation came as a reward for the long suffering and grief, wounds and bruises, widowhood and loneliness, loss and humiliation. Gudina Tumsa was in his eternal home; on October 12, 2014 Tsehay Tolassa joined him. The passion and selflessness with which

---

[149] Samuel Yonas Deressa, 214
[150] Samuel Yonas Deressa, 135 ff
[151] Commemorating the 15th anniversary of deposing Emperor Haile Selassie the new leaders declared an amnesty for 907 prisoners. On September 2nd 1989 Tsehay Tolassa and others were released from prison.

God endowed them – passion to take the gospel to all peoples suffering under the bondage of the evil one, passion to reach out to the poor and downtrodden, passion to bring the message of hope to the despairing millions – continues to thrive through the Gudina Tumsa Foundation and the Biftu Bole congregation.

### Her spiritual legacy

Tsehay often spoke about the book of Daniel. In the book God allows three young men to be thrown into the fiery furnace. But the fire did not burn them. In the midst of flames, God was with them. So many times she herself has been 'thrown into the fiery furnace' but God's hand was always there protecting her.

## 3. Lydia Larsson: 'We understood that we liked each other'

### A tough start in life

Lydia, the second youngest of six sisters, was born in 1913 and grew up in a small cottage in Sweden. At the age of five she lost her mother and *life became different*. The two oldest sisters had to start working to contribute to the family's livelihood.

When Lydia was 15 years old, her father also died, and the siblings had to support themselves by looking for work in different directions. Lydia was employed as a maid in Stockholm.

### The call and preparation for mission work

During her years in Stockholm, she attended services and Bible studies in the Bethlehem Church. The relationship with the congregation inspired her to join a Bible Institute where she had time to study her Bible and also learnt about mission work in different parts of the world.

Lydia was touched by the stories of suffering children and women and was very concerned about their pain and hardship. She shared her concern with fellow students and teachers. In her prayers she asked God what He wanted with her life.

After a period of inner struggle and reflection she was filled with a deep desire to make Jesus' love visible to the poor and weak. She was convinced that she wanted to serve as a missionary.

A long and thorough period of study and preparation began. First she spent three years at the nursing school, followed by a course in midwifery and finally a period of language studies in England.

On November 9, 1946, she was committed as a missionary for work in Ethiopia. She travelled from Addis Ababa to Mendi in the western part of the country. The 600 km journey was full of challenges. In the 1950s the road network was not developed and the availability of cars was limited. The trip took several days – first by truck, then by mule and on foot.

Lydia contributed an article about her work in a Swedish book by Dr Fride-Hylander in 1960:

## In place of a doctor – Serving the Great Physician

*To come almost empty-handed to a populous and remote district in place of a doctor, and not being able to ask any doctor to come and help, that fell to my lot.*

*Patients here have no other means of travelling than to sit on mule back for many days or a week to go to the nearest hospital. A feverish patient cannot travel in the scorching heat of the sun. And in the rainy season there is the risk of getting stuck in a muddy riverside. The grim reality is that most of the sick have no other option than to suffer without help, and to die, or to visit a witch-doctor. Those "doctors" use threat, superstition and blackmail as their methods of work.*

*In 1947 I came to Mendi for the first time. On the plot of land that was set aside for a clinic, there was only one tree. I started medical work in a tent under that tree.*

*In the mornings, my assistant Tareffa conducted morning devotion for the patients. Patients who came waited under a grass roof until they were examined in the tent. As I was a new-comer I did not understand the language, Oromo. By using the Amharic language and a kind of sign language, and an interpreter, I tried to diagnose the patients and give treatment to the best of my knowledge and conscience. Malaria, syphilis and horrible eye inflammations and tropical wounds on legs were common.*

*One morning, Abba Marga, the night guard for the mission station, came and asked for an advanced payment of his salary. What was the reason? Abba Marga looked very troubled when he told me that his oldest son was going to die. He was unconscious and the father had to buy a coffin for the funeral. I told the father to bring his son to the clinic. I felt very helpless. What could I do? But I felt the presence of the Great Physician and prayed for help. Could it perhaps be relapsing fever? I gave him an injection to stimulate his body. There was no place for the boy at the clinic, so the father had to carry him back to their home. Next morning I gave a new injection. On the following day the father was back with his son and said: "He was dead, but now he is alive." I was so grateful. It was great to be there and serve the Great Physician, the Wonderful Lord Jesus.*

*After one year of medical work in the tent a new clinic was ready. After some years, the earthen floor was replaced with cement slabs. A small hut was built, where patients could stay when needed.*

*A few years later, the chief judge in Mendi visited us. Secretly he had organized a collection of money to help build a better clinic. This new clinic, being the largest building in this area, was also used as a church. Orthodox Christians, Muslims and Evangelical Christians, all came and filled the 'church'. Many of those who came had been ill and got help from the clinic. But even others, who did not like our work, had given ten Birr each to the building. The money was handed over to the mission pastor. It was more than the equivalent of 1 600 Swedish Crowns.*

*Oh, this terrible malaria! Dr Fride Hylander says that in the year 1958, 250,000 persons died from malaria in the country.*

*We have had many improvements at the Mendi station. The microscope helps us to make diagnoses. We have electric light and a pump gives us water from the small stream at the base of the hill on which the mission station is built. I love this little clinic building and the patients and my work. Sometimes, however, I feel exhausted. But we serve the Great Physician. He has said that we can call for his help in time of difficulties*

*Now I am alone on the station. The Hansson family left for Addis Ababa, for vacation and the conference for the missionaries and for purchasing what is needed for the missionaries and the station.* [152]

Mendi was not the only place where Lydia lived and worked. She also worked at Nedjo, Bodji and Naqamte, to name some of the places.

---

[152] This text is a short version in English written by Eskil Forslund and based on Lydia Larsson's article, "In place of a doctor", in the Swedish book (Bortom Bergen), "Beyond the Mountains", 1960, Dr Fride Hylander (ed.), Stockholm, used by permission of Nils-Olov Hylander, son of Fride Hylander.

*Lydia Larsson on an outreach trip, courtesy of Nils-Olov Hylander*

Compassion for the weak and the sick characterized her work wherever she was sent. A deep desire to make Jesus' love visible to the poor and weak and the conviction that God had called her to this profession shaped her long and fascinating life.

## Pioneer missionary to the Gumuz people in the Blue Nile Valley

In addition to all other commitments and duties Lydia had a very special interest in and love for the Gumuz people in the Blue Nile Valley. The Gumuz are a Nilotic people living on both sides of the Blue Nile. For a long time Lydia had the hope to visit them. But her work in the clinics took most of her time.

Probably in 1957 she was able to leave her work at the clinic for eight days and go down to the Blue Nile Valley. Lydia and Biana, the dresser at the Mendi clinic, went on mule to the Valley, together with some persons who carried medical equipment, personal belongings and mattresses etc. To reach the valley took three days and the group had to make two overnight stops.

On the third day, when the company was close to the village of Sirba, their destination, it was already dark. Lydia had a small torch in her hand. Biana and one other man went just ahead of her. Then they heard someone in front of them shouting *"Who are you? What do you want?"* Lydia saw a man with a gun and another man with a spear. She was told to take away the torch. Again one of the men asked, *"What kind of people are you?"* Biana told the men that the *Hakim* ("Doctor") from Mendi had come and that he himself was dresser at the clinic. Then the men with the gun and the spear lowered their weapons.

Lydia said that she was too tired to be afraid, but she was sure, that if her dresser or someone else had had their guns with them, she and her followers would have been shot. She was told there had been unrest and disagreement between people on both sides of the Blue Nile. The people from Sirba and other villages were on the alert at night. The company then reached the village of Sirba, just half an hour's walk from the river.

Lydia brought small readers in Amharic hoping that the children would learn to read. One year after this, in the autumn of 1958, a few learners came to the mission school in Mendi: Deresu Dabana, who later became a dresser and worked at the clinic; Belo Demu became the first evangelist to the Gumuz and Rare Zenawe a teacher at the school of Sirba.[153]

Lydia was very eager to reach the Gumuz with the gospel by preparing students at the Mendi Bible School for outreach visits to the valley. Some Oromo evangelists learnt Gumuz and served them in their own language.

Lydia was one of the first Europeans who regularly visited the tribes in the valley and offered health care. The friendship between Lydia and the Gumuz people was evident. She described it herself in her humorous words: *"We did not understand each other's language – but we understood that we liked each other."*

---

[153] The text is an English summary from an interview in Swedish with Lydia Larsson, which Karl Erik Lundgren recorded on sound cassette in 1974. Eskil Forslund, Nov. 2018

Lydia died in November 1985 at the age of 72. At the funeral, the pastor made a summary of the qualities that characterized her: Loving but determined, calm but decisive.

## In the Steps of Sr Lydia

The EECMY saw the need to reach the Gumuz with the gospel and was searching for a mission partnering them in this ministry. It was Gudina Tumsa who, as General Secretary of EECMY, called the Norwegian Mission Society (NMS) to start work among the Gumuz and among the Mao and Berta people around Beghi and Assosa areas. In 1971 the first NMS missionaries arrived.

Sr Ingrid Sørensen, a professional nurse specialized in surgery, was among the first group of Norwegians. After studying Amharic and medical orientation at Aira Hospital she was based at Nedjo. She travelled mostly by plane and many times on foot to the valley of the Didessa and Blue Nile rivers, where the Gumuz live. Normally she was down in the valley for three weeks and one week up in the highlands at Nedjo.

During her first years she was working alone with a translator, walking from village to village giving medical help. She got local people in five villages to build small bamboo clinics.

Later permanent clinics were built in Agalo Metti and in Dalatti. In 1973 the medical work at Sirba in the Blue Nile valley was handed over to Johannes and Gudrun Austgulen. They lived and worked with the Gumuz in Sirba and other places over the period of 1973 to 1997. They keep visiting them until today and have published their experiences.

*I put my feet for the first time on the soil of Sirba 45 years ago.*

*Today Sirba is served by Rev Sudi Gote as parish pastor. She is the first female Gumuz pastor who was ordained. We remember Sudi as a little girl walking around in Sirba.*

The Austgulens met her in 2012:

*She told us that the next day she should walk for eight hours to perform a Sunday service which included baptism and sharing the Lord's Supper. A male person would accompany her, but according to the Gumuz tradition, she had to carry her*

*Rev. Sudi Gote, the 1st female Gumuz pastor, courtesy of J. Austgulen*

*baby herself on the whole stretch, and on the return walk some days later as well. A male Gumuz person cannot carry a baby on his back – that is for women to do.*

*I then asked her if she thought it was hard for her to walk that long distance to reach the church. My question was answered with a great smile which clearly told that she considered it to be a natural part of her ministry.*

*Her quiet answer made me think back to the years when I as a missionary walked from village to village in the same way as this young female pastor is doing now. All the good memories from that time will be preserved and will never be erased. Now this young female pastor is a missionary among her own people.*

*After having met both her and other church workers during our visit we could as previous missionaries clearly see that the word of God which had been sown in the past years had found its places in the 'good soil' – and plenty of fruit has been growing.*[154]

---

[154] Austgulen, Johannes: Ethiopia, Experiences and Challenges, BoD, Stockholm, Sweden, 2018, 206

# German Mission: A dream came true (1928)[155]

The German Hermannsburg Mission (GHM) is the fruit of an Evangelical revival movement in North Germany. Louis Harms (1808–65) was the pastor in the small village of Hermannsburg and founder of the GHM. For him being a Christian implied taking the Great Commission of the risen Lord to heart and engaging actively in the expansion of his church world-wide.

His sermons restored spiritual life in many congregations. Those below his pulpit listened to his teaching on spiritual renewal and on the Christian obligation to mission. He trained young craftsmen and farmers to become missionaries.

Louis Harms was inspired by reports of Johann Krapf who worked for the Church Missionary Society in Abyssinia. Krapf saw the need to reach the Oromo with the gospel and he shared his ideas widely. His communications were crucial in directing the SEM, the AUPM and the GHM to the people south of Abyssinia.

Louis Harms wanted to send his newly qualified missionaries to the Oromo. A sailing ship was built to take them to Africa and the ship was named after the queen of Ethiopia mentioned in Acts 8: Candace. However, attempts in 1853 and 1857 to deliver missionaries to the Horn of Africa failed and the GHM began work overseas in South Africa.

The dream of the mission founder would come true 75 years later. After World War I the GHM could not send missionaries to India any longer. Hermann Bahlburg, a home missionary, reminded the leader of the mission to reconsider Louis Harms' preference for an enterprise among the Oromo who were living then in Ethiopia. The idea was given an overwhelming response by the congregations supporting mission. Mission work in Ethiopia would fulfill the vision of Louis Harms.

---

[155] Arén 1999, Chapter 8, A Dream Came True – The Legacy of Louis Harms, 453–505
Bauerochse, Ernst: A Vision Finds fulfilment, LIT Verlag, 2008, 15–54

## Arrival in Addis Ababa and search for a mission field

In 1927 Rev Bahlburg as the leader of the group, Rev Wassmann, Müller and Grabe as lay missionaries and craftsmen left for Ethiopia. Bahlburg left his wife and five children behind and the other three men were yet unmarried. They took the train from Djibouti to Addis Ababa. Within a month they had an audience with Ras Teferi Mekonnen.

The German community in Addis Ababa numbered about one hundred people. They urged the missionaries to open a school and to form a congregation. A suitable building with spacious rooms upstairs was rented. Six weeks after their arrival the first German service took place and a school was opened. These were the beginnings of what would become the German Church and the German School in Addis Ababa. The house and big compound soon hosted an orphanage and was the headquarters for the activities outside Addis Ababa.

The missionaries had been commissioned to go to the countryside. But where could they start their work? As foreigners they could not buy land and Ras Teferi would not assign land for fear of the Orthodox Church and conservative nobility.

Kantiba Gebru Desta, a German speaking Amhara, attended a service of the new congregation and heard about their challenge to find a place for their work. He offered them a plot of land at Aira. Since other plans did not progress, they accepted his invitation, not knowing where Aira was located.

After many visits to offices a travel permit was given, valid for four weeks only. It was June and the rainy season had begun and normally nobody travelled during this time. It was no doubt taken for granted that they would not undertake such a journey. But the missionaries were eager to set off. Had not God answered their prayers and 'opened the door'?

## The long journey to Aira and construction of the mission station

Many preparations had to be made: purchasing pack mules and horses for riding, contracting caravan men and dividing all baggage into suitable loads.

In the meantime two more lay missionaries had joined and four missionaries left with an interpreter and a caravan of seventy mules. None of them was aware of the hardship it would entail to trek with a large caravan like theirs at that time of the year. Five weeks later they arrived at Aira, after a 600 km long caravan journey. They had been on the road twice the length of time they expected. Upon arrival they felt they could not have chosen a more beautiful spot for the establishment of their work.

Immediately they started clearing the land, erecting round huts and preparing the ground for a small vegetable garden. In the dry season the fiancée of Wassmann had come. They got married in Addis Ababa and went to Aira.

Louis Harms had instructed his missionaries to build up a model Christian community: all living together and living from the work of their hands. The mission community should be independent of support from home.

Finally – after the first child was born at Aira – the governor of the region gave permission for the construction of a permanent house. Unable to pay workers, the four missionaries did most of the work by themselves. The preparations for the erection of permanent houses kept them busy for a whole year and left little time for other activities. After two years the big house was ready, inaugurated and serving as residence, congregational hall and school.

The foreigners lived like a big family with Wassmann as their father. He was the pioneer missionary, working with heart and soul, tireless in his duties. Wassmann had the special gift of approaching people and he was a good reporter.

## A Bible reading congregation

The Evangelical movement was a movement of education from the very beginning. Wassmann gathered eleven adults and taught them reading. He wrote:

*In order to keep alive the small group's eagerness to learn, I had promised each of them a Bible as a present as soon as they passed their reading exam. And everyone succeeded except one man who lost confidence and thought his head was hard like the wood of a Kiltu tree; the lessons just did not want to go in. Instead he sent his wife, who understood. Our cowboy Turra and his wife were especially eager. When she had finished her work she went out to the field to her husband with the*

*Singing in the house of Rev. Wassmann, Aira*

*slate and practiced tirelessly. They were also the first who passed their exams and received their Bible. I had to give the husband an extra copy of the New Testament, because it wasn't practical to take the whole Bible while tending the cows, and because his wife wanted to read at home.*[156]

The first worship service at the mission house could be held at Pentecost 1932. Only a few people came, mostly Wassmann's reading and choir students. He wrote:

*One evening after Bible study, three men and two women stayed behind and wanted to speak to me. Our shepherd Turra was their spokesman, and stated the wish, in the name of the others, that I should give them more lessons. I first thought they meant language lessons, because they were interested to learn a foreign language, and I said that for that there was no need. They should practice reading so that they come to know the Bible better. But they didn't wish to learn a foreign lan-*

---
[156] Bauerochse, Ernst: A vision finds fulfilment, p. 66 referring to Wassmann, Dietrich (sen), Pionierdienst unter den Galla, Hermannsburg, 1938, 82

*guage; they wanted more lessons in the Bible so that they could learn more about God's language. I had stated in Bible study, Turra said, that God offers his gifts in two ways, through Word and Sacrament. One is not enough, one has to have both. For that reason I should give them more lessons, so that they could receive Holy Communion. They wanted confirmation lessons.*[157]

Three years later in 1935 the first public service was given. It was the confirmation of Dafaa and this left a great impression on everyone. From this day on the attendance at Sunday services increased.

At the end of 1939 the first group of thirteen confirmands completed their instruction in the Christian faith and was confirmed. Their education had taken five years of weekly Bible studies and teaching in the catechism. [158] Wassmann kept encouraging them to learn eagerly, because God was calling them. He was not after quick conversion; instead he wanted to give time for their faith to grow. Nobody under the age of twenty was confirmed. This group would be the foundation of an Evangelical Lutheran congregation, able to witness their faith to others and to respond to challenges. He wrote:

*An important duty of the congregation is to strive for and to ensure that they are self-financing as soon as possible. On the practical side, a monthly church member's fee and the fee for the church rites were set.*

In 1940 Wassmann baptized an old, almost blind woman together with her grandchild. She had attended the classes though she could not read. She was asked to learn a small part of the catechism. When the exam came she could recite the whole catechism almost without interruption.

### Language learning and Dafaa Jammoo

Language learning was certainly not easy. The missionaries possessed neither a wordbook nor a grammar. Onesimos, whom they had asked, was not able to come to Aira. They were forced to ask questions and take notes. Their small children picked up the language more easily and sometimes

---

[157]  Ibid, 35, referring to Wassmann, Dietrich (sen) s.a., 64
[158]  The teaching was interrupted when the missionaries had to leave Aira (Aug. 1936- Jan. 1939).

helped them. Every evening the missionaries read a chapter of the Oromo Bible together, translated it back to German and tried to analyze its structure and individual words, sentence by sentence.

Six months after their arrival they overheard one of their young workers praying with his peers.

*"God, a white person came. He says he wants to teach us the word of God. But he is dull. His head is hard like the Kiltu tree, our language does not enter. Therefore crash his head so that our language may enter and he starts teaching us your word".*[159]

The name of this young man was Dafaa. He recalls:

*My father died when I was 13 years old. I almost buried also my wish to learn to read, as there was now no money to pay the priest. While tending my flock I joined from a distance a class of deacons sitting in the shade of a big tree learning the Amharic alphabet from a priest. That is how I learnt the letters. One day I went to the market to buy a calf. I heard someone shouting: Who wants to buy a book? I was interested and bought it for the price of a goat. Slowly I read letter by letter: Kakuu Haraa – the New Testament, the only book in my mother tongue, translated by Onesimos and Aster some 30 years earlier. I kept reading and was deeply moved by the stories. A child born at night and the shepherds heard about it through angels. Behold I bring you good news . . . . What can that be – a saviour? I found a story that helped me to understand more: Jesus called the children. Such a saviour I would like to have too, someone who loved me, now that my father was dead and I was alone.*

*I could not sleep. I heard the shouting of apes in the trees, the sound of hyenas that were going around our houses, but in my heart I said: Come, dear saviour also to me and bless me.*

*Once I found a story that Jesus is not afraid of the most dreaded disease: leprosy. He sent ten people with leprosy to the priests. When they reached the priest, they were healed. No one ever heard that. One came back to Jesus to thank him. I thought that I would have done the same. And I thought if I had only known of Jesus before, when my father was sick.*

---

[159] Wassmann, Dietrich (sen) Der Durchbruch des Evangeliums im Gallaland (The Breakthrough of the Gospel in Galla Land), Hermannsburg, 1948, 51

*I read the whole book and had a lot of questions.*[160]

When the missionaries had arrived in Aira the 15-year-old Dafaa discovered their tents. Could he find answers to his questions with them?

After improving their Oromo language knowledge the missionaries established a school at the mission station with 34 students in 1932. The parents had to promise that they would get school supplies for their children. The objective was an elementary school supported by the congregation. The only book they had to practice reading was the Bible. Initially all subjects were taught in the local language; later secular subjects were taught in Amharic, the official language of the country.

## The Italian Occupation (1936–41)

After the German missionaries had been eight years in Aira only a few people had been reached with the gospel. The emperor had designated ten locations in Ethiopia at which Europeans were to gather in the event of impending war. One of these locations was Naqamte, the capital of the province of Wollega.

Wassmann offered the governor of the province the establishment of an infirmary in Aira for 150–180 wounded. The governor thanked Wassmann and reminded him of the emperor's instructions. Wassmann replied that the missionaries felt safe in Aira, did not have enough money to live in Naqamte and feared the station would be looted if they left it. In addition Fritz Bock and Wassmann's youngest daughter were sick and unable to travel.

Yet, when the English consul in Goree urgently requested the missionaries to use the last available ship from Gambeela to flee, Wassmann and Bock took their families and Sister Martha there. The families and Sister Martha travelled back to Germany via Sudan and Egypt, whereas the men returned to Aira. In Khartoum Helena Wassmann, just one year old, died and was buried.

---

[160] Wassmann, Dietrich (sen), Der Ziegenjunge von Aira (The Goat-shepherd from Aira), Hermannsburg, 1952, 4–5

## Dafaa gets a wife

Wassmann was on his way back from Gambeela and stopped at Dembi Dollo and spent some time with Rev West who was the last missionary of the American United Presbyterian Mission left. West confided to Wassmann the following matter. At his station there was a pretty girl named Qanaatu Karorsa who had been with them since she was very small. She was an orphan and her relatives had promised to give her in 'marriage' to a man she did not want to marry. However, that man hankered after her and had tried to abduct her. As he was a government official she was not safe from him even if she got married. West wondered whether Wassmann would offer her some work in Aira and suggested that Dafaa might be interested in marrying her.

Accidentally Dafaa's mother and his brothers had put pressure on him for quite a while. They insisted that it was his duty to marry and raise a family. But the girl whom they had selected for him was not a believer and Dafaa refused to marry a girl who did not share his faith in Christ. Wassmann and Dafaa made the question of a Christian wife their joint object of prayer.

West arranged for Wassmann to get a glimpse of the girl at work and gave him a picture of her to take along to Aira. Wassmann showed the picture to Dafaa, narrated his experience in Sayyoo and told him to meet the girl himself. In less than two weeks Dafaa was back from his trip to Dembi Dollo. He beamed with joy as he announced that Qanaatu had agreed to marry him. After Ethiopian Christmas in 1936 Qanaatu and Dafaa got married. This was the first Evangelical wedding of the area.

Dafaa and Qanaatu would also be the first Christians to go through mourning. Their first child, a daughter, got malaria and passed away. Many people had come to attend the funeral. Her small body was placed with flowers in front of the altar. She was the first to be buried at the funeral place of the mission compound. Wassmann pointed out that for a Christian death was sad, but to lose someone will not lead to hopeless crying, because of the Christian hope that the person is safe in the arms of Jesus. Dafaa and Qanaatu carried their grief in this spirit, which left the biggest impression.

Even the non-believers were quiet and listened. The grave of their daughter had a cross with a verse reading: I am the resurrection and the life.

## Ashana Nagade

Wassmann did not want to leave Aira – *'unless led away captured'* – but had to go in the end. From August 1936 until January 1939 Aira was without missionaries.

Dafaa and his friends protected the mission compound immediately after the missionaries departed. He led the work in the gardens and ran the mill in the valley. He conducted daily devotions and gathered people from the neighborhood for Sunday services.

After a while Dafaa came to know a small trader from Teegii by the name of Ashana Nagade. Ashana heard from Dafaa about the Christian faith.

Years earlier Ashana had come to Aira and attended a service by Wassmann out of sheer curiosity. Wassmann mentioned the name of Jesus Christ often and said that he was the Good Shepherd who loved all men and wanted to help them. He had come to destroy the power of the devil that was behind all evil.

Ashana had often heard the Orthodox priests mention the name of Jesus Christ, but none of them had stated that he was a loving God who wanted all men to live a good life and was able to deprive the *qallicha* of their power. Wassmann's words sank deep into Ashana's heart. This was the first time that he heard that Jesus was the Saviour. He was filled with an overwhelming joy.

Prior to the Italian invasion, Ashana came to know a man from Aira who could read. With his help Ashana realized that he had been cheated by the tax collector because he was unable to read the paper he issued. The man from Aira agreed to come to Teegii and teach him the letters. That way Ashana and his stepmother learnt the 236 letters of the Amharic alphabet.

To read or 'to make a paper speak' is not so different from witchcraft. Ashana's stepmother was a *qallicha* and hoped to improve her earnings by adding this new qualification.

*Ashana Nagaadee and Dafaa Djammoo*

In the end Ashana obtained a book from the man, who had been their teacher, so that they could practice reading. The book was the New Testament. In the weeks to come, mother and son exercised their new skills and learnt that the book was about a God.

Ashana became seriously sick. No qallicha could help. In the end they prayed to the God of the book. Ashana experienced a miraculous healing.

*"I experienced that a profound change had taken place. Nothing on earth attracted me anymore or gave me pleasure. My only desire was to speak about God, not about the things of this world. Yet I did not know anything about the gospel at that time."*

In addition, his fields and compound were saved from locusts and robbers, which he could only attribute to the protection of their new God. In response and full of thankfulness, Ashana promised to honor Sunday by keeping it free from work. Ashana read from his book to people he met and told them to live honestly and abandon fraud and robbery, which call down God's judgment.

## Conversion of a female qallicha

Ashana lived with his family at the place of his stepmother in Teegii. They liked each other and had a good relationship. In Teegii, an area with 1100 houses, more than 100 houses had a *qallicha*. Teegii was a famous centre of witchcraft.

Ashana's stepmother was one of the qallicha. Every day Ashana cried to God for his stepmother. She was convinced that if she would stop practicing witchcraft she would die. She struggled hard. Finally she decided to stop this work ... and she did not die. She began to read from the book for the people, who came to her. People came from far to see what they had heard and yet could not believe, that she had stopped witchcraft and was still alive. And all this happened close to Abbaa Magaal, the greatest qallicha of all. Because of her courageous act the reputation of witchcraft suffered, and the old faith was challenged. Her *galma* (ritual house) was replaced by a large building, where people assembled for prayer and biblical instructions.

The gospel played a significant role in the decline of the qallu institution and freed people from fear of it.

## Missionaries returned to Aira (1939–1941)

Germany and Italy were allies during World War II. In 1938 the GHM was granted permission to resume its work in Wollega, while it was planned to replace all other religions by Roman Catholicism, the state church in Fascist Ethiopia.

1939 Wassmann returned to Aira and was accompanied by Bahlburg. Wassmann wrote:

*The closer we got to the station the larger the crowd around us became. As we slowly drove down to our house from the market place, we saw how people were running down the slopes and were making their way to our house. We, however, were faster. We were able to greet the people of our location first. There was a lot of hand-shaking. Tears of joy glistered in all sparkling eyes... Brother Bahlburg himself admitted that tears had come to his eyes[161].*

Wassmann became the only Evangelical missionary in Ethiopia outside the capital. His family and some lay missionaries joined him after a few months. Many repairs needed to be made, but his chief concern was pastoral work. His Sunday services gathered seventy people and sometimes more than hundred. In addition to these services he conducted weekly Bible classes and taught his former confirmands three times a week. Some newcomers asked for instruction. He visited the Swedish congregations in Nedjo and Bodji. The two years he was able to stay were a very blessed period.

*We left due to the Italian occupation and came back 2,5 years later finding people coming from as far as Assosa (250 km away) to the services in Aira. Many people were faithfully attending the church services. There was one old woman who never missed a single service up to the day we had to leave. It would have taken a strong man eight hours to cover the distance from her house to Aira with three rivers that needed to be crossed. During the rainy season she stood at night at the river, waiting until someone took her over. When no one came she kneeled down, praying to the unknown God and passed by herself. This was not without danger to her life. There was nothing that could hinder her from taking part in the church service.*

---

[161]  Bauerochse, Ernst: A vision finds fulfillment, 42

The preliminary end of the GHM ministry came in 1941 with the arrival of Emperor Haile Selassie I and the British forces. Germany and Britain were at war. The missionaries were put in detention and Bahlburg and Rathje were only released in 1948, three years after the end of World War II.

When it became clear that the German missionaries had to leave Aira again they left a Christian community behind, which was functioning as one big family in accordance with Louis Harms' principles. A garden and a mill helped them to be largely self supporting. Dafaa was able to run the station on the income of the mill.

The GHM had not employed any Ethiopian, while the SEM had so-called Ethiopian missionaries in Nedjo, Naqamte and Addis Ababa: 18 women and 20 men in total. The AUPM had employed at least one evangelist: Gidada Solen.

Wassmann had begun to train Dafaa for the ministry. It is possible that the missionaries had planned to leave without ordaining Dafaa as the ordination took place on the eve of their departure. A request urging them to ordain Dafaa came from one of the outstanding ladies among the Evangelical leaders in Ethiopia: Nasisee Liiban. She asked Wassmann what would happen if the Germans had to leave like the Swedes. Without a pastor the young Christians would be without a shepherd. She had experienced in Nedjo that congregations without a pastor missed official recognition. Wassmann later said to Dafaa that it was her request that made him ordain him. Dafaa was entrusted with the congregations that had been established in the Hermannsburg and Swedish Mission areas in West Wollega.

Who was this far-sighted and wise woman?

## 1. Nasisee Liiban: Capo Protestanti

Nasisee Liiban (1886–1968) is also known as Hadhaa or mother of Gammachu. She grew up in Bodji and heard the gospel from Samuel Danki[162].

---

[162] In 1911 Samuel, one of the first converts went to Imkullu for his confirmation classes. After his return he became the Godfather of Abraham (father of Emmanuel Abraham) and Danuu (father of Gammachuu Danuu), personal communication Qes Gammachuu Danuu.

Later Nasisee lived in Nedjo, a town at the cross-point of two caravan routes and with the central market place of the region. Swedish missionaries had started a school, which was the only school in the region and students came from far places. Boarding facilities were attached and Nasisee became the warm hearted matron. In addition she provided lodging in her own house, for those from far and without a bed in the boarding[163].

Nasisee was confirmed in 1936, she was much older than the others. This was the first confirmation group at Nedjo with nine confirmands; four of them were girls.

The Swedish missionaries had to leave when the Italians occupied the area. Martin Nordfeldt, the missionary who had built up the mission station in Nedjo entrusted the evangelism work to Nagaasaa Silgaa. However, the Italians employed Nagaasaa, a literate young man, sent him to Assosa and promoted him to *Belata*. The Evangelical church and boarding school at Nedjo were closed down.

## The congregation in Nedjo in time of persecution

Two women in particular emerged as leaders.

Wolete-Sillasse led services in the hut she had erected earlier for this purpose in her courtyard. Nasisee ran a small 'trattoria' (restaurant) in town; besides food and drinks, she also served devotions.

The members of the Evangelical congregation were disdained as an assembly of heretics, suspected of engaging in subversive activity under the cloak of Bible study and prayer. Many young men like Nagaasaa found jobs with the Italian administration and were scared to be loyal to the congregation, which had been reduced to a small group of elderly people. Their worship had to be kept secret. Eight families took turns to hold services at their houses.

Nasisee became the spokeswoman of the Evangelical Christians and a dedicated evangelist. She boldly opposed the Italian government officials as they turned the church in Nedjo into their office. She went and said "*The*

---

[163] Nedjo and Dembi Dollo were the only places with schools in West Wollega. Students were sent from places, like Gimbi, Aira, Gulisso, Bodji, Jarso Gambel and Mendi to be educated in Nedjo, see Gammachuu Danuu, 60–61.

*forendji (white people) gave us Christ and built this house for him. Why do you take our church and use it for a worldly purpose? Are you not a Christian"?* Lieutenant Mario became angry and inquired: *"Are you Capo Protestanti, head of the Protestants?"* This name became her name of honour. Indeed, she was the heart of the small congregation in Nedjo during the time of occupation.

## Church founder in Challia Eka

Nasisee suffered from asthma. For this reason she spent some weeks every rainy season in Challia Eka approximately 40 km from Nedjo, to recover in its healthier climate. During her visits she stayed at the place of Balambaras[164] Gammada Urgeessa, the judge of Nedjo sub-woreda. She did not pass these weeks in idleness. In the daytime she taught some women and children to read. In the evenings she gathered the members of the household and neighbours for devotion and for instruction in the Christian faith. As more and more people attended the meetings, the chief ordered a bigger house to be constructed. One part served as a prison, the other part as school and house of prayer. Nasisee led the meetings and sang new songs with her beautiful voice. That was special. It is reported that she contributed to the construction of the first church building in Challia Eka in 1938.

In Challia and surrounding there were many qallicha and their drums were heard throughout the nights. Nasisee spoke out against this cult. *"Don't be afraid of them"* she said, *"they are no gods. Not even Abba Magaal, the greatest of them. He is also just an ordinary man."* She was instrumental in helping many people abandon the qallicha belief and adopt the Christian faith. After a while five qallicha turned to Christ. A small church replaced one of their shrines. As the qallicha cult decreased Challia Eka became the centre of the Evangelical movement in Western Wollega.

Nasisee also went to Teegii, where Ashana had been accused of illicit church building. She and Balambaras Gammada convinced him to move to Challia Eka.

---

[164] Military title, Commander of the Fortress, basically a man entrusted with imperial commands

She had experienced the weakness of the Christians in Nedjo without a pastor. Her advice to Wassmann to ordain Dafaa was far sighted. Dafaa was very faithful in visiting the congregations, preaching and administering the sacraments to the young Christians in Aira, Tegi, Bodji, Nedjo and Mendi.

Nasisee, a mature lady by that time, encouraged and mentored Dafaa throughout the five years he was the only pastor and without support of missionaries. In need of money and in order to support himself and his family Dafaa started teaching for the government in Mendi. Nasisee told him to leave that job and to continue being a pastor. He followed her advice. The boy who once tended the goats of the missionaries had become the pastor of the young congregations.

Later Nasisee moved to Addis Ababa.

Further information on Nasisee is to be found in the Encyclopaedia Aethiopica.

*Nasisee was a person who lived by faith and Bible reading. She taught many people and travelled far distances to bring the gospel of Christ. Worldly talks she did not like, she only wanted to talk about the Bible. Her faith gave her strength and courage to stand up against occupying forces, qallus, priests and partisans – a strong woman who deserves to be called 'capo Protestanti'.*

## 2.  Qanaatuu Karorsaa: '… worth far more than jewels'

Qanaatuu Karorsaa Bamsaa was born near Dambii Dooloo[165] on September 20th, 1921. She is now 98 years old and taken care of by her daughters in America.

### The way she grew up

Both parents passed away when Qanaatuu was a little girl. Mrs. Blair from the American Presbyterian Church took the responsibility of helping her as the girl was born into an Evangelical family. Thus Qanaatuu grew up in a

---

[165] The Oromo spelling of Dembi Dollo is used

*Qanaatuu Karorsaa, portrait by her son Samuel Daffa*

Christian environment and got the chance to learn. Being the firstborn[166] it was her duty to help her younger siblings even though she was still a child herself. Mrs. Blair encouraged the twelve-year-old to give Bible teachings to adults and to attend evening prayer meetings. She also led her brother and sister to Christ.

## Marriage and family

Qanaatuu got married to Dafaa Jammoo[167], who was not ordained at that time. It was God who led them to each other so that they would be able to live together as husband and wife on this earth. Their wedding took place in 1936 and was the first Evangelical wedding in the area. Rev Bock, a German missionary who had arrived in 1932 conducted the ceremony. Qanaatuu got married to a man of God who served him all his life.

Their marriage was blessed with four sons and five daughters. The first child passed away. The other children grew up, completed school in Addis Ababa and reached higher levels of education. One of them did his PhD and worked as a professor in Germany. Sadly he and one of Qanaatuu's daughters, a nurse, died some years ago. One son is living with his family in Addis Ababa. All other children are in different States of America.

## Her personality

Qanaatuu could easily engage in gospel teaching because she had the experience from Dambii Dooloo. Dafaa Jammoo was responsible for many new congregations and he earned five Birr per month. His wife supplemented the family income by doing embroideries, platting hair and handicraft. She was running the house, feeding and educating their children and taking care of them in all aspects.

Qanaatuu was locally known as a good gardener. She sold mangos and oranges from the trees she had planted around her house, and she looked after a coffee plantation, which was the biggest source of income.

---

[166] Qanaatuu had a brother, Faajjii and a sister, Elizabeth. Both of them have gone to the Lord. Faajjii left Dembi Dollo and lived near to Qanaatuu in Aira. Elizabeth, see Elizabeth Karorsa.

[167] Luba (Rev) Dafaa Jammoo was the founder and first president of the former Western Synod

She was known as a noble Christian woman in whom people had confidence including missionaries who found in her a self confident woman and friend. After she had accompanied her husband on a trip to Germany she understood even better what it meant for female missionaries to live in Aira.

### Her participation in church work

In various ways she contributed towards the development of the church. Many elders came for Dafaa's advice. His strategy was to train fifteen people from different areas to read the Bible and to learn songs. They stayed for three months in Aira. Qanaatuu, Dasta Bogasa and the wife of Rev Ashana[168] provided food for the large group and the neigbouring women brought firewood and water. Qanaatuu taught them the Amharic alphabet[169], the Ten Commandments and songs. At the end of the training they received Holy Communion and Dafaa sent them home to proclaim the gospel.

Many times her house received guests from congregations and she provided a sleeping place for them. Hosting guests was not easy without a grinding mill, everything was done by hand and Qanaatuu worked day and night preparing food.

However, she was a strong woman and was happy to serve them on top of giving birth and taking care of the already born children. When church business required, her husband was away for weeks or even months and she had to manage the big household alone. That was not an easy job, but God the Almighty helped her.

She participated in the women's work of the congregation, by organizing them to do handicraft. The sale of their products was an important source of income for the congregation. Qanaatuu taught women to know their Bible well; she taught them to pray and to lead a good Christian life.

At special occasions she took time for prayers. Morning and evening prayers were compulsory and Qanaatuu used them to give spiritual support

---

[168] The wife of Rev Ashana Nagade said: *My tithes are to cook one month in a year for free at the bible school.*

[169] The Bible in Oromo language was available in Amharic script only.

to Dafaa and other pastors and evangelists so that they could do their work in a more effective way.

When Rev Dafaa got tired his wife uplifted him. Missionaries felt comfortable in her company and left her house encouraged and cheerful.

Thus through practical hospitality, prayers and counseling she had a great contribution to the growth of the evangelism work from the initial stage to the Gimbi Awraja Board and later to Synod level, the former Western Synod.

## A capable wife is ...

What is written in Prov. 31: 10–31 can be applied to her life in many ways: A capable wife is worth far more than jewels. ... She brings home food from out-of-the-way places, as merchant ships do... She gets up before daylight to prepare food for her family and to tell her servant girls what to do... With the money she earned she plants a vineyard... She is a hard worker, strong and industrious ... She spins her own thread and weaves her own cloth... She is always busy and looks after her family's needs... ... A woman who honors the Lord should be praised. Give her credit for all she does. She deserves the respect of everyone.

Qanaatuu was a model Christian woman in many regards. This time she is very old. May God bless her and be with her the rest of her life.

**Shifarraw Sadii (Rev., Dr.)**

# 3. The women missionaries: Their invisible ministry

Women missionaries are either single missionaries or wives of missionaries. The proportion of women missionaries grew rapidly in the beginning of the 20th century. By the early 1920s, women represented about 60% of the world's missionary core. No doubt, they played a central role in the progress of mission work.

## The wives of missionaries

The wives like their husbands cut ties with family and home country, though in their heart they were still part of their home society. However, due to their physical absence they gradually became outsiders. In the new country their lifestyle made them as being different. Such status created a strong bond of togetherness between those who belong to the same group.

The wives of missionaries were often tied up with children at home and had fewer chances learning and practicing the language thus they often had a more difficult start than their husbands. Language learning is crucial for integration and communicating in the local language helps to bridge the gap between cultures. Whoever could speak some words had found the key to the hearts of the people around them and this often marked the beginning of integration.

They faced the daily struggle for food and its preparation without electricity and running water and had to accept a simple life style. In this respect their situation was similar to that of their Ethiopian sisters. They trained young people to support them in their various household tasks. Thus boys and girls earned the money for their school fees or were able to support their families. Many educated men and women from the countryside started their career as garden boy or kitchen girl in a missionary's household.

The bond with local women was strengthened when missionary wives gave birth. Bringing up children in a foreign culture was another challenge they mastered. The support of nannies freed them for other tasks. Missionary children usually had a happy childhood. In their first years their mothers often taught them but when they reached school age and higher grades, the issue of schooling came up and many parents had to send their children to a boarding school in Addis Ababa.

The following story illustrates what such times of separation could mean for a family. In 1940 the Wassmanns left three children with a German family in Addis Ababa, so they could attend the German primary school. The vacations were too short for the long trip to Aira and back and the children did not see their parents for 1.5 years. After the birth of another child the family was reunited for two weeks. The happiness of this time was quickly over. The parents struggled with the decision to send their children back to Addis Ababa. The political situation had become unstable. When the car came to take the children to Addis Ababa, the children had disappeared and were nowhere to be found. The car had to leave without them. Several hours later one of the workers told the children who were hiding to go home again. The parents were angry, but the children said: *We did not want to leave you and we saw that you were also not happy to let us go again.*

The wives at home were the ones to live Christian hospitality. Pastors and colleagues, beggars and sick people, schoolchildren and neighbours knocked at their doors trusting someone would open and attend to their requests. Their houses were open; they had guests at the table and guests to stay overnight.

The husbands were sometimes absent for longer periods of time, leaving their family behind. Being foreign their wives might have suffered from homesickness, particularly when no other missionary families were nearby. Communication with families and friends in Germany was by letters which could take 1–2 months. When the Missionary Aviation Fellowship started flight services in the 1960s radio communication was available. In times of need these women could often not care for their old parents and were unable to attend their funeral.

Mothers had to cope with the sicknesses of their children. This is always distressing, even more so, when there is no medical help nearby. There are reports that women of the Ethiopian neighborhood came and prayed; they knew such situations too well. Such experiences created a deep sense of solidarity.

Only few wives of GHM missionary could practice their profession. Most of them assisted wherever help was needed, e.g. in administration, in the schooling of their children, in clinics or at schools. In the congregations missionary wives formed women's groups and taught sewing and other household skills. They also organized and taught at Sunday schools.

This service required a high degree of humility, as their contributions were neither paid nor recognized by the sending mission society. A number of them suffered from not being appreciated for their commitment while the achievements of their husbands were praised and celebrated in public. Moreover, the limited role of women missionaries significantly shaped the role of Ethiopian women in the EECMY.

Two missionary wives are mentioned by name as example of many others: Christa Launhardt and Regina Schönherr. They visited Tsehay Tolassa and other prisoners for many years and organized weekly support visits, in place of Ethiopian women for whom it was more dangerous to do so.

**Women missionaries: From a small hut to a general hospital**

In his first letters Wassmann reported about the sick that were being brought to him and closed his report with the words: *Yes, a nurse would find ample work, if the sick in the houses were given more care.* People had heard that a nurse was working at the Swedish mission station and asked him if there was no woman in Aira who could practice medicine as in Nedjo.

The Mission Board reacted promptly and sent out Wassmann's sister Deaconess Martha Wassmann. When Sr Martha arrived she needed to go to Dire Dawa to get used to the climate. In 1930 she began her service in Aira. Many times she was called to the houses of sick people, she often rendered first aid to fighting cases and she opened a small clinic on the compound. 922 ailing people sought treatment in her clinic in the first quarter of 1931[170]. From 1930 to 1936 Sr Martha laid the foundation for the medical mission at Aira.

As of 1956 Aira hospital was served by an all-female mission cadre of nurses, midwives and doctors. They reached out to people beyond the hospital and built up a network of clinics. One of the doctors came every month for supervision. They promoted health through community based services. They trained local people as dressers, health assistants and nurses. Many of these women missionaries did not marry and gave their entire energy. Dr Elisabeth Knoche and Dr Susanne Harms, Sr Tine Albers and Sr Annemarie Weseloh dedicated their professional lifetime to serve and heal the sick in Ethiopia.

Many times the experience of healing led to conversions and new congregations in far away places.

In 1972 the mission institutions were integrated into the EECMY. From then on an international team worked at Aira hospital. 1978 was a critical year, because many missionaries had to leave due to the unpredictable polit-

---

[170]   Almost one third of these (290) had received wounds from spears or firearms; 260 suffered from venereal diseases; 181 were treated for eye infection; less than one fifth of the 922 cases came because of other ailments, Arén, 1999, 436 from GHM/AE 1.31.

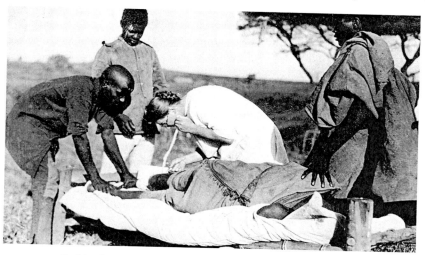

*Sr. Martha examining a patient, who was brought on a wooden bed*

ical situation. Without doctors and nurses the hospital was endangered to be closed down. Dr Hanne Larssen from Norway and Sr Tine Albers remained and guaranteed the continuity of the hospital. Soon later Dr Doorenbos and his wife came to Aira.

The LWF funded the construction of a modern hospital, which was inaugurated in 1991. The hospital was upgraded to a General hospital in 2016.

Today Aira Hospital is run by national staff. The last expatriate staff, a surgeon, left in 2014. Half of the hospital staff are women. The dresser school has developed into a nursing college. General practitioners receive training at Aira General Hospital. The hospital is known and appreciated all over the western part of Ethiopia.

## To be seen

Mission after World War II is widely female, though most of their ministry remained *hidden*. This 'culture' may have contributed to the general invisibility of women in the EECMY.

God, however, has eyes and sees (Gen 2, 31). Seeing shows appreciation and to be seen renders dignity.

God has ears and responds when people cry. He heard Hagar's desperate crying in the desert and revealed himself to her. Hagar testified: You are a God who sees (Gen 16, 13).

God looked upon Elisabeth and was kind to her when she still suffered from the public disgrace attached to her as a childless woman (Lk 1, 25). Mary praised God for he remembered her, his lowly servant (Lk 1, 48).

In the same spirit Jesus reversed the Jewish culture of excluding women, by insisting to listen to the Canaanite woman (Mt 15. 21–28), by teaching Mary (Lk 10, 38–40) and by welcoming women and blessing their little children (Mt 19, 13–15). Jesus at the end of his earthly life wanted the deed of a woman to be remembered; he dignified her service and kept her memory (Mt 26, 15). The teaching of Jesus changed male-female relations.

Respect is at the heart of Christianity. Jesus always gave attention to the forgotten ones. That is why missionaries went far to bring the gospel to unreached people and to heal the sick.

Diakonia is an expression of Christian love and many women are found in this ministry. Have they and their uncountable acts of love been recognized?

## 4. Annemarie Weseloh: Pioneer in Public Health & in HIV/AIDS

The interview took place after her last visit to Ethiopia in November 2018.

**Question 1:** *Sr Annemarie, you came to Ethiopia 60 years ago. As a professional nurse midwife, you had seen many women and mothers. What do you remember of your first years in Ethiopia?*

At first I worked at Aira Hospital. I remember a wife who, after 35 years of childless marriage, came to the hospital and gave birth to a baby boy. I suggested naming him Kenesa, meaning 'his gift' and so she did. I never met her again, but a few years ago I received a letter. The writer said that his mother had told him about the circumstances of his birth at Aira Hospital and she had mentioned my name. The letter was signed by Kenesa. Unfortunately the letter had no sender' address.

People who were sick came with unspecific complaints and it was often difficult to find a diagnosis. Amoebae and parasites were common and also diseases we knew from Germany. I still saw cases of small pox and we did vaccination campaigns. Typhoid fever was much reduced over the years.

We were often invited out; sometimes there were several invitations in one day. We always went, so as not to disappoint anyone. There was not a lot of energy left to learn the language, because we were deadly tired in the evenings.

In the years 1969–77 I was the only nurse at Dapo Gatcho clinic, a remote place 70 km away from Aira. I had to deal with all medical situations by myself. Once I delivered conjoined twins, the mother survived. The Missionary Aviation Fellowship (MAF) started its service in Wollega in 1960. I could ask them to come to Dapo Gatcho for emergency cases that could be treated in hospital. But before that a runner had to take a message in which I described the case to the doctors at Aira Hospital. The one-way trip took the runner one and a half days. The response would be transmitted by radio during a set time the following morning. In the beginning the station at Dapo Gatcho was able to receive but unable to transmit messages, later two-way radio communication was established.

In 1976 the situation in Ethiopia became very unpredictable and the Western Synod told us to leave Dapo Gatcho.

**Question 2:** *You attended a course in Public Health at the University of Liverpool. 1978 was the year of the Declaration of Alma-Ata which underlined the importance of Primary Health Care (PHC) to achieve Health for All. The need for urgent action by all governments and the world community to protect and promote the health of all people was expressed. This approach differed from treating diseases in a clinical setting. How did you implement what you learnt in Liverpool?*

When I went back to Ethiopia I was assigned to Challia clinic, where Dr Elisabeth Knoche was already working. She had started the medical mission work at Aira Hospital together with Dr Traute Freimann.

Later Dr Knoche left the hospital to supervise the church run clinics in remote areas. We divided the tasks among ourselves: Dr Knoche was the supervising doctor going monthly from clinic to clinic, while I was at the clinic in Challia.

We went out to all the villages around Challia clinic, which built trust between the population and us and the service we offered. At churches we taught women about health, hygiene and nutrition and we gave vaccinations to small children. We started our outreach programmes always with a devotion. These were the days of the socialist regime with closed churches and imprisoned pastors. After everybody had been attended to we were served a delicious meal and enjoyed the fellowship with people of the congregation before returning home.

We also trained Community Health Agents and Traditional Birth Attendants as part of the government health programme. Malaria was the major disease and killer in our area. Therefore we trained people from the congregations in diagnosis and treatment and supplied them with anti-malarial tablets, which they bought and then sold later to patients. Getting community members involved made a big difference. The number of patients and critical cases at the clinic dropped dramatically. These so called *malaria agents* also learnt how to diagnose and transfer people with suspected resistant malaria and cerebral malaria.

Female Genital Mutilation was commonly practiced. We told women not to have this done to their daughters. But the women responded that when their daughters grew up, they would ask for it themselves, as they did not want to miss the celebration and all the presents they got on this occasion.

Dr Knoche and I had a nice fellowship. She returned in 1985 to Germany after almost 30 years of service in Ethiopia.

**Question 3:** *Sr Annemarie, you were among the first health workers in Ethiopia to implement PHC. In the 1990s you were among the first to respond to the HIV/AIDS epidemic. Please, can you tell us more about that?*

When I reached pension age in 1994 I moved to Naqamte. My task was to give support and social services to people with HIV. It was not easy to reach the affected people, because fear and stigma led to denial.

Medical doctors have to keep diagnoses confidential. The young doctors in particular had problems to deal with these cases and their suffering.

*Sr Annemarie attending to patients at Challia clinic, courtesy of J. Launhardt*

But some doctors gave consolation and encouragement and they referred people who were diagnosed HIV positive to our office run by the Organisation of Social Services for AIDS (OSSA). In order to follow those who had come to our office I went to their villages. Except for one case all the people were very thankful that we came and did not forget them.

One woman, <u>Almaz</u>, became important for our awareness raising programme in schools and other places. She was born to a school girl. Her mother feared her parents might kill her, when they realized that she was with child. In her despair she gave Almaz away to the care of another woman.

Almaz grew up in a family with children. She knew that the mother was not her biological mother. Almaz said she had to wear the clothes of her brothers and sisters all the time and therefore she dreamt of having something new just for herself. Almaz left that family and the village in search of her own life.

When she reached Naqamte she ended up in a buna-bet[171] and worked as a prostitute. Over the years she became very rich with *one golden ring on each finger.* When Almaz got sick, she spent all her money on doctors until nothing was left, but no one could help her. In the end a doctor told her the diagnosis: AIDS.

This became the turning point in her life. Almaz came to our office and I met her. Like other clients she received minimal support, not enough to live on, so people had to find another source of income. Almaz volunteered to go with us to schools and tell her story to students and that left a strong impression on the young generation. She showed courage by coming out with her diagnosis, as almost all kept their status secret for fear of stigmatization by the society.

**Question 4:** *At the age of 90 you are still visiting Ethiopia and keeping the contacts alive. Now you are preparing the Christmas bazaar and the income from that will benefit work of OSSA at Naqamte. My last question brings me back to the beginning of your lifelong mission adventure. Can you explain what made you, as a young woman, go to Ethiopia and how could you stay faithful to that country for so many years?*

---

[171] Literally a coffee house, practically a bar

When I was ten years old I was allowed to accompany my aunt Grete Rathje to her farewell at the harbour. She was leaving by ship to join her husband in Ethiopia. For medical reasons the family was not allowed to continue their ministry in Ethiopia after World War II and this was very hard for them.

I became a deaconess, which was a difficult decision for me to make. One day my uncle, who was not allowed to return to Ethiopia, suggested, *"Why don't you go to the mission field?"* This idea made me happy.

As a single missionary in Ethiopia it was good to belong to a fellowship. One reason was that I could decline proposals of marriage.

For the first five years I was very happy in Ethiopia up to the point that I said, *"I want to die and be buried there."* A woman I was friendly with pointed out, *"When you are old, we cannot take care of you!"*

It had been my vision to start a deaconess house after retirement, but I realized at the age of 65 you are too old; you need to be younger.

In all ups and downs I had prayer fellowship with a few Ethiopian Christians and that was the continuation of the spirituality that I had come to love as a young Christian woman in Germany.

**Christel Ahrens**

Jesus was called *Rabbi*, teacher. His disciples were learners and Jesus ordered them to go and teach.

Education is another field women missionaries were pioneers in. The school in Nedjo was founded by Onesimos (1904) and re-established under his son Gammachis and Rev Nordfeldt (1927). After the Italian occupation the school was reopened by Stina Ljungberg (SEM) who was gifted with a strong personality which helped her to overcome many challenges and obstacles. She had two female teachers from the area on her side: Wodinesh Ayele and Gumeri.

In Aira Christel Rebin (GHM) became the school directress. She went out to visit the local chiefs and convinced them of the importance of education. She insisted they did not send just their sons, but also their daughters. Mrs Rebbin's cheer appearance: tall stature, low voice and strong determination did not leave much room to reject her proposals, thus girls started to come out of their compounds. In Challia Eka Balambaras Gammada build a school for boys and girls and his daughter <u>Magartu</u> became a teacher.

Many schools were built by missions. The EECMY is still running some schools, e.g. Lalo Aira Secondary School (LASS), where <u>Margaret Doorenbos</u> served as teacher for almost twenty-five years.

### 5. Margaret Doorenbos: Called to the classroom

Margaret's father was a pastor, so she grew up hearing the gospel and Margaret became a believer at a young age. She met Harvey Doorenbos at Hope College and together they were led to consider career Christian service: Harvey, in medicine, Margaret, in teaching.

The Doorenboses came to Ethiopia via missionary service in the Arab world. They were assigned to the Arabian Gulf as missionaries of the Reformed Church in America. They arrived there, with sons Dirk and Keith, in 1965. After language study, they made their home in Muscat, Oman.

Harvey wrote that they *thoroughly enjoyed the challenge of that work. However, oil revenues began to stimulate a very rapid and needed development in Oman, and, after 1974, my service was no longer essential to that country's medical program. We therefore accepted transfer in July 1975, to Dembi Dollo, Ethiopia* – even though they were told that it might only be for two to three months because Americans were not appreciated by the new regime. However, they were able to stay for two years and made significant contributions in their fields of expertise: Harvey at the hospital, and Margaret, as a teacher at Bethel Evangelical Secondary School. She taught mathematics to grade 7 through 10. Dirk and Keith were students at the Good Shepherd School in Addis Ababa.

Soon after they arrived, Margaret expressed their reactions: *The whole family has fallen in love with Ethiopia and are grateful to have been transplanted here. The wonderful mission family in Dembi Dollo has made us feel at home. We pray that each of us may bring praise to the Lord through our lives and service.*

In June 1977 the family was able to go to the United States for a brief furlough. They did not know what the future held for them. During this interim, the EECMY requested that they relocate to Aira to serve in the hospital and school there. The village of Aira was the site of a former German mission station that served the medical and educational needs of a large rural population. They unhesitatingly accepted this challenge, though they were aware of the growing political tensions throughout the country as the communist regime tightened its control over all aspects of life.

In Aira, Margaret became involved with the Lalo Aira Secondary School (LASS), which, at the time, had seven hundred students. When 'Education!' became the political slogan, she found herself also having to teach night school classes. Her students included pastors, health workers; primary school teachers who had not completed 12th grade, and a number of political cadres.

Even the poor peasant farmers were required to learn to read and write. Because the communist authorities had not prepared material for literacy classes, the church happily distributed excellent and simple Bible readers for adults and Margaret used these in her classes.

For Margaret, the years in Aira under communism were a time of remaining faithful to God's call. *We moved carefully, spoke guardedly, trusted very few friends or coworkers, seldom traveled or entertained guests from abroad, and lived with restrictions.* As the local congregation underwent persecution, she and Harvey were a source of hope and encouragement. In addition to their leadership in the school and the hospital, they were thoroughly involved in the day-to-day lives of the community members. Margaret viewed everyone as a member of her extended family and could recite the current joys and sorrows of nearly anyone in Aira.

One way that Margaret influenced an entire generation of church leaders was by paying the school fees of promising students, so they could complete their education. Through her classroom work, she identified students who would benefit from support and made sure the need was met, either paying or approaching other missionaries to sponsor the students. Over the years, her generosity changed the lives of countless students, and mightily contributed to the mission of the church.

Finally, in 1991, the Derg was overthrown and the church could once again openly resume its ministry opportunities. Tragically, during the turmoil, their son Dirk died in a motorcycle accident in the U.S. in May 1991. It was several days until the word got through to Harvey and Margaret on

*Margaret and Harvey Doorenbos, courtesy of Leena Nieminen*

their mission radio, and by that time, Addis Ababa was surrounded by the takeover troops and travel was prohibited. The Doorenboses' great comfort was the assurance that *'when Dirk was born we had placed him in God's hands, and we know that he remains there forever.'*

Life for the Doorenboses went on. In 1994 the secondary school opened with a good enrollment, though not enough teachers. Margaret was disappointed to realize that, as under the communists, the new government was not friendly toward Christian ministry.

*The secondary school director has been told that we must follow political lines in our teaching and our curriculum, and the government curriculum does NOT include the teaching of the Bible. School has been functioning for a week, and Bible teachers are still not appointed. The stockroom shelves have two hundred forty beautifully bound Bibles for use in the classes – a gift from a partner church in the U.S. Will they be used?* (Sept. 26, 1995) Margaret was later told that this order was never received in writing, so they ignored it. An Ethiopian pastor was appointed to the school staff, and Bible classes were being taught.

Completing her eighteenth year of teaching twelve-grade English, Margaret wrote in 1996:

*There were thirty students in my first class; there are ninety-one seniors in two sections this school year. In some respects, it has become boring. The curriculum has been the same for eighteen years, and the students have become less and less capable as the years roll by. Why is that?*

*The government put more emphasis on quantity than quality in education. Without high enough standards to meet the university entrance requirement test and without any alternative industry or craft shops to which to turn, high school students began to see education as futile. Thus it is very difficult to motivate the students to inquisitive pursuit in the sciences, to creative writing in the arts, or to wider vistas through reading material outside their assigned curricula.*

With retirement looming, Harvey and Margaret expressed their love for the work at Aira and the need for someone else to catch the vision, whether national or expatriate:

*We left Michigan for the mission field thirty years ago. We have lived in Bahrain, Oman, and Ethiopia... What a privilege we have had to work with the churches and their outreach into unevangelized areas! But now this privilege will end in this decade. Who will meet the many needs we see as yet unfulfilled? It does not have to be foreigners. However, expatriate missionaries bring with them not only their particular skills, but also connections with the worldwide fellowship of believers. Through that connection, Bibles get printed for tribal people, literature is sent for young Christians, supplies for special medical or educational needs are provided, and the local church is richer for its fellowship with the international network of Christian people.*

*Who will meet their needs? Meanwhile we will continue to educate here, so that young Ethiopian doctors, new teachers from Aira, newly trained health assistant students and young Christians may become tomorrow's leaders in Christ's work.*

They "retired" from serving the Reformed Church in America as missionaries in 1999, but until 2012 offered their services eight months each year as a missionary surgeon furlough replacement and Margaret as teacher. That work took them to India, Kenya, South Sudan, Malawi, Cameroon, Zambia, Ethiopia and Liberia.

From letters published in *The Call of Africa*[172], additions by **Carl Toren**

### Tribute to Mrs. Margaret Doorenbos by her colleagues and students

Ragaa Abdissa, her colleague and neighbor for more than 20 years, wrote: The Doorenbos came during a difficult time to Ethiopia, because when the emperor was overthrown by his military the hate and envy was on the foreigners mainly Americans. Workers at Dembi Dollo hospital signed a petition that made the foreign workers to quit their service and evacuate. The Doorenbos did not go home but came to Aira.

Mrs. Margaret Doorenbos served at LASS with enthusiasm as and taught English and Mathematics. Most of the pupils in grade seven did not understand English. She prepared teaching aids from local materials and her students caught up easily. In a very short time her students started to do better in listening and understanding. There are still some teachers who imitate the way she taught. After each topic she evaluated her students by giving quizzes and tests. This way she continuously assessed her pupils.

She was a workaholic par excellence; always busy in the class room and at her seat in the staff room and at home on her writing desk.

During seasonal changes from rainy to dry season when one complains she used to comment *"when it is hot we want it cold; when it is cold we want it hot; always wanting what is not."* She used to walk to school, half an hour away, she rarely complained of the rain, mud, dust and tumbling stones. The advice she provided to the school director, concerning students and teachers made the school to

---

[172] Morrell F. Swart Morrell, Historical Series of the Reformed Church in America, No. 29. Subtitled "The Call of Africa"; the Reformed Church in America Mission in the Sub-Sahara, 1948–1998." Wm. B. Erdmann Publishing Co.; Grand Rapids, Michigan. Copyright 1998

stand at a highest level in the 1970s and 80s.

**Ragaa Abdissa**

Mrs. Doorenbos taught English and Mathematics to grade seven, eleven and twelve students. She also sponsored the poorest but brilliant students. I remember three boys and one girl who are now in very good positions. Furthermore, some of the students were supported in the University, too. Many students from LASS, were so successful at the university, because they had learnt English from a native speaker. She also taught mathematics in a way that students got a good understanding and foundation for their further studies.

My own English improved by being her colleague for about four years. In Aira she brought books for me to strengthen my stand concerning my belief, also books such as '1984' and 'Animal Farm' by George Orwell. The last book informs about socialism in the Soviet Union and tells the trick of people propagating socialism and equality. Another book I remember was the true story of a Christian girl in a socialist country who was killed because of her faith in Jesus Christ; and a book about Mary Magdalene and Jesus. Mrs. Doorenbos was a counselor, too, to students who had psychological problems.

She invited a few of us, the Christian teachers, to her house for prayer and Bible study. I was supported in my spiritual life, as I was the Chairperson of the women's association at that time and at risk because of going to church.

**Ebise Ashana**

I did not know English well, when I started my first job as high school teacher at LASS in 1988. It was Mrs. Doorenbos who provided me every week with a new English book with a Christian message. Thus I improved my English language skills.

**Tsegahun Ayele**

For three years I worked together with Marge at LASS. Patiently, she guided me into the details of English lessons and the Ethiopian school system. She also supported the other members of our department and beyond according to their needs. She was extraordinarily reliable and loyal even in politically difficult times. In spite of the classes' huge size, she always took each of the youngsters as an individual and lovingly kept them in her phenomenal memory.

**Annette Marung**

It always amazed me that Marge knew the names of all or at least most of her students in her classes and often I saw her coming from school carrying a big pile of exercise books to be corrected at home. Every two to six weeks our mail came with travelers in big sacks. It was distributed and it surprised me that the lion's share went to the Doorenboses. How did they manage to keep such a wide circle of friends after so many years abroad?

**Christel Ahrens**

Margaret was very dedicated to her work; happy, encouraging, and unselfish. She spent much of her free time correcting student's exercise books, in order to follow their individual progress. Many students have told me how much they appreciated and loved her. Many of her students at LASS have now important positions in the country. She has helped many poor students.

**Leena Nieminen**

With regard to Mrs. Doorenbos, I am very happy with her personal style. She listens carefully and corrects you one by one. She knows who has economical problem and is concerned for his or her future. She loves all levels of students equally in terms of academic ability. If somebody has trouble learning a subject, she tries to reason out the difficulty and then takes a different approach.

**Dr. Tariku Waquma**

I really have good memories of Mrs. Doorenbos. When I started secondary school in LASS, my parents were able to pay school fee for grade nine only. For grade ten I approached Mrs. Doorenbos and she paid my school fee for six months and later introduced me to the Finnish family who supported me in high school and all the way through medical school.

She taught me English in grade 11 and 12. She made us love English as a subject. It was an incredible experience with Mrs. Doorenbos: a gifted teacher and mother for the poor. May God bless her!

**Dr. Samuel Bora**

# Norwegian Mission: The seed bore fruit (1948)

This chapter is based on a book by Tessama Zewde: The Seed bore Fruit, the Beginnings of Evangelistic Work in Sidama, Oslo 2010.

## Topography and climate

A special feature in Ethiopia is the East African Rift Valley, a continental rift crossing from north to south and dividing the highland into east and west.

Climate and lifestyle of people varies according to altitude. Pastoralists live in the hot lowlands, below 1500 metres above sea level, where they may grow maize and sweet potatoes. They are vulnerable to malaria and other lowland diseases. The midlands with an altitude between 1500 and 2400 metres are fertile and people grow different types of cereals, enset, banana and coffee as cash crop. In the highlands, above 2400 metres, people grow enset, a thick soft stem from which main staple food is made.

## The Sidama people

In prehistoric times the Sidama and the Hadiya were migrating side by side and settled in highland areas west of Bale while the Somali and the Oromo settled in the lowlands south and east of Bale. All four groups are Cushitic and they share many similarities in language, culture and socio-political organisation.

Among the Sidama elders regulated family and community affairs. The democratically-led discussions allowed all participants to reach a consensus during their weekly meetings. If no consensus was reached, the decision would be postponed. Conflicts were resolved by reconciliation or by paying a lump sum of money. In case of continued opposition the offending person would be excommunicated. Death penalty was prohibited. Tessama concluded that generally the administration by elders functioned well and had served as grass root democracy.

South Ethiopia and its people were unknown to mission organisations until the second half of the 19$^{st}$ century. The people in that vast area were hardly evangelized by the mid 20$^{th}$ century. NLM missionaries were the first to settle among the Sidama.

### The beginnings of the Norwegian Lutheran Mission (NLM)

NLM, established in 1891 was initiated by a group of women within the Church of Norway, who then invited influential laymen to assist them in the great task of bringing the gospel of Jesus Christ to unreached countries.

The mission developed independently from the official structure of the Church of Norway, who did not favour the establishment of independent mission organisations and therefore did not recognize NLM. The spirituality of NLM focuses on the priesthood of all believers and lay ministry.

The first NLM missionaries were sent to the mainland of China. They evangelized urban areas, by working among business people and other people with education and work. The work of NLM expanded and flourished over the following 60 years until Mao Tse-tung came to power in 1949. His communist authorities regarded any mission work as dangerous for the development of their communist ideology. NLM was forced to withdraw its missionaries. From 1891–1949 NLM had sent 240 missionaries to China.

### A new mission field in Ethiopia

The leaders of the SEM were busy evangelizing and running schools and health services in Eritrea and in West Ethiopia. Who could respond to the open doors in the south, east and south west of Ethiopia?

It was in these circumstances that NLM missionaries came to Ethiopia to place their desire before the Emperor. In 1948 they got official permission to work and to start schools and clinics.

The South of Ethiopia is home to a number of peoples like the Guji, the Boorana, the Gedeo, the Burji and the Sidama. The work of the NLM spread to all these groups in addition to the province of Gama Gofa in the south west which has an unusual high number of different peoples.

Twelve Norwegian missionaries, some came straight from China, settled in Yirga Alem, 330 km south of Addis Ababa.

The day after their arrival the missionaries began to preach the gospel under the shadow of a big zigba tree at the Ras Desta School compound. Services continued on the same place every Sunday until it was possible to move to the newly leased compound.

Most residents of Yirga Alem were followers of the Orthodox Church and were unhappy about the coming of the missionaries. Their resistance made it difficult for NLM to find a place for their work. Despite this opposition a local follower let his house and a part of his site to NLM. Before the leasing contract was signed the missionaries moved their tents and started renovating work on the existing building. Afterwards they established elementary and secondary schools and strengthened health services.

Kristine Svensen and Mamite H/Wolde visited the homes of government officials, landlords, clergy and others and invited women to join their classes at the station. Many women wanted the tracts which contained portions from the Bible, but only few could read them. Kristine and Mamite taught them Bible stories, reading, writing and handicraft.

## The first missionary to Sidama

The Sidama kept their traditional religion for thousands of years. Islam and the Ethiopian Orthodox Church entered the Sidama homeland before the first missionaries arrived. Prior to the arrival of Norwegian missionaries Dr Lambie and other missionaries sent by the Sudan Interior Mission (SIM) had come to Sidama in 1929. They studied the language. With the assistance of local Evangelical believers Christian booklets were prepared and printed. Literature became an important aid in spreading the gospel.

Kebede Erbeto remembered in 2005:

*"While we were unknown to them, Dr Lambie and his fellow missionaries came on foot to our place like our Lord Jesus Christ did when he lived on this earth two thousand years ago. The Lord also provided them with knowledge and wisdom to live with us in love without showing prejudices against anyone. They ate what we ate, they drank what we drank, they slept where we slept, and they spoke what we spoke. The Lord himself must have worked with the missionaries so that they accepted us as we were."*

Because of the rapid growth of the mission work, followers of traditional religion, the Orthodox Church and the local government authorities began to oppose the SIM activities and forced Dr Lambie to leave. Despite all these problems the evangelism work grew steadily among the people in Sidama, Wolayta, Kambata and Hadiya areas.

## Cooperation failed

The first mission societies came with the aim to co-operate with the Ethiopian Orthodox Church (EOC). The EOC baptized and gave Holy Communion to the new converts who became members of the local orthodox churches. The growing group of Evangelical Christians brought a change in attitude among local people. When the number of indigenous converts grew beyond the expectation of the EOC they refused to baptize them and denied funeral places for Evangelical converts on their cemeteries.

This led to severe conflicts and divided the EOC believers and the Evangelical converts. The EOC did not accept to cooperate with foreign mission organisations. The missions had to change their policy. The Evangelical Christians understood that they had no future in the EOC and started discussing about their future destiny and how to establish their own organisation in Ethiopia.

## Evangelists from Kambata and Wolayta

Shamebo Kelbero remembered that the new religion was the main topic everywhere on the markets. *There was real fighting between believers of the traditional religion and Evangelical Christians. Young people were more eager to accept the new religion than old ones.*

Shambeo was born in East Kambata. He and his two wives were the first young persons who received Jesus Christ as their personal saviour. Before that his three children had become seriously sick and he had paid a lot of money to witch doctors, but his children died. As a Christian he received a call to serve among the Arsi people, but they did not accept the gospel.

Shambeo was known to be a very honest and humble man. Because of this and his wonderful message, he was welcomed by the Guji and the Sidama of the Wondo Genet area.

Shambeo knew that he was not able to carry out this big work and returned to Kambata asking the church to send more evangelists. At the end of a two days prayer meeting, the elders of the congregations laid their hands on five young evangelists with basic bible knowledge from Bobicho SIM Bible School and commissioned them as their messengers to the neighboring people. The elders promised to take care of their families and their farms.

Despite serious persecution the number of believers grew. One of the causes could be that people were suffering from a serious epidemic and those who turned to Jesus experienced healing. Another cause was the awful feudal system that reduced their living standard below poverty line. In order to struggle against such a system, other men joined the Christian brothers.

Eventually they were brought to court. The judge at the Provincial High court in Yirga Alem reasoned that preaching Christ was no crime and set them free. This was a day of victory for the prisoners and for all the Christians in the Wondo Genet area.

When Shamebo was transferred to Gidole he was arrested and brought before the landlord. The landlord asked him, *What are you doing here? Who gave you permission to build on a place that was not blessed by the EOC?* Shamebo was in a situation similar to that of the Apostles Peter and John. He replied boldly, *I am here to preach the Kingdom of God to people who were worshipping Satan and living in darkness! You are one of them! Believe in Jesus Christ who died for you, and you will get forgiveness of your sins.*

From the time Shamebo began to preach the gospel in the second half of the 1940s until he retired in the mid-1980s, he faithfully served the Lord and the EECMY in Sidama, Gamu Gofa and Borana.

Lejebo Madebo was born in 1923 in Kambata. His uncle had become a believer and for that reason he was hated and condemned by non Christians. Lejebo's uncle passed away and his death gave the family great fear that no one would come to his funeral. When the Christians of Kambata and Hadiya lands heard about his death, they came in great numbers on horseback from various directions to be present at his funeral. They buried him after preaching and conducting a great funeral service.

It was at this funeral that Lejebo and many others received Jesus Christ as their personal saviour. Afterwards an evangelist was sent to teach the word of God and literacy. He stayed for one year and the people provided food and covered his stay.

On a market place Lejebo bought the gospels of Matthew and Mark in Hadiya language. The books had been printed by SIM missionaries. The cover of the gospel books were in green, yellow and red; the colours of the Ethiopian flag to attract the attention of people and authorities.

Lejebo worked in Kambata and Hadiya. After two years he went to Addis Ababa, joined the SIM Bible School and went to Homacho in Sidama to preach and teach without salary, but with food and housing assistance by the congregation.

He went to Yirga Alem, applied for a job with NLM and was employed in 1951. The missionaries were very satisfied with his work and asked him to go to his home country and recruit evangelists and literacy teachers[173].

### Why did Evangelists from Kambata/Hadiya and Wolayta come to Sidama?

The above mentioned pioneer evangelists were the main tools the NLM had during their first ten years. But why did the evangelists come to Sidama land?

One reason was that these evangelists believed that the Holy Spirit had touched their hearts to go and preach the gospel to their neigbouring people, namely the Arsi and Sidama. The second reason was to get legal protection from the authorities who were persecuting them. NLM as a foreign mission

---

[173] An illiterate person was considered a person who lived in darkness. Though modern education reached people in the Sidama towns, the mission schools included both academic subjects and Bible teaching. In 1948 there were schools in towns, attended by children of privileged people. Every congregation wanted their own literacy school. The mission faced problems to finding teachers and this was resolved by employing evangelists who also served as literacy school teachers in every congregation.

organisation had got legal permission from the Imperial Ethiopian Government to work in Sidama and Gamu Gofa provinces. Thirdly, when the evangelists had been trained at the SIM Bible School they were sent back as voluntary evangelists without payment. Some of them went to new areas leaving their families behind. They had no resources to live on. When they heard of the NLM in Yirga Alem they approached the mission and applied for paid work. The fourth reason was that farm land was available in Sidama so that they could bring their families and live an ordinary family life.

Some of these evangelists had been working until the 1980s, but most of them were replaced by Sidama evangelists.

## Disagreements between SIM and NLM

The fact that NLM had employed evangelists that SIM had trained for voluntary service caused problems between the missions. Lejebo recalled the two conditions the missions agreed at the end of several discussions:

1. Instead of recruiting trained evangelists without the consent of SIM, the latter is willing to train evangelists selected by NLM.
2. The work areas of NLM and SIM in Sidamo were to be divided as follows: The western side of the road from Tikur Woha in Awassa to Moyale in Boorana should be allocated to SIM and the eastern side of the road to NLM.

In the end however, the agreement was not respected by either mission.

Merkina Meja was another person born in 1923 in Wolayta outside Soddo town, who went to evangelise among the neighboring Sidama people. In Addis Ababa he was engaged in street evangelization. NLM ordained Merkina Meja as the first pastor of Yirge Alem and he went back to Wolayta to recruit evangelists from outside Sidama.

## Evangelists trained by Bible Churchmen Missionary Society (BCMS)

NLM also recruited evangelists, who were trained at the BCMS Bible School in Fitche: twenty male evangelists, one female evangelist (Rachel

Wato), one nurse, and six coordinators, teachers and interpreters. Some became teachers, others evangelists or interpreters, many had multi-purpose tasks.

Among them was Memhire Sileshi Wolde Mikael who was sent to Yabelo and later served as Executive Secretary of the synod. Ato Alemu Derseh, a teacher and evangelist also served as an interpreter to the missionaries. Later on he was transferred to Urael congregation at the NLM's compound in Addis Ababa and became the leader of the congregation.

Haile Damte and Tuffa Deressu and others served in Negelle Boorana, Wadera and Mega districts. Haile Damte was transferred to Tabor Seminary, Awassa and later served as pastor of Awassa Mekane Yesus congregation.

Engidawork Egualebirhan, a former witch-doctor living in Wolisso town, about 100 km south west of Addis Ababa got basic Bible education and was assigned to distant places to sell books. In this service he travelled on foot to Hadiya, Kambata and Wolayta areas. Later he started his work as an evangelist in Agere Mariam District together with Sandved, who was the head of mission work in the area. Next to Dilla district, Agere Mariam was a very difficult place for mission work. The landlords, the traditional authorities and the EOC were great obstacles for the ministry of Engidawork and other evangelists, who often were arrested, beaten, thrown into the landlord's custody or the local police jail. Despite all these difficulties, Engidawork travelled all over Agere Mariam district with love and joy, often on foot, and carried out his work as an evangelist, literacy school teacher and literacy school supervisor.

Teshome Yifrashew another trainee by BCMS went to Agere Mariam as a school teacher and interpreter. After some years he was transferred to Yirga Alem Elementary School.

To sum up, the narratives of the evangelists show how the work spread to various places in the South, where then NLM established one mission station after the other.

### The change the gospel brought

People started to read and write and they began to send their children to school. The way they dressed changed. They began to wear clean cotton clothes instead of greased and buttered skin skirts. Every Sunday men and women used to go to the congregational meetings and shared the word of God. Evangelical Christians refused to stick to the traditions of the traditional religion.

The monthly and fortnightly assemblies of Evangelical Christians from different places helped them to develop fellowship with Christians who were living in other parts of Sidama regardless of social order such as clan, sub-clan, high or low caste groups. All came to worship the Lord Jesus Christ and to eat together. More than any other act this signified that Evangelical Christianity had brought equality between non-artisans and artisans and between men and women.

However, Tessame Zewde realized that pride in one's own group and contempt for others is still deeply rooted even in educated Christians. He interviewed a graduate from the Mekane Yesus Seminary in 2005. An unwritten law followed by both Orthodox and Protestant Christians in Sidama is that tanners and blacksmiths do not intermarry. The young graduated and yet unmarried fellow agreed that isolation of these artisan groups was wrong and a sin before God as well as before men. Tessama asked him personally: *Can you marry a girl from these groups?* He responded, *"To tell you the truth I cannot."* Tessama continued asking, *"What are your reasons for not marrying a girl from these groups?"* He said, *"It is the oral traditional law which forbids it. You have to remember that I am a Wolabicho and because of that I have to follow my traditional law which I have inherited from my fathers and ancestors and that law prohibits marrying any girl from these groups."*

Certainly, many Sidama condemn this tragic attitude, which is a sign of what Christianity has done over the years. Development and modernization have brought about many changes. It is now possible to observe that Hawacho (tanners) and Tunto (blacksmiths) find spouses outside their groups.

## 1. Women pioneers: Rahel Wato, Elsabet Gulti and Mariam Dicha

These three women bear witness to their Christian faith during a difficult time in the history of Ethiopia. Two scholars reflected on the influence women had in the church during that period.

Dr Øyvind M. Eide[174] on the role of women in the EECMY in the years 1974–1991:

*When you deal with EECMY during the Derg period, you must be aware that the persecution was generally aimed at Addis Ababa and West Ethiopia. In the Southern Synods there were difficulties, particularly in Gemu Gofa, but for two reasons these areas managed better, because few church buildings were closed and because of their structure of lay ministry of Word and Sacrament. In the three synods of the EECMY to the west of the country at the time (the Central Synod, the Western Synod and the Western Wollega Bethel Synod) almost all church buildings were closed, and pastoral and evangelistic ministry was forbidden. In spite of this some of the elderly pastors functioned. They were invited to private homes to baptize and administer Holy Communion.*

*The crucial role of women was that they, at great personal risk, created a space in their homes for Word and Sacrament, the lifeline of the church. I give them credit for saving the church.*

**Dr Øyvind M. Eide**

Daniel Worku in his thesis about the role of women in mainline Addis Ababa Evangelical churches (1960–2012) [175]:

From 1974–91 Ethiopia was ruled by a military junta (Derg). The political terror came close to every member regardless of sex, age and ethnicity. The fact that the church was in the midst of persecution meant the gender issues vanished. The charismatic revival in the EECMY expanded women's ministerial boundaries and this period turned out to be a real blessing for women's ministry. When religious freedom returned with the fall of the

---

[174] Rev Dr Øyvind M. Eide was a missionary in Ethiopia during the time the country was ruled by the Derg, His book: Revolution and Religion in Ethiopia, Ohio University Press, 2000 records this time of Ethiopian history.
[175] Daniel Worqu, The role of women in mainline Addis Ababa Evangelical churches 1960–2012, AA University, MA

Derg, women were pushed away from their position. After 1991 women's noble ministry was forgotten and they were obliged to their former service giving position.

The following short biographies give evidence of how women took courageous initiatives to keep the light of the gospel burning during these dark years.

### Mrs. Rahel Wato – a tireless evangelist

Mrs. Rahel Wato Sode was born in 1926. As a child she lived in Yabelo and in Mersabet, Kenya where she was introduced to the Gospel by Mother Sara and accepted Jesus Christ as her saviour. Rahel studied one year at the BCMS Bible school in Fitche.

In 1951 she joined the Norwegian gospel outreach in Moyale. *She touched the ground of the place and gave that land to the Lord*[176] and moved to another places.

In 1952 Rahel was assigned to work with Norwegian missionaries at Nagale hospital. She translated the gospel from Amharic to Afaan Oromoo thus enabling several people to hear the gospel and accept Jesus. She served at the women's section and as gospel ministry leader in Nagale congregation.

After 1975 the gospel spread rapidly. From 1978 to 1994 Rahel put all her efforts in church planting in Boorana and Guji and together with the missionaries she founded more than 20 congregations[177]. She preached the gospel of Jesus Christ with love and courage, lived a life pleasing God and set an example for others.

During the time of the Socialist regime, she was asked to deny God, but she refused and suffered imprisonment. Despite all the challenges and problems she walked from home to home and encouraged women groups through prayer and preaching.

---

[176] Touching the ground and giving it to the Lord is done when there is a very important issue people want God to deal with.

[177] Nagale Boorana, Bura Dhera, Dekakela, Semento, Dabe Adama, Hara Qalo, Wadara Ganale, Hiddi, Yabelo, Mega, Moyale, Kibramengist and Shakisso – to mention some of them.

She worked with many people including Sister Oslog from Norway.

Rahel Wato served Nagale parish from 1951 to 1994 and retired after 43 years of service. At her retirement ceremony the Church, awarded her with a gold medal, and different certificates of appreciation from South Ethiopia Synod.

She was devoted to the church even after her retirement and brought many people to the Kingdom of God. Rahel passed away in 2011 aged 89 years.

Rahel gave birth to twelve children and saw twenty-seven grandchildren and nineteen great grandchildren. In addition she raised another three children. Her children are serving the Lord where they are living. One daughter and two grand children serve the Lord full time.

**Bereket Tesfaye,** translated to English by **Ebise Ashana**

### Elsabet Gulti[178]

My name is Elsabet Gulti. I am a Secretary of Women's Service in the South Ethiopia Synod. I am a mother of three children.

I received the Lord Jesus Christ as my personal saviour at the time of the revolution in the former Gamo Gofa District, Konso Congregation and became a choir leader. Every Sunday we were ordered to participate in what they called work campaign. Although it was expected of us to perform something that is useful for the well-being of the country, we first gave the spiritual service in the church and then went to the work place and performed our duties. But the principal aim was to take us Christians out of the church and teach us atheism. One day people from the "Revolutionary Ethiopian Youth" came to our residential school saying, *At this time people are struggling for their country Ethiopia till death and you are saying you die for the gospel truth.*

By the help of the Lord I could escape their beating and I went to Arba Minch where persecution was waiting for me. One day during a high political meeting in town, while we were going to the church for a choir service,

---

[178] Women's Ministry Coordination Office, The EECMY Women's Ministry, 2001, page 17

they wanted us to participate and the police was sent to take us to the Kebele office like criminals.

It is difficult to list all that we faced and I will only mention a few commands which led to my three-month imprisonment: *Throw away this useless Bible! Say the slogan of the revolution! Do not go to the church! Do not gather for prayers! Do not spoil the youth with your preaching!*

However, God helped me to stand the beating, the rolling over the rocks, the hunger and the thirst and I could come out of prison. After I had completed my high school, I was assigned to the Synod duplication office and soon later to the Christian Women's Office. A three month course in Addis Ababa, an English course in Kenya and a one-month administration course by the Women's Office prepared me for my new job. Later I was sent to Mekane Yesus Seminary to study Leadership, Management and Communication and I graduated with a diploma.

It is my 16^th year now to serve the Women's Office. My wish is that my sisters in Christ get the opportunity for service, work and education equal with that of their brothers. Then they can give service in their respective congregations and to the church at large.

The women's service of the South Ethiopia Synod includes: Sermon and prayers on Wednesdays and Thursdays; leading choir services and other programs; preaching the gospel and serving in various committees; raising income for their congregations by producing and selling different handicrafts work and diaconal services.

## Mariam Dicha[179]

I am married and a mother of five children. I was born in 1955 in the former Gamo Gofa District, in Genta Ocholo. There was a school in Arba Minch town but no private or government school in my area. Since the people in our area concentrated on farming, they did not have the thought of sending their children to places where there were schools.

One day in 1966 the EECMY sent some people to our area to give basic education. I and others got the chance to have our eyes opened for educa-

---

[179] Women's Ministry Coordination Office, The EECMY Women's Ministry, 2001, page 19

tion. The person was teaching us the word of God, and I accepted the teaching and the Lord. When I reached grade five my parents received requests for marrying me from different directions. Accordingly I was married to my present husband being a student of grade six, while he was in grade seven. The marriage took place according to the church tradition. Even after my first child I continued with my education by the assistance of my husband who replaced my father for me. Then, I continued for seven years like this combining the work of motherhood and service in the church as a choir member and by witnessing to Christ.

God helped me to join a bible school in Hagre Selam for one year. After graduation I gave free service until 1981 when I was employed as Arba Minch Christian Women coordinator. Now I have 16 years work experience, and while giving service to the church I completed my high school education in evening classes. I have got different short trainings and a two-year diploma level education at Mekane Yesus Seminary Leadership Department which helped me a lot to improve my knowledge. I have a strong faith and hope to be in service of the Lord and God's people during my remaining lifetime.

## 2. Jorunn Hamre: From Kvinesdal to the end of the earth

### The expedition to serve in unfamiliar conditions

Sr. Jorunn Hamre was born in Kvinesdal, Norway in 1931. After graduation as a nurse and midwife she joined the Norwegian Lutheran Mission (NLM). She was also trained in music and played the piano in church.

In 1948, NLM started working in Ethiopia and established several mission stations as centres for evangelism, health and education among indigenous communities in remote and least served areas in the south.

Sr. Jorunn first arrived in Ethiopia in 1959. Since there was a shortage of Ethiopian health personnel, NLM used their missionaries, who received short language courses in Amharic, the national language of Ethiopia. Yirgalem Hospital, one of the two hospitals established and run by NLM, had an acute need for a nurse, and Sr Jorunn was sent straight to the hospital without any language course.

Once she embarked on the highly demanding work, she had no chance to return to study the language. However, patients and the neediest became her teachers and she learnt Amharic and Oromo, from her day-to-day communication. Sr Jorunn was always willing to be among them.

Having filled a crucial gap at Yirgalem Hospital, she was then assigned to be in charge at a clinic in Mega, a small town close to the border with Kenya and 665 km from Addis Ababa. This was where I got to know her, being a child of six years and between life and death, severely wounded by Somali cattle raiders. She has been my guardian ever since as I lost my father in the incidence and also his herd of cattle, all the property my father had.

Coming to a remote clinic with a large catchment area had its challenges and lessons. There were completely unfamiliar cases and various tropical diseases; she was there during times of local armed conflicts by rival pastoralist groups resulting in serious wounds like what happened to me. Such cases came to her clinic as there was no equivalent health institution in the vicinity. Transport to distant health facilities was often no option, because vehicles were hardly available, transport costs were high and the roads were in poor condition.

In addition, complications at birth caused many maternal deaths. Mega, the district town, used to be visited by a private lorry once a month. The next NLM doctor lived 400 km away at Yirgalem. He visited her clinic once in three months with mission land rover. The children in town received the rare vehicles passing by with amusement and songs.

## Reaching out to pastoralist communities

In such conditions and an unwelcoming environment mainly due to under-development, Sr. Jorunn decided to reach out farther afield to communities in the countryside. She came with the word of God, with her midwifery skills and with medicines. Thus, pastoralist communities in Boorana received health services. Their places were out in the wilderness; to be found only with the help of a guide on small foot paths. In addition, villages were far apart from each other and Sr Jorunn had to learn to ride a mule.

Even more dangerous was that most of those communities had not heard about the word of God, and they were ruled by nonbelievers, witches and those worshipping big trees and making offerings to them. Any teaching against their belief system could be life-threatening.

Preparations for a field trip started with careful planning of items to be transported: medicines for the most prevalent diseases such as malaria and eye diseases; bandages and medicines for wounds and delivery equipment. Everything was packed on mules. On top of the medical luggage, large posters with picture to illustrate biblical teachings were fixed. Finally, camping equipment for a journey that might take a week was added. One or two assistants would lead the way and serve as interpreter.

These journeys have their own long stories including some striking ones which Sr. Jorunn still remembers, e.g. once she confronted a number of people possessed by evil spirits; another time, during a fight, a husband was beating his wife severely, Sr Jorunn intervened to prevent a tragedy.

The main objectives of her holistic service were to respond to physical and spiritual needs of vulnerable people and to treat and heal the sick. Thus, she served the pastoralist communities in Boorana society, while she was in Mega. Many people, who were struggling economically, received support and became productive citizens. She continued serving in the same committed and self-sacrificing manner when she was transferred to other clinics in remote communities elsewhere in southern Ethiopia.

### Shift in the emphasis of service

Sr Jorunn has always been interested in communities that struggle on their own and in many ways are left behind in human development. She is convinced that the spread of the Gospel will make people free from the power of evil spirits and from backwardness. She has worked hard for that to become a reality wherever she could reach.

While her professional service as a nurse midwife continued during most of her active working life, she gradually shifted her focus to strengthen evangelists in preaching places, to support the establishment of congregations and to plant churches.

Naturally this was not without problems and she even faced life threatening situations. One was in Neghelle town; where her opponents tried to murder her at her home on the church compound and God miraculously saved her. The second attempt to murder her was in a place called Oborso in Bale Zone. Sr. Jorunn usually parked her car in their clinic compound and stayed overnight sleeping in it. One night murderers broke into her car thinking that she was sleeping inside. The day before she had left by mule for a locality called Gurra which was her preaching place. God saved her life ...

Sr Jorunn was the first person to proclaim the Gospel at Gurra, a place inaccessible by car. She had to cross a big river called Iyya on a suspension bridge which is a pedestrian crossing made locally from thin tree branches interwoven together with sisal ropes. This was very risky, if the hand-made bridge was to break those crossing would fall into the river and go for good without any trace.

## Her service after her retirement

Sr Jorunn reached retirement age at 67 and had to give up her regular work for NLM and returned to Norway to start her pension life. But, she could not give up the objective that she had built up over many years and had to continue on her own. Trusting God and with moral and financial back-up from groups and individuals in Norway, she returned in 2006 after five years of rest as a pensioner. Against all odds, she decided to continue until God says: *"You have done enough."*

Although she has been occasionally ill and undergone surgery and medications; she came back and still serves. Thanks to the Lord! God has allowed her to continue over many years and she has achieved so much, particularly in Gudji zone.

Earlier, she has had hymn books printed in Gudji Oromo dialect and supplied EECMY congregations in both Gudji and Boorana zones with cassettes as these hymns are widely sung in churches. She has raised funds and planted churches in Gudji zone, strengthening spiritual revival in the area and neighboring communities.

Coupled with these main activities and spiritual projects she has supplied the Bible, other spiritual books and reading spectacles to those who
cannot afford them.

For the last five years, she has been busy building a big church in the
suburb of Shakisso town. The building is bigger than most churches and
constructed with expert help from abroad.

While the church building was well on course with a sufficient supply of
funds and local contractors, a dispute over the land between EECMY and
the nearby Adventist church was brought to court. The court case started
when the construction was half-finished and this conspiracy-like move took
more than three years to be resolved with a win by EECMY. Meanwhile the
construction work had to stop until the court case was finalized.

This had caused her much grief and affected her health. Nevertheless,
she did not give up. She cried to God every day on this huge setback until
the case was won. She was delighted to see the construction work being
taken up again and finalized in a master piece manner including curtains
and sound system.

### Recognition and award by the EECMY

Back in 2008, on the commemoration of the fiftieth anniversary of the
EECMY, the church recognized several notable services of her national and
missionary workforce. Sr. Jorunn Hamre got the highest award and received
the medal from the hands of the President of the Federal Democratic Republic of Ethiopia.

This award was not what Sr. Jorunn expected or looked for; but the
recognition has further encouraged her to go ahead, doing what she always
loved to do even though her physical strength and health are of concern
for people around her, including myself. Despite brief periods of ups and
downs, so far God has helped her to continue and blessed her.

### Is she now wrapping-up her extraordinary ministry?

Sr. Jorunn, the long serving and persistent servant of God and His church is
now 88 years of age and getting frail as time goes by. There is so much to
thank God for: For her coming so far with a strong desire to serve and with

*Sr Jorunn Hamre and Deed Jaldessa, courtesy of D. Jaldessa*

a lot of shining achievements on record. She has bravely worked, prayed and at times wept for the spread of the Gospel. Many people were saved. She has reached the poor, they have been served and saved by receiving Christ; things devoted Christians like to see in life.

But there is always a limit to how far a human being can go. This limitation seems now to be appearing rather sooner than later. Sr. Jorunn has to make a decision consulting her creator that her work is done and thank Him abundantly.

## Closing Statement

First of all, I praise the Lord Jesus Christ for the heroic Christian work and life of my beloved and respected guardian who became a mother to me and many others. I extend my due respect to all efforts that her work and that of other women who lived heroic lives for Christ and unprivileged people will be made known. I hope many will follow their example.

I strongly feel that Sr. Jorunn needs a breathing space now, something which she has not enjoyed so far, even in her late retirement age. I want to take care of her as much as I can in the remaining part of her life. She has spent so much; her time, talent and her whole life for me, my fellow citizens and country without expecting anything in return.

She has left us a huge witness, a debt that we cannot pay back. What remains to be done by me is try to keep her happy in the Lord; for which I commit myself and my family to be on her side as much as possible, thanking God who has given me her wonderful motherhood with incredible blessings to my life. May our Lord and Savior Jesus Christ grant her joyous remaining time and a happy passage to eternity. Amen!

*Sr. Jorunn Hamre is a heroine of the Gospel and an extraordinary woman. Throughout her long life she has combined strong faith in Christ with love for humanity and commitment to serve those in acute need in the unreached areas. She has completed 55 years of service in Ethiopia and continues serving voluntarily aged 88. May God abundantly bless her!*

**Deed Jaldessa Kontoma,** her adopted son

## Hirut Beyene: 'The way God wanted me to be'

Hirut Beyene is the coordinator of the Hannah project and shares her story:

I am a disabled woman from the Konso tribe. I was born in Patengalto, a village in the south-western part of Ethiopia. From every generation God calls individuals to fulfill his will. I am one of them, called to be a servant for his kingdom.

My father, Beyene Gunna, was an evangelist and later became a reverend. My mother, Oshe Kusiza, brought up nine children and all are serving the Lord.

At the age of six I was attacked by polio and became unable to walk. I got depressed and felt inferior to my peers, since I could not run and jump any longer. This was the way God wanted me to be, the way he had chosen to work through me.

My father could not afford to pay for the operations. God raised missionaries from Norway who covered the costs for two hospital admissions and as a result my leg improved.

Starting from my preschool age I had a close relationship with God. He filled me with joy, visions and songs at a time when Christians stepped back from their faith and others were persecuted because of their Christian faith. God was with us and gave us a burden to pray for them.

I became a member of the youth committee and a choir leader. We established many choirs in Konso Parish and a translation committee at the main congregation. Years later God used the members of this committee as Konso translation team.

During the communist time (1974–1991) we visited different villages. We sang songs and shared the word of God; we encouraged each other and prayed for those suffering from persecution. Our faith grew and matured.

I did my Elementary school in Konso and my Secondary and High School in Awassa. The government did not allow me to go to college nor to get a job, because of my leg. While those doors were closed, the doors to voluntary service at the house of the Lord were wide open. I served in Arbaminch by praying, singing and teaching at Sunday school and by preaching and teaching new believers. This continued for five years until I was called to join a team to translate the four gospels and some epistles into Konso language. From then on I earned a salary.

## Giving the Bible to people in their own language

The spirituality of Konso people changed after they received the New Testament in their native language. *God became part of our culture and now he speaks our language.* In the past people would say, *So and so said this ...* But after getting the New Testament they said, *The Word of God says ...* Isn't it a blessing that believers start to live according to the Word of God? Isn't it a joy that the Word of God changes the mentality of believers? And the economic status of the Konso people changed too. Herdsmen carry the New Testament and read while taking care of their cattle. People are now longing to have the Old Testament in Konso language also.

After ten years of working for translation God opened the door of marriage for me. He gave me a God-fearing and handsome husband. We got one daughter and one son.

I was send with my family to Nairobi to study for my bachelor degree in Bible translation. At that time many Ethiopians left Nairobi and were going to America. My husband and I also decided to go to America. We would have gone, if God had not spoken to my heart through Gen 26, 12–25: If I would go back to Ethiopia he would bless Ethiopia 100 times like he blessed Isaac, the son of Abraham. In Nairobi our life was better than in Ethiopia. A call from God is better than a good life in safety. Sometimes it is difficult to listen to the voice of God. He calls and he gives the ability to survive in the midst of his ministry.

I returned to the South West Synod and coordinated the Bible Translation and Literacy Team, which is a very respectable and lovable ministry. From the start funds were lacking. My coordination included translation into eight languages. My salary was very low. When I could not survive on it any longer I left to Addis Ababa.

When I was called for the translation ministry, I told God that this work was not my gift. But the response I got from him was different. On an Analysis Grammar course my boss, Mirjami Uusitallo from Finland and I shared the same room. While sleeping bright light suddenly filled the room and a voice called my name three times, *Hirut, translation work is gospel work, it is a 24-hours work not an 8-hours work.* This was a call from the Almighty God. It was hard to coordinate all these translation projects but the power of leading was from God. It is not my intention to boast, rather to testify that God calls someone for his work and that is how he worked through me.

I have a message to the church leaders, since I don't have a chance to discuss with them. My appeal is that God gives the leaders a burden for Bible translation and literacy. Every tribe and nation should have their own Bible and read it in the language of their heart. Then they will sense God is theirs and part of their culture, because he starts communicating to them in their own words and they will fully understand.

*Hirut Beyene, courtesy of H. Beyene*

## A heart for Sunday school

A Norwegian missionary taught me Sunday school and I benefited from her teaching. In the last twenty-five years I have taught Sunday school children in different places. The church lacks teaching materials which help kids to grow mentally and spiritually. I decided to fill the gap and wrote text books and teacher guides.

Over the years I also realized the importance of a good family background on the development of children. The church through good teachers and biblical lessons can play an important role and exercise a lifelong influence in those kids.

The name of the books I am writing is: Building a New Generation and each of the books has its own sub-title. Ethiopia has more than 80 languages; Amharic can fit for many but not for all. If I can get the budget I hope we can translate the guides for parents, church leaders and Sunday school teachers into different languages.

# The ministry and visions of women today

# Women leaders

Women through their role in families pass on values to the next generation. In the same way faith has been handed down during biblical times. Paul testified about Timothy whom he considered his spiritual son: I have been reminded of your sincere faith, which first lived in your grandmother Lois and in your mother Eunice (2. Tim 1, 5).

In 2005 Aberash Dinssa, the Women's Ministry Coordinating Office Coordinator wrote:

*When we look at EECMY, from the beginning, there were pioneer mothers and sisters who first became Christians themselves, then persuaded and brought their husbands and other family members to Christianity. They contributed a lot to the spiritual growth of the church through their ministry of prayers, opening their homes for church services, caring for the sick and others in need, by contributing their personal knowledge and skills.*[180]

However, the lack of women in public life and as persons in key positions reinforces the stereotype that women cannot fulfill these tasks.

Bekure Daba, Elsabet Gulti and Sophie Gebreyes are examples of women leaders today. Their stories reveal the challenges they faced, the support they received and their achievements.

## 1. Bekure Daba: The first ordained woman pastor in Ethiopia

### Her struggle for education

Bekure Daba was born into an Orthodox family in 1961. Her parents were farmers in Kiltu Kara. At an early age she was attracted by the only book in the house. No one read it, but she used to cuddle it and carry it around like a doll. When someone asked what she was carrying, she would say, *this is my book.*

---

[180] The EECMY's Women's Ministry, WMCO, Development, Major Undertakings. Future prospects, page 5

At the age of six Bekure went to the local primary school. Most girls did not attend school at that time. Her father did not approve of her going to school and chased her away. Her elder brother had a positive view of educating girls and took her into his house. With his economic and moral support she completed grade four, which laid the foundation for the educational ladder she would climb up.

During her junior secondary school years Bekure came to know an Evangelical congregation. She attended confirmation classes and became a member of the EECMY. Later, when she was in her final years of secondary school she got an invitation letter from her congregation to sit for the entrance exam for theological studies. Four girls sat for this exam, Bekure passed.

## Women students at the Mekane Yesus Seminary (MYS)

Bekure left the area of her childhood in order to study theology in Addis Ababa. Four years later she graduated with a diploma in theology from the MYS. Two out of twenty-eight students in her course were female. She recalls: *We were loved and respected by teachers and students alike, there was no discrimination against us as women students.*

The MYS at Mekanissa was inaugurated in 1960, shortly after the EECMY was registered as a national church. The objective of the seminary was to train theologians. In the first twelve years (1960–72) there were only a few students and a number of them went for jobs outside the church.

Rahel Kidane from the South Ethiopia Synod was the first and only female student in the 6th diploma course together with thirteen male students. Why had female students not been admitted before? The reason is no mystery. The cultural trend of the day was that the Ethiopian society at large had low regard for the education of women which had an impact on the church as well.

Hirut Magarsaa (Central Synod) started her studies in the following Diploma Course in 1975 together with ten male students. The following Diploma Course had two female learners: Bekure Daba (Western Synod) and Tenagne Niguse (Kaffa Illubabor Bethel Synod). Abebech Shamebo (South Ethiopia Synod) was the fifth female student, admitted to the 11th

Diploma Course in 1981. These four Synods encouraged women to join theological education.

Over the decades the percentage of female students has been steadily increasing from 2.4% in the seventies to 11% from 2010–2018. Overall 6.7% of theologians trained at MYS have been women.

Unlike the graduates of the 1960s, most graduates in the following years went back to their respective synods to serve in any position offered to them. Male theologians were ordained and became pastors with chances of promotion to other positions in the church. Almost all Synod Presidents, Executive Secretaries; Evangelism Department Directors, etc. were MYS graduates. The women served in positions such as Women's Secretary of the synod.

## First assignments and further studies

After her graduation Bekure served for more than ten years as Women's Secretary leading all affairs of the Western Synod related to women. This was during the time of the Derg. In her synod churches were closed and a number of pastors were imprisoned.

During this time Bekure and her fellow student Rev Tesso got married. She gave birth to their three children and shouldered the double responsibility of a working mother with small children.

In 1993 Bekure and her husband were awarded a scholarship to the UK to do their master studies. They left with their children and obtained a masters degree in Christian/religious education from Liverpool University. Afterwards they went home to serve their church. Bekure was assigned the same position that she had held before she left for the studies.

Ten years later both Rev Bekure and her husband had another chance of a scholarship. Rev Bekure was granted PhD studies at the University of Liverpool. Her experiences as the first ordained women pastor in Ethiopia guided her in the choice of her research topic: The role and status of women in the holistic ministry of the EECMY.

## Challenging the role and place of women in the EECMY

Male graduate theologians of the Mekane Yesus Seminary were ordained; female students – despite exhibiting more dedication than some of the men – were not ordained because the question of ordination of women was not raised in the EECMY.

During her theological studies a journalist interviewed Bekure for the LWF and asked: 'Do *you want to be ordained?'* Her response was clear: *"No, I do not want to be ordained, but according to 1. Peter 2, 9 there is nothing to prevent women from taking up that ministry."* At that time none of the four female theologians had asked for ordination.

The reason given for not ordaining women was that they were not educated enough. The attitude prevailed that men are the only capable and powerful people for leadership and decision making.

Five years later, in 1985, Bekure asked: Now women are educated theologians and they have experience, why are they not ordained?

## The Western Synod takes the initiative

Immediately after Bekure graduated, Rev Mergersa Guta, the director of the Evangelism Department of her synod told her: 'You *are equal to the men who graduated with you. At our next church officers meeting we will discuss the ordination of women and we will apply to the church.'* The Western Synod brought ordination of women to the agenda of the EECMY and made sure that this issue stayed on the agenda for the coming years.

Although it seemed to be a new subject, women's ministry is as old as the age of the church. Christ himself chose Mary Magdalene and said: *Go and tell the disciples that I am returning to my father (John 20, 17).*

Thousands of women have played important roles in God's salvation history. Likewise in Ethiopia, women were among the pioneers of the gospel. In the 1980s, the years of the communist regime, churches were closed and their leaders imprisoned. Women secretly met in their homes for prayer and their courage kept the light of the gospel burning. They raised funds, kept the church economically alive and took care of the families of those who were in prison.

The legacy and the witness of women contributed to the openness of the Western Synod to a new role and status of women in the church different from their role and status in society at large. Finally the Western Synod was also the pioneer in taking the major step of calling the first woman theologian to become a pastor.

## The long road to the ordination of women

In 1981 the EECMY Evangelism and Theological Commission discussed women's ordination for the first time. A series of consultations, workshops and seminars were conducted at all levels of the church. This took quite a long time with several ups and downs.

Tenanje Negusse of the then women's section of the EECMY and one of the first female EECMY theology graduates was the first to encourage women ordination against the strong opposition from within the EECMY. Fear of opposition by the EOC, by other denominations and by missions that do not ordain their ministers were other factors that needed to be overcome.

The breakthrough came in 1997 when the Assembly resolved to ordain qualified women with a call from God and from a congregation to be ordained and serve as a pastor.

Implementation of the decision required a careful approach. It demanded more workshops and sensitization programme to transform the church by bringing awareness, a change of attitude and understanding about women's ordination and participation in the ministry. This project was financed by the LWF.

After 20 years Bekure Daba was ordained and became the first woman pastor. The EECMY was the first of all churches in Ethiopia to accept and support the ministry of women, faithful to their mission statement of 'Serving the whole person' by all persons. The ceremony of this historic moment took place on 16.5.2000.

## The first generation of ordained women

In Ethiopia the various cultures share the idea that women's place is at home and men should be out in the public arena. However, there may be

*Rev. Bekure Daba, courtesy of B. Daba*

intercultural differences with regard to the status given to women in their respective societies. Traditional wisdom as expressed in proverbs gives less respect and value to women and their stories are rarely told, they simply are forgotten. Secondly, the Orthodox environment manifests the same male-centered world view. Members with such background bring this view to the church. The third discouraging factor may have been the lack of female missionary pastors and the subordinate role of women in their own mission societies. Women in the EECMY had no foreign role model. So it was a big step to assign a woman to the leading position of a pastor.

The first ordination was soon followed by the second one that of Hirut Megersa, a woman theologian from Naqamte. She had been the second woman theologian trained at the MYS. After her ordination she became the leader of the Evangelism Department of the Central Synod in Naqamte.

In the following years only few women (10) were ordained. Either the congregations did not come forward with candidates or women theologians were not willing to be ordained. A number of synods were skeptical about this new development.

From 2014 onwards the number of women pastors increased. In 2018 there are 89 womenpastors and 4.271 male pastors[181] (2%). Almost all synods have ordained women theologians. This shows that there is a change and the obstacles are gradually being overcome.

### Reverend Bekure Daba

Rev Bekure Daba's first assignment was to be the pastor of a congregation. One year later she was transferred to Gimbi Jorgo Synod, a newly established synod, and became the head of the Evangelism Department. After a few months she was elected as the first female Synod president of the church for a term of four years.

Besides her normal responsibilities, she initiated a project on female genital mutilation (FGM) in one of her parishes. She was respected among her colleagues for her firm stand in the administration of church matters.

After she completed her term of office she joined Liverpool University to do her PhD in theology. Rev Bekure examined and assessed the role and status of women in the 'holistic' ministry of the EECMY on congregational, district and synod as well as on national levels. This is the first comprehensive research to be undertaken on that wide field.

Finally the little girl that had cuddled a Bible had become a woman holding a PhD in theology.

### Investigating women's roles in the EECMY

In recent years women in the EECMY have become a research topic. Rev Debela Birri, then one of the staff of the MYS wrote his master's thesis on: Women and Ministry in the New Testament: Ordain them or not? (1986)

In 2007 a paper on the role and status of women in the holistic service of the EECMY in three districts of the Western synods was submitted by Melkamu Dhunfa. The paper concluded that women play a significant role in choirs and prayer-groups, at Sunday school and in youth ministry;

---

[181] From the 29 synods of the EECMY 18 synods have ordained female pastors.

they clean the church buildings and they serve guests. Their contribution to the economy of the church and church construction activities is significant. Church owned pre-school education is rendered by women.

Preaching is one of the central activities of the EECMY's spiritual services. Women play only a very minor role in this. For a long period they have been excluded from getting theological education. The lack of women teachers in church owned schools (5%) is significant. This is known to have a negative impact on the academic performance of female students.

In short, women's roles are limited to serving, which is still considered of low status, even though Jesus had a different view about service. Though they play an active role in the church, their service often remains invisible. In preaching and teaching women's contribution is minimal. The study concluded that the status of women in the EECMY is rather low.

## The research of Rev Bekure

A number of policy decisions have been passed to authorize women's involvement in different Church ministries, e.g. the decision in 1973 that they should constitute 25% of decision making bodies. But still women are silent in the EECMY. Why is this? This was the research question Rev Bekure examined in her PhD paper.

From the abstract:

The study reveals that women are denied opportunity to participate fully in four key areas of decision-making, evangelism, leadership and ordained ministry because of theological and cultural reasons. Women experience exclusion through under-representation and restricted participation in various areas of EECMY's holistic ministry, but particularly in top leadership roles. Findings show that theological arguments are used to subordinate women with the effect that in the home, church and wider public spheres they are relegated to domestic rather than strategic roles.

The study then seeks to respond to the cultural and theological barriers by proposing a theology that is inclusive and liberating. It does this by means of biblical texts and Gospel stories. Some texts such as 1 Cor. 14:34–35, 1 Tim. 2:11–15 and Gen. 2, 3 are often used to legitimize men's authority over women and keep them in submission. Women can find a scriptural basis for their full involvement in the ministry of the Church by using different texts, such as 1 Cor. 11:5, Gal. 3:28 and Gen. 1:27, as lenses through which the other texts may be read.

The thesis proposes adoption of a series of principles, including con-scientization, engendered theological education and partnership. Embracing these principles will lead women in the EECMY to develop and engage in practical strategies to gradually bring about positive change so that the barriers of patriarchy will be dismantled and women will achieve full representation and participation in public, strategic and valued areas of ministry.

### Dr Bekure's service at EECMY head office

After Rev Bekure graduated with the PhD in Theology she was assigned to the head office. She is heading the women evangelism section of the Women's ministry department and is responsible for capacity building.

Rev Dr Bekure returned with funds from the UK to strengthen 300 women economically and to train 36 women: 2 Masters, 30 Bachelors and 4 Diploma graduated from 2013–18.

Twenty years after the first ordination, the EECMY is still the only church in Ethiopia with ordained women pastors; however it seems gender equality in the EECMY has still a way to go such as assigning appropriate positions and salaries to qualified women.

**Christel Ahrens**

## 2.  Elsabet Gulti: Big challenges, but God provided

### Background

Elsabet Gulti Dibaba was born in Wolisso in 1962. Soon afterwards her family moved to Konso in Gamo Gofa. Elsabet did not grow up in a Christian family. One day, when her Mom had sent her off in an errand she used the opportunity to peek inside a church. This led to more frequent visits and one Sunday, when the preacher called people to come forward and receive Jesus as their savior, she stepped up and proclaimed her faith.

When her parent decided to move on to a new place Ms. Eva Djupvik, a Norwegian missionary serving in Konso at that time, arranged for her to stay at the hostel. Elsabet moved into the hostel only twelve years old, and continued her education while working as a part time babysitter for an Icelandic missionary family. She was sent to Gidole to continue at High School. Elsabet was active in the church and the youth ministry. After finishing High School she moved to Arba Minch and later to Awassa where she got a job at the EECMY Synod center.

Elsabet was working as a secretary when she was asked to join the Women's Ministry together with Norwegian missionary Ms. Jorunn Sorbo. Having served for thirteen years, she was sent to Mekane Yesus Seminary for a two-year leadership program. Later she continued her studies by distance education and now she has a Bachelor in Theology.

When she returned from her studies in Addis Ababa, the South Ethiopian Synod had been divided into several new synods, and Elsabet was asked to join the synod in Hagere Maryam. She accepted and led the Women's Ministry there for sixteen years, traveling back and forth between her family in Awassa and her ministry in Hagere Maryam.

## Contribution to the Women's Ministry

During her many years in ministry Elsabet has equipped and empowered women both spiritually and socially. Elsabet's approach to ministry has always been holistic and she has purposefully addressed all areas of women's lives both within the church as well as in the society.

In Hagere Maryam there was no budget for the Women's Ministry office at the synod, and though there were many things to do, it was difficult to get things done without funds. At that time Elsabet received an invitation to attend a Women's Conference in Germany to represent Ethiopia. People from ten different African countries discussed in Berlin how best to empower women in church and society.

Elsabet returned back with funds to carry out awareness training for women on the issue of Female Genital Mutilations (FGM). But instead of using the money for the training she invested the fund in building a cafeteria on the synod compound in order to secure continuous income for the women's ministry. When the cafeteria was up and running, the income was used to give training to create awareness about FGM and many other things.

*Elsabet Gulti, courtesy of R. Osmundsen*

Regarding FGM, Elsabet shares that she has a very clear stand in this matter, and she has on several occasions prohibited FGM from taking place within her own family as well as among neighbors.

Elsabet has traveled around in the synod, shared the word of God and arranged different kinds of training for the community. She has addressed the issues of Harmful Traditional Practices in regard to the role of women and wives in the society and trained men and women about these issues.

She has also trained married couples about marriage and family life.

A number of men admitted that they had caused extra burdens on their wives. Due to not doing their share of the work at home and participating in the responsibilities of the household they had failed to support their women.

## Challenges in the ministry

The budget limitations for the work in the Women's Ministry Office continued throughout the years even though there was income from the cafeteria. That and the little support from the leaders in the synod most of them men, were the biggest challenges for Elsabet. The constant fundraising and struggle to get the issues of the women on the agenda at the synod office were tiring. Additionally, the geographical area of the synod was vast and transportation was often scarce when Elsabet was traveling around to visit the congregations and give training to the church members. Twice she has been in motorbike accidents, but both times she has seen God's interference and she was able to continue with only minor injuries.

Something that often made Elsabet consider quitting was the issue of serving so far from her home. Due to the distance between Hagere Maryam and Awassa, and weekends being the only time when church members were available for training, Elsabet was not able to spend time with her children on a regular basis. Often she experienced that when she had been home for some time and was about to leave, one of the kids would fall ill, and it was a tough decision to have to leave a sick child at home in order to return to her ministry.

## It is an honor to serve

What kept Elsabet going for all these years were a clear calling from God and an understanding that it is a privilege to serve in His kingdom. And then the unwavering support of her faithful husband. He carried a lot of the responsibility for the household and the children, making it possible for Elsabet to be a fulltime minister. Elsabet has always considered it an honor to serve God and she is grateful for the opportunity to serve and for how God has provided for her and her family all these years. Elsabet's history is a story of God's provision and care for His children, and Elsabet is filled with gratitude seeing her children succeed academically, and knowing that her parents and siblings too have become Christians.

**Ruth Osmundsen**

### 3.  Sophie Gebreyes: 'Know what you want and work towards it'

As of 2013 the Office of the Lutheran World Federation (LWF) in Ethiopia is directed by Sophie Gebreyes. She was interviewed by Ebise Ashana, a colleague working in the same building at the Development and Social Service commission of the EECMY.

**Question 1:** *Sophie, please tell us who you are and how you managed to get to this position!*

My name is Sophia Gebreyes, born and bred in Ethiopia, now a Canadian citizen. I am 51 years old, single and have no children. I am the second of three children born to my parents Gebreyes Haile and Fantaye Berhane.

The position was a long time coming and in the most indirect way. My childhood dreams were not an indication where my life path would take me later on in life. I remember that my dream as a child was either to become a stewardess on Ethiopian Airlines or to become a multilingual interpreter for the United Nations. Those were the two ways that I could imagine would take me places and speak many languages, two things I was passionate about. Looking back, I came to live out my dream, in a totally different way that I had imagined as a child.

My father worked in development all his life and on vacation and when school was out, I used to travel with him to the field, very remote areas of the country, during my adolescent years. Looking back I think that those field trips left a huge impression on me but did not know at the time when and how I would end up in the same field as him. That started to change when I left the Addis University Law faculty in 1987 and joined a French NGO, Action International Contre la Faim in Addis for whom I worked for three years. It was my first job ever, but one where I would cut my teeth in development. Straight out from university had no professional skills and I was basically hired because I was literate but most of all I spoke French fluently. Having studied at the Lycée franco-éthiopien Guébré-Mariam School, I was trilingual and most of my time was spent as a go between the French senior staff and the local staff. I also did everything, from correspondence to filing, and reviewing project documents. Really I was what one would call a Girl Friday. I did that for three years and then I moved to Canada in mid-1990. There, I worked as a Secretary Receptionist in Winnipeg, Manitoba for an organisation called Canadian Lutheran World Relief (CLWR). I worked or CLWR for a total of seventeen years and held many positions starting with Secretary/Receptionist, Program Assistant for Asia and Asia programs, Alternative Trade officer, Program Director for Latin America Programs.

During my years in CLWR, from 1990 to 2007, I learned and grew a lot professionally. I was working full time and going to the university part time (evenings) which took several years. I studied French Literature and International Development Studies. Those years were the years that prepared me for what I am doing today. It was also during those years that I met several of my mentors, persons who significantly contributed to who I am today. They are many but will only mention six who left an indelible imprint on my life.

1990–1992 First and foremost was the then Executive Director, Rev Dr. David E. Hardy, who gave me my first break back in 1990 and who made my first years at CLWR memorable. There, I met and worked Mrs. Ursula Lange, a German Canadian, survivor of World War II and immigration expert who became instrumental in my settling-in in Canada. Another person who took me under her wings was Mrs. Dorothy Lamberton who basically became my Canadian adoptive parent. Dorothy and I started in CLWR the same day and that became the tie that binds us still.

Mid 1990s to early 2000s after Rev Hardy left his position, CLWR welcomed its first woman representative, Ms Ruth Jensen. Ruth having lived in India and in Nepal for many years was very welcoming of refugees and immigrants. She also had an uncanny ability to spot talent and to nurture them. This is how I remember her as she was the one who gave me my first executive position in CLWR. During those years, I count myself lucky to have met and worked with two special persons, my mentors: Susan Walsh, who was the Manager of the bilateral Andean Program in Bolivia and Peru and also doubled as International Program Director and Mr. Erling Nielsen, a Dane who was the Finance Manager.

Of course I worked hard also; money however was never my motivation. I worked for many years earning a low salary, paying my way through school, taking the bus to and fro work every day. I was aware that what I was getting working along such people was better than university and more than anything I enjoyed the international travels I was afforded due to my position that took me to exotic places such as India, Mozambique, Haiti, Peru, Bolivia, Switzerland, Zambia and Zimbabwe. My childhood dream was now slowly coming true.

Before my mentor Susan left to take up a position in Ottawa in 2004, she groomed me to take up the position of Director Latin America Program along with one-month Spanish language training in Sucre Bolivia.

After seven-teen years, in 2007, I decided to work overseas and I accepted a position of Program Coordinator for the LWF in Kigali, Rwanda where I stayed for 2 years. This was four-teen years after the Rwandan genocide, and the country was clearly consigning that sad chapter to history and moving on and so did the LWF program in Rwanda. I oversaw the close out process of the program and applied for a position of Program Officer for Latin America and the Caribbean in Geneva, Switzerland where the LWF headquarters were located. I had picked up Spanish during my work as Director for Latin America Program in Canada and so obtained the position. I held that position for three and half years. During that time, Angola, Mozambique was added to my portfolio so was supervising a total of eight countries: Angola, the Regional Central America Program including El Salvador, Guatemala, Honduras and Nicaragua), Colombia, Haiti and Mozambique. In 2011 I went to Salvador, Brazil for Portuguese language training which was a dream come true. The most notable experience during my three and a half stint in Geneva was the Haiti devastating earthquake in January 2010 which occurred just a few months after I assumed the position in October 2009.

In 2013 the Country Representative for LWF Ethiopia became vacant and I decided to move back to Ethiopia after more than two decades of living abroad. I felt that I could bring my career spanning two decades and all the experience that took me to various places and various positions to bear on the work that I do today.

**Question 2:** *How do you see the position of women here in the Ethiopian society?*

I come from a family where the women are very strong so from my early childhood, I believed that women can do anything. I give that credit to my Mom and Dad. So I don't have any personal experience of struggle as a woman in Ethiopia and even less in Canada and/or Switzerland. I remember one time my father was visiting in Canada and my Ethiopian friends were astonished how we were friends with my father, which to me was very strange. 'How can you speak to your dad like that' they would tell as I was not using the polite form of 'irswo' addressing him, but joking and teasing him. To me that was the most natural thing to do. But be that as it may, working development so I am very familiar of the plight of women, the injustice they face in meeting both their practical and strategic needs. This is why I really think that we should include men in gender equality training, but most importantly socializing them differently from boyhood. However, sometimes women in the Ethiopian society are also complicit in what is happening by perpetuating social norms that keep boys and men away from certain roles like taking care of small children, cooking and cleaning and the like. I agree with Gloria Steinem who once said: "The first problem for all of us, men and women, is not to learn, but to unlearn."

But overall, I am optimistic; the wheels of change are turning. I see more women graduating from university, more professional women engaged in traditional male occupations, more women in Parliament, in diplomacy and in aviation. That gives me hope.

**Question 3:** *What are some of the challenges you faced by being a woman and a leader? Is there something specific to Ethiopia?*

Both CLWR and LWF are equal opportunity employers par excellence, so I have not faced challenges being a woman leader due to my gender working for both. However, women leaders can be exposed to sexual harassment and abuse of power just as any other women especially when working in the field. I had that happen a couple of times. This is not specific to Ethiopia, it can happen anywhere.

I think that many think that women leaders are soft, 'motherly' and therefore expect that they can get away with misconducts without so much a reprimand. It is important that women set the tone the first day of work and send a clear message about ethical and accountability standards that

*Sophie Gebreyes(right) and Ebise Ashana, courtesy C. Ahrens*

all should uphold as well as show that women can take tough decisions, establishing from a get-go a rapport based on mutual respect.

There is no shortage of women leaders in Ethiopia, but sometimes to break the glass ceiling, besides personal perseverance, one needs an enabling environment to thrive in and support to unleash the untapped potential to the fullest.

**Question 4:** *You are working within the LWF – What do you recommend to women in the Lutheran churches?*

My recommendation is perseverance and to be in it (fight) for the long haul. It took me seventeen years to finally do what I wanted to do, go to the field and manage programs. It takes time to break the glass ceiling but one needs to know what you want and work towards it. Be fearless, believe in oneself and never take no as an answer.

**Question 5:** *What would you like to see happen within the EECMY with regards to women?*

I would like to see a Woman President of the Church someday but I have a feeling that might be a long way off, but to start with I think the Church should allow women in leadership to be in charge of departments beyond gender, women and children affairs. I really do believe the world would be a better place when men are in charge of women and children's affairs just like women can thrive in traditionally male occupations.

*Thank you very much for this interview and all words of encourage-ment!*

**Ebise Ashana**

# Projects by and for women

In most congregations[182] groups of women meet regularly. They put Hebr. 13, 16 into practice: *Do not forget to do good and to help one another, because that are the sacrifices that please God.*

Their financial contributions seem small and insignificant. Compared to well-funded church projects theirs is rather like the two copper coins in the Temple treasury (Lk 21, 1–4). They do what their biblical sisters Mary Magdalene, Johanna and Susanna did (Lk 8, 1).

Their contributions benefit all. But who takes care of their needs? The following four projects target women as beneficiaries.

## 1. My Sisters: Support for destitute women at Nefas Silk Lafto

### The beginning

Marit Bakke recalled in an email how it all began:

*My family had spent thirteen years at the Mekane Yesus Seminary in Mekanissa, Addis Ababa. We left for further studies. Several years later when my husband and I were to return to Ethiopia, there was one thing I dreaded: the begging women in front of the door of our house. I knew they would come, one by one, to greet me and to tell me about their problems. Each of them could only think of her own misery and was blind to the problems of her neighbor. I asked myself: Will it be the same all over again? I knew I had to do something about this situation. Could they learn to see each other as sisters, who support each other rather than as competitors for aid?*

*My Sisters started without any great visions and glorious plans. I wanted to get the begging women on my doorsteps a bit away from me. I wanted them to take some actions to better their own lives, ambitious? Maybe, but with God's help, it succeeded. The women had resources I never had expected.*

---

[182] According to 2019 statistics the EECMY has 9003 congregations

*We were not yet organized and established in 1988. For two to three years we just came together, twenty-five women in my home. Aster's mother* <u>Suriash</u> *served coffee and cakes, she was eager for this. Nothing important happened, but something invisible had made a change.*

*In 1994 the day came we could open My Sisters' first place, a second-hand clothes shop and a shop for renting out wedding outfits. With the small income from that we had the opportunity to give medical assistance to some poor women and children. We see this as our official opening. During the ceremony, one of the twenty-five women asked if she could be allowed to give a speech. She formed it as a prayer* "Heavenly Father, I thank you that you have made me rich. Now I am wealthy enough to help those who are needier than me." *She and most of the other women, I had felt a burden to me some years before, are now members of My Sisters Association.*

<u>*Aster Haile-Michael, Aster Negassa, Hajima Beyene, Ayantu Shiferraw*</u> <u>*and Sr Tihun Tola*</u> *have all carried the work forward together with all the staff, they are all important."*

Marit concluded her email with gratitude: *God gave me My Sisters, a gift and great blessing!*

## The organisation

My Sisters Women's Welfare Association, a non-profit, non-religious, humanitarian and development-oriented organisation, was officially registered in 1999. The objective is to alleviate the problems of young and adult destitute women, including their vulnerable children, youth and local communities in Addis Ababa, at Silk Lafto Sub city, Woreda 02 and 03.

The vision is to see a poverty and disease-free, active, empowered, and productive society, by assisting marginalized segments of the community such as destitute women, children and youth to improve their life including health, education and social and economic wellbeing.

My Sisters has five specific goals. These are to build the economic capacity of vulnerable women, to enhance the lives of vulnerable children, to strengthen the skills of youth, to increase the awareness in the community and to strengthen the capacity of the organisation.

## My Sisters in 2019

The association is operating four branches each with a day care centre for eighty-two children from six months to four years of age. Thus their single mothers are enabled to go for training or work. Tutorial services are offered for children from grade three to eight and students from grade seven to twelve can make use of reading room facilities. My Sisters facilitates a sponsorship program for targeted children and provides scholarship support for high school girls and university students. Most children are doing well in their academic career and the organisation is proud of two students who graduated in medicine, one became a pilot and several students studied engineering.

My Sisters facilitates training in child care and hair dressing to increase opportunities of young women and their chances to get employment.

Poor people who are sick are supported to access and afford medical treatment. Home visitors give awareness on health, hygiene, nutrition, HIV/AIDS counseling and child care.

The capacity building project focuses to enhance the organisation's capacity and accessibility of its service to the vast majority of destitute women and orphans in its project area.

Every year more than two thousand families are receiving services from the above mentioned activities.

## The people behind

Mrs. Marit Bakke and many supporters in Norway formed a Foundation in 2007 and raise funds. Marit wrote: *My Sisters in Ethiopia does not spend more money than necessary and most of all; they give the clients first priority.* On the Ethiopian end currently forty-two full-time and five part-time employees, almost all women, are running the work. A local board oversees the general activities while an international board in Norway is following on fundraising and fund spending.

### Aster Haile Michael

Aster Haile Michael was born in 1973 in Makanissa. She knows Mrs. Marit from her childhood. As a high school student she was helping her as a translator.

When My Sisters moved from Mrs. Marit's home into a container, there were three people; a cashier, a salesperson of second hand clothes and a guard.

Aster has a diploma in Management, a Bachelor in leadership and a Masters Degree in Development Management from the MYS Leadership College. She is married and the mother of two children.

What is special about My Sisters? Aster said their different activities are integrated whereas many other organisations give either sponsorship or HIV services only.

I have been visiting My Sisters several times over the last twenty years and I always felt the friendly approach of the employees. So I wanted to know 'the secret behind'. Aster responded, *Seeing that what we do is vital for poor women and children motivates every staff, most of whom are born in the same area. It is a pleasure to work for one's own community. Most of all God brought like-minded people together; all are eager to serve the poor.* The staff has morning devotions and twice a week a prayer programme at lunch time, participation is voluntary.

**Christel Ahrens**

## 2.  Biftu Bole congregation, Gudina Tumsa Foundation and Terkanfi

### Biftu Bole EECMY Congregation

'*I will give you a spacious compound, where you will reside*' These were the words of the second promise Tsehay Tolassa received while in prison, a promise fulfilled fourteen years after she was freed. Tsehay entered the 'promised compound' and vowed to set up a church right there to serve and honour him who answered her in the days of her distress, who never forsook her as she walked through the valleys of the shadows of death. Tsehay lived on that compound until she was called to her heavenly home.

During the memorial event following her burial Marta Kuwe Kumsa, a former inmate who had spent ten years in prison with Tsehay, stood up and testified: *This church did not start in this compound but in Kechele prison. Every night after the guards had left she called the women prisoners, read the bible, sang hymns and prayed with us.*

Bibles entered the prison secretly; to be found with Bibles was deadly. This underground ministry was the nucleus of the Prison Fellowship Ethiopia, an NGO later founded by Tsehay and Rev Birhanu Tedese.

Being older than most other prisoners, Tsehay was regarded as a mother and allowed to move around in the various barracks. She initiated small scale industries, so that the prisoners could support their families with the income of the sale of their products. Tsehay served fellow inmates as nurse and midwife. During those years she attended grade 9–12 and completed her high school education.

At Biftu Bole congregation that spirit of holistic ministry is alive. Times of worship embrace elements of culture and art, as these are God's gifts. The gospel is expressed in the context of a modern city in the 21st century, e.g. the young generation presents her songs and choreography and may lead a service. Christian literature in Oromo language is promoted. Many churchgoers stay behind after Sunday service for lunch at the church run restaurant and thus use the opportunity to have fellowship in a town where anonymity grows. The income generated from the sale of foods is used to support social projects of the congregation.[183]

## Gudina Tumsa Foundation

The Gudina Tumsa Foundation (GTF), founded in 1992, is run by Aster and Leensa Gudina. They named the NGO after their father Gudina Tumsa, the late General Secretary of the EECMY who was martyred by the communist government in 1979.

GTF took up a mission to the Karayu. The Karayu are pastoralists in Fantalle, only 200 km from the capital but deprived of any type of service

---

[183] Street children are fed and cared for by the diaconal team of the church. The mentally ill from rural areas are brought to compound where they receive spiritual and physical nurture. The poor are economically empowered through income generating activities.

including schools, water and health clinics. This arid land lies in the depths of the Great Rift Valley and receives an unreliable 400 to 700 mm of rainfall per year. Fantalle goes for long seasons without rain and in recent years the region has been suffering through a merciless drought.

Workinesh Begi was among the first employees in the GTF and served for more than a decade. In an interview she talked about the beginnings in Fantalle:

*Out of forty five children who were enrolled at the school there was only one girl. The Karayu were reserved in sending their female children. It took her father courage to stand alone among his community and resolve to send his daughter to school. On the occasion of the inauguration of the school the girl's father testified saying, "sending my girl to school meant becoming like an out-cast in my own community. I knew that if I educated my daughter she would come back to her community just like Aster, Leensa and Workinesh who set good example for us."*

GTF offered separate workshops for elders, men, women and girls. Some girls confided to GTF staff that their parents force them to get married. *"We told them that the men should get an HIV test first."* When two of the future husbands tested HIV-positive and the grandfathers still insisted the girls should marry them, three girls ran away and stayed on Karayu Mountain for one week. Thereafter the girls were kept in Addis Ababa until a girls' boarding was opened in Fantalle. The local police promised to secure their safety.

Twenty families sent their girls and even more were begging for a place in the girls' boarding. In the end thirty girls were admitted; today some of them are electric engineers, nurses and lawyers.

The word the Karayu used to express giving their girls in marriage was "selling a girl". Workinesh said they made sure the people agreed never to say again that they sell their girls. The Karayu were concerned if anyone would marry a school girl. GTF staff told them that boys who went to school may come to know them and marry them.

Fantalle is a very dry area without trees. GTF recruited volunteer women and trained them on environmental issues and the importance of trees. The women received donkey carts to water the plants. The outcome of their work is a place with many trees providing shade.

Though GTF can no longer run the school the number of educated Karayu has gone up to thousands. What is even more surprising: girls outnumber boys in school.

Workinesh said that Mama Tsehay was a source of inspiration for her; *always positive, never giving up and often saying, 'this will pass.'*

### Terkanfi

Workinesh Begi studied Community Development in the United States, the country where her daughter is living. Back in Ethiopia Workinesh founded Terkanfi, meaning steps. The motto of Terkanfi is:

***Start where you are, use what you have, learn what you need ... and start walking.***

Workinesh lives in Dukem, a transit town on the Eastern highway. Seeing the streets full of young girls from all over Ethiopia after 8 pm was a shock for her. She talked to the Social Affairs Office and began to train women and to provide seed money, so they could break the cycle of poverty, prostitution and AIDS. Eighty women were enabled to start a new life.

Currently Terkanfi is educating and supporting one-hundred destitute women in a nearby camp for displaced people from Somali region.

Workinesh belongs to the EECMY. She sees her church slightly more progressive than other churches, as the EECMY is ordaining women. According to her long years of experience the potential of women and their visions cannot develop because of their poor economic situation, the lack of encouragement and opportunities.

When asked to compare leadership styles of men and women she answered, *women are perfect leaders, because as mothers they care and they have listening and mentoring skills; these are the characteristics of a good leader.*

Workinesh welcomes the move of the government towards 50% representation of women at all levels. She said, *Christian women tend to go after spiritual issues and are usually not interested in politics. In general taking up responsibility in politics is not encouraged by the church, but this needs to change. The life of Moses is a good example and there are many others in the Bible."*

## In the steps of their parents

Aster and Leensa continue the ministry of their parents. They described their family life:

*Our father was often absent, but whenever he was home he spent time with his family. He discussed issues with his children. One of his most frequent prayers was:* Help us to live to the good of others and to the glory of God. *He lived what he prayed for.*

*Our mother used to get up around 4 o'clock in the morning. After cleaning the house and having a shower, she burnt incense and prayed for hours while standing. We remember some of her frequent prayer phrases:* Waqaayoo, moti motoota (God, king of kings ... ), *words we heard many times while half asleep. She had a calling herself and feared God in a loving and submissive way.*

*When our father addressed us he would say: "Your mother and I ... " He expressed his appreciation for his wife by saying, that our mother was the most beautiful woman.*

*Our mother was his driver and accompanied him many times. They had friends together, not to themselves and they enjoyed each other's company. Being highly intellectual our father would share many ideas with her at night, such as ecumenism and moratorium by using words she understood.*

*We consider their marriage as ideal like the marriage of Isaac and Rebecca and the marriage of Aquila and Priscilla.*

*In our childhood we received a spiritual training at home, by the daily bible reading and singing from the hymn book in our mother tongue.*

*Aster and Leensa are talking with their children about passing on the heritage and challenge them. God gives children so they become godly off springs. Parents have to raise them in a godly way and promote their potentials.*

**Ebise Ashana and Christel Ahrens**

## 3. Women of Hope: Project Hannah

*"Should not this woman be set free from what bound her?"* (Luke 13, 16)
The person Jesus talked about had been sick for 18 years; she was bent
over and could not straighten up. Many women in Ethiopia are bent over,
because of the burdens they are carrying.

Trans World Radio – Women of Hope (TWR WOH) was founded in
1997 with the name Project Hannah. Their vision is to bring hope to women
through radio programs. Radio messages reach people in places where others cannot reach, e.g. to women in prison and to maid servants in the Arab
world. Their mission statement is to educate, encourage and equip women
to pray, listen, learn, grow and to give by using media, small group interac-
tion and leadership development.

TWR WOH operates worldwide and sends messages in over seventy
languages. When in 2008 two Ethiopian women went for training to Nairobi
and shared the burden and tears of women in their country, the Ethiopian
branch of TWR WOH was born. Yemissrach Dimts[184], the EECMY communication service and a joint program of their synods, is their partner. Radio programs in Amharic and Oromo are recorded at the Yemissrach Dimts
radio studio and transmitted weekly.

The information below is from the bulletin on the occasion of the 10-
year anniversary of Women of Hope in Ethiopia, 2019.

### Radio and prayer, advocacy and mercy

The TWR WOH is a service in which women learn from each other, know
and comfort one another, edify and help one another. The teachings by
TWR WOH have brought awakening and fellowship among women of different churches and among women of different generations.

Next to radio the second pillar of TWR WOH is prayer ministry. The
project staff in Ethiopia dedicate Wednesdays to prayer. Every three months
members of the EECMY churches in the capital and outside meet for a day
of prayer. TWR WHO's international prayer letter is translated and unites
women in Ethiopia with their sisters around the globe.

---

[184] = Voice of the Gospel (Amharic).

Advocacy, the third ministry, has been a challenge, since the previous government did not permit NGOs to get involved in advocacy. But the Ethiopian staff found ways to raise controversial issues by asking challenging questions in churches, *Chasing a pregnant girl away from church and family, is that justice or injustice? If a young man rapes a girl, does his family keep quiet or search for justice and punishment?*

Realizing the importance to help destitute women and their families Women of Hope in Ethiopia has added Mercy as their forth pillar of service. For Mercy ministry all support is raised locally. They collect clothes, soap, Bibles and radios and visit women in prisons. The suffering of women with uterus prolapsed was recognized and many of them were operated.

## Project Hannah

In Ethiopia Women of Hope is rather known under the name Project Hannah, because their activities are based on the prayers of Hannah, (1. Sam 2, 1–29).

Hannah was a woman without hope. In her Jewish culture women who do not give birth were considered cursed. Hannah was without child and considered herself cursed; she was criticized for not giving birth. This created a deep sorrow in her heart. She got depressed and cried many times. Though her husband used to love her very much she could not be comforted. She became a woman of sorrow and her heart was broken.

There are many women with us today who are without hope and these are targeted by Project Hannah.

Who are the Hannah's of today?

The Hannah of today is the barren woman; she is attacked in her home and sexually exploited by her relatives; she is kidnapped and married before she reached the age; she is forced to become a prostitute and held as hostage in dark places. The Hannah of today is isolated due to fistula and uterine prolapse. She is the victim of HIV/AIDS, slandered and stigmatized; she is suffering and languished in prison without justice. She and her children live in poverty. She has fallen under the yoke of the dominion of the devil.

Womanhood is a precious gift given by God. Since the time sin entered the world sin has been destroying the relationship between men and women. It has become customary to look down on women in the society. When we look at the negative impact of sin, it seems there is no hope for them. That is why Paul wrote in Eph 2, 12: *At that time you were far away from the kingdom of Israel, you were apart from Christ; you lived in this world without hope alienated from God and without Christ.* Humankind got a living hope through Christ. Now there is hope for all, even though there are difficult situations in which people find themselves.

Hirut Beyene coordinates TWR WHO in Ethiopia and wrote:

*It is now my turn to show the way of salvation to others, so that the lives of many women could flourish, their hope be renewed, the tears of the mourners be wiped, the forgotten ones be remembered, those who are in prison set free, husbands and wives live together in peace, those who are in dispute get reconciled, those who are on the street be remembered by the society and get service. What I came to understand from this ministry is the call to lift up those who are quarreling, who are hated and despised, who are forgotten, those who are naked and those who are starving. We need to be diligent in prayer so that the Lord goes into the life of people and fills up their identity that has become empty.*

## 4. The network of female theology students: Let her

In the Women Theologians' Network women share their stories and their daily life, and they reflect on God and his presence in their situations. The network encourages women to do theology from their own perspective and to challenge the challenges they face in their contexts. It also works to uplift the forgotten, to include the outcasts and to make visible the invisible.

Since 1997 the LWF took the initiative to bring women doing theology together, e.g. in the African Women Theologians' Network in Tanzania. The aim of this network is to strengthen the church's mission by acknowledging the gifts of women and men.

## LWF – African Women Theologians' Network

In 2012 the LWF coordinators of the Office for Women in Church and Society gathered women theologians and suggested to start women theologians' networks in their respective regions. Representatives of LWF – Women in Church and Society offices in the African region reached a consensus to establish a female theologians' network in Africa facilitated by the Women in Church and Society Department. Its purpose should be to address issues hampering leadership qualities of women theologians in their respective churches. The network would enforce mutual empowerment, support and sisterhood. LWF – Women in Church and Society is the coordinating point to sustain the networks and give them a collective voice. The need for a platform of academic writings and publication was emphasized. In 2014 the LWF in collaboration with the EECMY organized a workshop for African women theologians in Addis Ababa.

## The network in Ethiopia

The female theologians at Mekane Yesus Seminary (MYS) were motivated by that LWF workshop in 2014 and initiated their own Network of Female Theology Students.

Besides weekly meetings they celebrate the International Women's Day on March 8th with the MYS staff and students.

In 2019 the topic chosen was: Let her! (Jn 12, 7) Ebise Abdissa is a lecturer at the MYS and presented a keynote on John 12, 1–8.

[1] Six days before the Passover, Jesus came to Bethany, where Lazarus lived, whom Jesus had raised from the dead. [2] Here a dinner was given in Jesus' honor. Martha served, while Lazarus was among those reclining at the table with him. [3] Then Mary took about a pint of pure nard, an expensive perfume; she poured it on Jesus' feet and wiped his feet with her hair. And the house was filled with the fragrance of the perfume.

[4] But one of his disciples, Judas Iscariot, who was later to betray him, objected, [5] "Why wasn't this perfume sold and the money given to the poor? It was worth a year's wages." [6] He did not say this because he cared about the poor but because he was a thief; as keeper of the money bag, he used to help himself to what was put into it.

[7] "Leave her alone," Jesus replied. "It was intended that she should save this perfume for the day of my burial. [8] You will always have the poor among you, but you will not always have me."

Jesus and his disciples were in the home of Mary, Martha, and their brother Lazarus. This family was very close to Jesus during his earthly ministry.

In the preceding chapter we read the story of Jesus raising Lazarus from the dead. Hence, the family prepared a special dinner for Jesus. Martha, a practical woman who loved Jesus showed her love by serving dinner.

Mary showed her love by bringing Jesus a gift, a very expensive perfume. She took the most precious thing she possessed and spent it on Jesus. The value of the perfume was equivalent to the annual wage of a worker (Mt. 20, 20). What a person does with his or her money reveals what is inside his or her heart and Mary demonstrated her love for Jesus by spending all what she had. She treasured Jesus more than the cost of the perfume. Not only that, the way she expressed her love and adoration is also remarkable.

It was a sign of honor to anoint a person's head as the psalmist says; you anoint my head with oil. But Mary would not look at the head of Jesus, she anointed his feet and she wiped his feet with her hair. Mary expressed her love with humility.

In Jewish culture no respectable woman would ever appear in public with her hair unbound, because it is a sign of an immoral woman. But Mary never even thought of that. Her greater concern was Jesus rather than what the culture stresses or what other people think.

John tells us that as a result of this extraordinary adoration "the house was filled with the fragrance of the perfume." From the style of John's writings we know that his statement has double meanings; one which lies on the surface and one which is underneath. So he wants to show that the whole church was filled with the sweet memory of Mary's action, as something which time cannot ever take away.

Unfortunately, this amazing action of Mary was not appreciated by the apostles and especially not by Judas Iscariot, who perceived Mary's extravagant love as extravagant waste for two reasons:

Firstly John tells us about Judas' greed: He really wasn't concerned about the poor, but he was a thief. He had the money box and used to help himself to the funds (V. 6). If Mary had given her perfume to be sold for the money to be given to the poor, some of that money would have ended up in Judas' pocket. For Judas, money is the most important thing more important than Jesus.

Secondly, Judas and the other disciples opposed Mary's action due to their culture. Jewish women were treated as second class citizens, for example they were not allowed to testify in court and they were separated from men in public and in religious life. Jesus on the other hand had a theological discussion with a Canaanite woman (Mt 15, 22–28).

However, Jesus shattered this darkness by offering his teachings freely to anyone who would listen, whether they were women or men. In the gospels, we see Jesus healed the sick and he forgave women as well as men. Jesus valued their fellowship, prayers, service, financial support, testimony and witness and he honored them, and ministered to them in thoughtful ways.

Accordingly, Jesus acknowledged Mary's action and told Judas to leave her alone so that she keeps her thrill, her gratitude, her amazement, her worship, even at his death.

Every time we encounter Mary in the gospels, she is at Jesus' feet; first, learning from Him (Lk 10, 39); then pouring out her sadness on Him (Jn 11, 32). Mary discerned who Jesus was more than the apostles did. It seems she also knew about Jesus' impending death when none of the disciples had noticed, even though Jesus had told them three times. Mary got this personal knowledge of Jesus, by sitting at His feet.

Today is March the 8th, the International Women's Day. I want us to be challenged and encouraged by Mary's relationship to Jesus and her good actions. She gave her ear and heart to Jesus, and experienced that this led her to serve God's purpose for the human race! In giving her all, we see Jesus standing up defending her. We all have part in the same joy, if we just give our ears and hearts to Jesus.

***Picture 38:*** *Let her, International Women's Day 2019, courtesy Ebisse Abdissa*

Dear brothers and sisters, I also encourage and challenge you to follow in the footsteps of Christ, to encourage and defend women so that they freely exercise their spiritual gifts and talents in their service at home, in church and society.

**Ebise Abdissa**

# In the diaspora and at home

Many Ethiopians for various reasons live abroad. The bond to the home country is always there. The three women below all earned a PhD in various fields. Now they reached pension age and each looks back on the journey of her life. Their contribution to the church and to the lives of women in Ethiopia and worldwide deserves appreciation.

Belletech was born and brought up in Nedjo, a place blessed by Evangelical women pioneers, of whom Aster Ganno and Feben Hirphe, Nasiise Liiban and Tihun Tola are mentioned in this book. Chaltu was born near Dembi Dollo and spent part of her childhood in the house of Chawake Alabe. Gennet grew up in Addis Ababa. Her parents came from Eritrea, where the Evangelical movement had its roots. She was a member in the AAMYC and treasures this bond until today.

## 1. Belletech Deressa: From Ethiopia to seventy countries

### Her Early Life (1954–1972)

Belletech Deressa[185] was born as the 7th child to Bussa Karayou and Deressa Sasiga near Gimbi.

Her maternal grandmother understood the value of education and moved from Bodji to Nedjo to send her five children to the new Swedish Mission School. Belletech's parents were among the first children who attended the school. Her father attended the higher grades in 1936, when Italy invaded the country. Her mother, babysitting for the Nordfeldt family was in grade four. She was one of the first eight people confirmed Lutherans.

Her father, a teacher and school developer moved from town to town to start schools. He died when Belletech was just two years old. Her mother

---

[185] Belletech earned PhD, MS, MBA, MHA and B.S. and published many articles "Oromtitti: The Forgotten Women in Ethiopian History", (2003), IVY House Publishing Group, Raleigh, NC 27612, USA. The book is available online. References are made to. Arén Gustav (1999), Envoys of the Gospel in Ethiopia: In the steps of the Evangelical Pioneers, EFS, forlaget, Stockholm. (Arén 1999: 330, 485 + 486).

gave birth to four boys and four girls. Three of Belletech's brothers died before her birth in 1954 and the fourth passed away after her husband's sudden death.

It was the most difficult period for her mother and family. Stricken with grief she decided to move back to Nedjo and built a house next to the Swedish Mission School. Her mother earned some money by working at the boarding school. The family had additional income from a coffee farm planted by her father. This plantation was confiscated by the Derg government in the late 1970s.

Despite the challenges of a widow with four small children she was determined to send her daughters to school and even took in relatives' children who needed a place to live to attend school. Belletech and her three sisters were able to get schooling, thanks to their mother's hard work, perseverance, resilience and courage and with the assistance from some Swedish missionaries, who paid her schooling from grade 1–12.

Belletech had a happy childhood. Unlike many girls in her home town she rode bicycles, had dolls to play with and climbed trees. She enjoyed the company of her neighbor's Swedish children whom she visited and learnt their language. She grew up in a caring community that loved and protected children. Her mother assigned different responsibilities to the daughters. Belletech's duty was to bring their donkey home from grazing before six o'clock in the evening, a task she enjoyed.

As a child she also observed how women supported the church. Her mother served as a volunteer and led the group of women who met on Wednesdays. She conducted Bible studies, taught handicrafts and the products were sold on auctions. The income of their sales went to support evangelism work.

Like her mother Belletech attended the SEM School in Nedjo. After grade eight she was sent to the Ethiopian Evangelical College in Debre Zeit and lived in the boarding school, but Belletech missed her mother and cried often. Being away from home at a young age taught her to become independent. At high school, she joined the Welfare club, a group of students who on Saturdays went out to build shelters, clean streets, and help poor people in Debre Zeit.

## Bako project, Egerton College and Western Synod (1972–1979)

Belletech became the deputy Head to Home Economics School at Bako. She spent her free time educating herself. The age gap with students older than her did not intimidate her. She was determined to offer the best training so young adults could find employment and have a better standard of living.

Two years later the Swedish Women's Political party sent her to Egerton College in Kenya to study Agriculture and Home Economics with the objective to serve as director of the school at Bako Project. While in Kenya, the project at Bako was nationalized. Rev Gudina Tumsa, the General Secretary of EECMY asked her to serve as Women's Work Secretary of the Western Synod, where she served under the leadership of Rev Tasgera Hirpo.

Belletech was the first national woman in this position. Her responsibilities included supervising the women work activities and preparing teaching materials. She travelled and educated women and girls all over the synod while advocating for the rights of women and gender equality in both church and society. She enjoyed working with church women of Western Synod.

In 1978 she and another young women from EECMY attended a three months training on Advanced Leadership Training Program for women leaders of LWF member churches in Switzerland, which enlightened her perspective on the role of women in the church.

## Working with Lutheran World Federation (1979–1981)

The LWF requested the EECMY to release Belletech to work at their Women's Desk as a Research Assistant and she worked two years in Geneva. Besides organizing conferences for Lutheran women in different continents she conducted need assessments, led workshops, prepared resource materials and carried the responsibility for the publication of the newsletter WOMEN.

The most important issue for theologically trained women in late 1970s and 1980s was the ordination of women and their participation in leadership. Even in developed countries very few women were ordained. The Women Desk and Department of Studies of the LWF initiated discussions on ordination of women with member churches. Although women are the pillar of the church, ordaining them was implausible for some churches.

## Student and Assistant Professor (1981–1987)

In 1981 Belletech completed all courses for a bachelor's degree in the United States. Prior to her graduation, she requested LWF and EECMY to extend the scholarship for one more year to do her master's degree. The decision, however, was not to endorse the extension even though the scholarship fund was secured for three more years. Without endorsement of the EECMY scholarship committee LWF could not provide funds towards her education. The scholarship committee of EECMY suggested for her return to Ethiopia, yet the political situation in the country was getting worse.

During 1979–1989, many EECMY congregations were closed and many of their pastors, church members, leaders and employees of the church were in prison. The General Secretary of the EECMY had been kidnapped and his whereabouts was unknown. Therefore, it was not feasible for Belletech to return during those dangerous years.

The president of EECMY, his Excellency Dr. Emmanuel Abraham on his way to LWF meeting held in Canada, he called her and told her not to dismay but find alternative means for her education. Taking his fatherly advice at heart she pursued her studies. Her financial condition was distressing.

In 1983 her mother got seriously sick and medical doctors in Addis Ababa recommended treatment abroad. Belletech arranged for her mother and her sister Zawditu, who is a nurse to come to the US. Unfortunately, their mother passed away six days after hospital admission in Iowa. Belletech was devastated by her loss. Unable to accompany her sister and the coffin because her passport had been cancelled the situation got even worse for Belletech. She was stateless and a refugee. Two months later she defended her thesis and received a master's degree.

1983 was the darkest year in her life, yet she did not give up hopes and dreams for a better tomorrow. The death of her mother affected her perspective in life. Although she performed well in her grades at the University, she exhibited signs of depression for more than two years until one of her professors counseled her and she overcame her grief. During those difficult years, she was consoled by reading her favorite text from the Bible Psalm 23: *the Lord is my shepherd, I have everything I need* became her everyday prayer. She got advice and encouragement from some American friends and the late Elizabeth Karorsa whom she considers as her mentor and a second mother or Adada (aunt). Fortunately, in 1984, the US of America granted her permanent residence status which led to citizenship.

When realizing that she may never go back to her country, she changed her major field of study to consumer economics and family environment. Part time work as research enabled her to do her doctoral degree.

## Serving at the Evangelical Lutheran Church in America (ELCA), (1988–2008)

In 1987 she received a call from the late Rev Dr. Mark Thomsen for a job interview. After that she was elected to serve as a director for development, an official call to church wide service by the Board Chair Person.

ELCA is a merger of three Lutheran Churches that established its' corporate office in 1988 in Chicago. Belletech became the first African woman, to serve in that capacity, a professional field dominated by men. The position was new; the organisation did not have a policy on sustainable development or humanitarian response. She was humbled for being elected to serve at the head quarter of such a big church. Rev Dr. Mark Thomson was her immediate boss, mentor and her spiritual leader and she was blessed to have such a supportive executive director.

At the ELCA, she led the international development and disaster response program from infancy to global recognition. Their financial assistance expanded to more than 70 countries. She wrote guiding principles for international development programs and set priorities for funding of projects.

The job involved collaboration with many partners: LWF, ecumenical organisations, partner churches in Asia, Africa, Latin America, USA and Europe to challenge poverty, hunger, diseases environmental degradation, and injustice through sustainable development. She directed multimillion-dollar per year for economic development programs such as water resource

*Dr. Belletech Deressa, courtesy of B. Deressa*

development, agriculture, income generating projects, health care, support for HIV/AIDS victims, orphans of AIDS and relief programs in developing countries.

## Advocate for social justice

Her position as director for International development gave her access to many non-governmental and faith based development organisation. During her career with the ELCA she served on the governing board of ecumenical organisations including Church World Service, Heifer International and Action by Churches Together. Representing ELCA she used opportunities to address the needs of impoverished people.

As the elected Vice president for Program Committee of LWF World Service and advisor to the LWF Council she asked sensitive questions at the LWF council meeting regarding the '*the silent approaches*' of Lutheran Church leaders on HIV/AIDS endemic in Africa and South East Asia. The

LWF General Secretary asked her to draft a resolution paper. Some church leaders expressed discomfort to adopt the resolution because of the stigma attached to the disease, but the LWF Council for the first time openly discussed and passed a resolution on HIV/AIDS as a disease; called upon leaders of Lutheran churches to educate its constituencies on prevention and care and to provide support for people affected by the disease. Following a visit to the centre of AIDS epidemic she reported to the conference of ELCA Bishops and Church Council in 1999, on the negative impact of HIV/AIDS on development. As a result, in 2000, ELCA endorsed a fundraising campaign for HIV/AIDS prevention and care referred to as *'Stand with Africa – Campaign of Hope'*.

She often expressed her views at international forums regarding lack of peace and civil unrest initiated by some governments that contribute to internal and external displacement of people e.g. human rights violation in East Africa including Ethiopia. As of 1992 Africa Watch and Amnesty International issued press releases on violations of civil and political rights in Ethiopia indicating that many professionals and political opposition groups were arrested, tortured, disappeared and killed by government. In 1997, AI released an emergency appeal regarding sixty-five prisoners of conscience that included her nurse sister, another nurse and a medical doctor who were alleged to have supported Oromo Liberation Front or provided medical treatment to opposition group members. AI indicated the imminent danger in detention especially of the sixty-five Oromo prisoners of conscience and called for fair trial or to release them. Belletech expressed her concerns about human rights violations at various meetings despite the indifference exhibited by some representatives of the region.

With supporting data at hand, she requested LWF and churches in the US to ask the Ethiopian government to produce evidence of alleged crime committed by these prisoners. Belletech mobilized churches and NGOs in the US to write a letter and appeal to the Ethiopian government for the release of prisoners of conscience. Many people in the US were appalled by the imprisonment of medical professionals for treating patients in particular. Thousands of letters were sent to Ethiopian Prime Minister and Justice Minster demanding their release. Eventually many were released in 1999.

Belletech was alarmed by what she saw in Rwanda during a visit three months after the genocide. She often articulated the danger caused by human rights violations during the civil wars in Liberia, Sierra Leone, former Yugoslavia, Kosovo, Colombia, Nicaragua, and the Middle East including Israel and Palestine. In 2006, Church World Service organized an ecumenical delegation of African American Religious leaders to visit Israel and Palestine and to discuss a peace initiative with the leaders of the conflicting governments in the Holy Land. She was the only woman among eleven bishops.

She believes that development work can flourish where there is peace and justice. During her professional life as development director she travelled to more than seventy-three countries to monitor, evaluate and conduct need assessments.

### Appreciation for the Opportunities she had in life

Her experience in Ethiopia and third world countries prepared her to comprehend the needs of people living in poverty. She has seen negative effects of extreme poverty and children dying of preventable diseases. She considers education as basic human rights which can change the world for the better. She believes that Christian and faith-based organisation are obliged to provide services needed for marginalized people regardless of their faith, gender, ethnicity, and country of origins.

As a woman who came from a humble background, she is consistently reminded of what could be possible given an opportunity for education. She has unconditional love for her home country as well as her mother church EECMY. She thanks God for many opportunities over the years and is aware that most women and girls around the world do not get such chances. She is indebted to her adoptive country the USA and to her progressive church the ELCA for the trust and support rendered to her and the opportunity to serve at international level.

She acknowledges that her success in life was primarily because of her mother, Swedish missionaries and her faith in God. She is thankful to those who gave her the opportunity to serve in the USA. She expresses her gratitude to her loving husband who stood by her side, rendering advice along the way and to her two older sisters who looked after her when she was growing up as well as her younger sister who remained to be her best friend and confidant.

Belletech admits that life is full of surprises, struggle, disappointments, and at times challenging especially for African women who live and work in the Diaspora. Nevertheless, with perseverance, courage, determination and support from compassionate and morally decent individuals it is possible to overcome the hurdle of life and be a productive citizen in any country. Belletech enjoyed working for the church and believes if you make use of your God given talents and skills you can make a difference in the lives of people.

After more than twenty years she left the ELCA and worked for a non-governmental international organisation as director of international development operations in Baltimore, Maryland.

Belletech is married to her best friend and compatriot Dr. Bahiru Gametchu who also comes from her home town Nedjo. Currently she is enjoying early retirement and lives with her husband a few miles outside Washington, D.C.

Although, they lived for more than four decades outside their home country, they often talk about their home town, their childhood playmates, their old neighbors, and memories of their joyful years as children.

## 2. Chaltu Dereessa: 'Together we are stronger'

The interview took place in the home of Chaltu in Burayu.

**Question 1**: *In my country we have a saying: An apple does not fall far from the stem of its tree. Dr Chaltu, can you tell me about your parents and the influence they had on your life?*

When I was born my father became Abba Chaltu, the father of Chaltu. My brother Igazu was his second child. After his birth people called my father Abba Igazu, as is the customs, a father is named after his oldest son. My father protested and insisted on being called Abba Chaltu saying: Chaltu is my first child. His response was a booster to my self confidence.

He wanted a better future for me, whereas my mother asked him: *Why do you want to send her to school, a girl has to become a good housewife.* He said: *I do not want her to grind flour on stones like you are doing; I want to send her to school until she can read the Bible.*

After 2 years of schooling I was able to read the Bible and my father decided: *Now this is enough!* Again my mother disagreed: *You started sending her to school and now it is impossible to stop; she has to continue.* From grade three on every child needed to leave our village and attend school in town. My father was worried and argued: *You can't send small girls to town.*

One morning my family went for a prayer programme and I left secretly by following someone who was going to the market in Dembi Dollo. I stayed at someone's home and continued my schooling.

After grade four I lived with Chawake Alabe and became part of her family. Her older sons had left her house by that time. I took care of her when she was in hospital. I assisted Aster, her daughter, whenever needed.

My father used to say: *Yes is yes and no is no – everything else is a lie.* He was a man of conviction and lived according to this principle.

My father's mother was the daughter of a landlord and she was an only child. Twice she had travelled on foot to Addis Ababa, a distance of more than 600 km, to seek justice from Haile Selassie. In the capital she saw educated women and wanted me, her grandchild, to be educated too. She said: *I have land and can fund her* and so she did.

**Question 2:** *After grade eight you became a health assistant, why?*

At the National Exam I scored first in the Awraja. Brilliant students were offered manager training by the Commercial Bank of Ethiopia in those days; they got a good salary, a car and high status. I wanted to take care of my mother, my younger sisters and a brother who was sick and so I refused to go to Addis Ababa for that training. I married and became a health assistant at Dembi Dollo hospital. The second year of advanced health assistant training was difficult: it meant working regularly for eight hours and studying for four hours in class and three hours private study time. Including the two years of training I worked for six years at the hospital.

In 1978 workers wrote a petition to be signed by all hospital workers. I insisted on reading the paper before signing. The paper contained false accusations against foreign staff; I refused to put my name to that paper. There was peer pressure from my colleagues, but I said: *I'd rather live with a clear conscience than do what everyone else is doing.* I continued my schooling when I was 25 years and much older than the other learners.

**Question 3:** *Your school had foreign teachers. Was there equal education for boys and girls?*

In grade nine girls had to do home economics and typing classes. I asked: *Why are only girls here? Why do we not learn woodwork, metalwork and car mechanics – who prevents us?* The teacher had no answer. I went to the director, Mr. Thompson and said: *Boys go to car mechanics etc, but girls are limited to home economics and typing, which keeps us at home and in the kitchen. Why?* He called an urgent staff meeting and informed us later about the outcome: *Well, we don't know who decided that, it was just a tradition. From now on all fields are open to girls.*

The situation is like this: At home I am with my mother in the kitchen; my brother sits in the next room and near the light. Even today it is women who are always around the food, they are cooking and serving people to eat and drink. We are like Martha. In the church that's your place as a woman, you are always in the same area.

There is a saying: Girls can't do Mathematics, Physics and Chemistry. At school I said: *I can do it!* And I scored 100% in Chemistry and > 90% in Mathematics and Physics, with the bonus questions I got more than 100%. My advice to girls today is: Do not believe it when people tell you, girls are good at Geography but not good at Mathematics. It is simply not true.

**Question 4:** *After you received the advanced Diploma in Community Health in Canada in 1984, you did your Masters and a PhD. In my experience it is difficult for women to access a scholarship from EECMY. How did you manage to get that?*

I worked for 20 years in Bako and in Naqamte in the Mother and Child Health Clinic and for the family scholarship programme. My name was on the scholarship list of the synod and church. In the 1990s Swedish women had received my paper on harmful traditional practices and wanted me to extend my education. They realized being a woman I stood no chance on the scholarship quota either of the synod or of the church. The Swedish Church Women's Association sent me to the UK to do a Master's in Primary Health Care in Manchester.

Upon return to Ethiopia new challenges came up. My previous position was given to someone else. The synod said they had no place for a person with my qualification. My sponsoring organisation insisted that I should be given an assignment. After four months without work I got a job with a 50 ETB salary increase while male MA holders of theology degrees got a position and a double salary with their new qualification.

In Manchester a Finnish fellow student wanted me to apply for PhD studies in Finland because in her country there are no tuition fees. However, I was determined to work in my home country but my new job situation was frustrating and discouraging. My Finnish friend facilitated the process and in the end I went to Finland for my PhD in Health Policy and HIV.

**Question 5:** *Staying abroad means long times of absence from your family. How did you manage that double responsibility?*

I did not sacrifice my family to follow my career. My husband supported me and took care of our four children. Once I even came back from Finland, because there was a problem with my teen-aged children that needed my presence to find a solution.

When I married my husband was in grade 10, I was in grade 6. People said: *'Karaadha si deebise!'* meaning now he limited your growth. But on the contrary he was a big encouragement for me to study more. Turn by turn we went to school and further education.

**Question 6:** *After returning you worked for the LWF. You have served as a board member on the Executive committee of the EECMY (2005–2009) and at DASSC (2008–2012). Probably this was also a pioneering role for a woman. Were there also other female members and how did you cooperate?*

We were five female members on the Executive committee of the EECMY at my time. All of them were bold and spoke out the truth without fear, even though this had no impact on decisions. In the end five members resigned, three of them were women.

*Dr. Chaltu Dereessa, courtesy of C. Ahrens*

**Question 7:** *Now you have been retired for a couple of years. Can you share the vision for your retirement age?*

I conducted some mini research in Naqamte town and found out that many pensioners soon after leaving work get sick and many of them even die. On the other hand a lot of young children hang around their homes before entering school, and many youngsters without jobs are idle. Why not start a day care centre? Old and retired people who are often lonely at their homes could go and meet others, share their capacity and experiences with each other and with the younger generation. That would give quality life up to the end. They could discuss, read and work together. They could instruct TVET students practically to obtain skills that are needed in the market. It would be a pilot project and restore the bond between generations which is broken in our days. It would be an initiative that would create community fibre.

**Question 8:** *Why do you choose to live in Ethiopia?*

My roots are here. Even when I was victimized and imprisoned several times and once even tortured I still called Ethiopia my country. There are thousands of people here who need me. For my own conscience my presence is more important, I am physically participating in their pain and

searching for ways to overcome it. I want to hear others to say: I can do it
... that is why I am here with them in day to day contact.

**Question 9:** *Women generally have a strong sense of care and solidarity.*
*Ethiopians in the diaspora send a lot of support to their families at home.*
*A slogan by Hilary Clinton in her competition for presidency in 2008 was:*
*Together we are stronger. How do you see women in Ethiopia and in the*
*diaspora joining hands in solidarity on behalf of their sisters at home?*

"*We are separated by walls; let's build bridges*" as Dr Abiy Ahmed,
the Premier Minister of Ethiopia says. To build a network of solidarity, that
is so important, but not so easy if you are far away. But just to give your
hand to one person to lift her up, so she can continue by herself means
a lot. Nehemiah returned to restore the wall of Jerusalem and life in that
town could prosper again. If we stand together, next to each other, we can
become a protecting wall for our Ethiopian sisters.

Thank you for this interview, your pioneering work and the visions you
shared!

**Christel Ahrens**

## 3.  Gennet Awaloum: A stranger still and yet, God is the same everywhere

Gennet writes:

My name is Gennet Awaloum and I was born in 1934 in Addis Ababa
from Eritrean parents.

In 1954 I graduated from Empress Menen Girls' school, the first high
school class of girls that graduated in the country. After two years of college studies, one year at the University College of Addis Ababa and one
at the American College for Girls in Cairo, I went to the USA in 1957 on
LWF scholarship. It was, however, while I was in High School that I started
to attend the AAMYC and participated in the youth and Sunday school activities. In 1955, just before I left for Cairo, I was confirmed by Kes Stjärne
and became a member of the congregation.

In 1959, I received my BA degree in Home Economics at Concordia
College in Moorhead, Minnesota. While I was attending the Lutheran Bible
Institute in Seattle, Washington (1959–1960), I was asked by LWF if I

*Dr. Gennet Awaloum, courtesy G. Awaloum*

would be interested to study communication in view of coming back to work with Radio Voice of the Gospel which was to start in 1963. I accepted the call and enrolled at Boston University where I received my MS in Communications. I returned home in 1962 to start working at Radio Voice of the Gospel and later with Yemissrach Dimts Radio.

My years with the radio, where I worked mainly with the production of women's and children's programmes was a pioneer work where we had to do everything from scratch: write manuscripts, translate hymns and articles, and even sing to meet the need of the newly established work. It was a very engaging, meaningful, exciting and rewarding work. Hopefully, many have been helped through the various programs.

In 1962 at the third General Assembly of EECMY held at Mekanissa, I was asked to present a paper on the place of women in the church. As the national church was established only three years earlier, there was as yet no women's desk at the head office.

In 1963, I was sent to attend the LWF pre-Assembly Women's Conference held in Germany where I was elected as member of a women's work committee. The same year I attended the Fourth Assembly of the Lutheran World Federation held in Helsinki, Finland. When I came back, however, the absence of an organized women's work at the national level did not allow the immediate follow up of the recommendations from the conference. It took some years before the women desk became a reality.

Women have always been the backbone of Addis Ababa Mekane Yesus Church at Siddist Kilo. Hundreds of them have faithfully served the congregation in the last 93 years, both in good as well as in bad times. They were always there carrying on their work diligently. The support and encouragement from many Swedish women missionaries and missionary wives throughout the years, have been an invaluable help to these groups. I happened to be one who appeared on the scene just for a short period, between 1962 when I came back from the USA and 1970 when I left for Sweden with my family. When we left, Mekane Yesus, as a national church, was then only 11 years old preparing itself to meet the unknown challenges, successes, joys and sorrows waiting ahead.

As my husband, Kes Ezra, was pastor of the AAMYC, we lived in the church compound. The four years there gave me a close and good opportunity to observe the work of our dedicated women who came to church every Wednesday afternoon in spite of weather or wind. They made beautiful embroideries, baskets, span cotton for gabis and various other products which they sold once a year to bring an income to the congregation. They did diaconal work as well by visiting the sick, the mourning, the aged and helping the needy in the congregation in every way they could. We, the working women, did not have a chance to see these women at work, although we knew they were there faithfully carrying on their work. It was then we began to think about the role of the working age group. A number of us got together and discuss the possibility of involving ourselves in the women's work. We started to meet once a month on Saturdays. Although I was not there long, I knew the group continued and a number of them later served as active leaders of the entire women's work.

In spite of my early departure to Sweden, my interest for the work of the women in our congregation had not diminished. I am grateful for the continuous contacts I have had (and still have to some degree) with the group over the years. Fortunately, my work with the Church of Sweden Aid, the Swedish Section of the LWF, during a period of 20 years had given me an outlet to continue my interest on the question of women, this time even in a wider sense.

I have traveled a lot, in Africa and Latin America. In my capacity as the head of the Child Sponsorship Program, it was only obvious to see that dealing with the problems of children could not be tackled without taking their mothers into consideration. Unfortunately, fathers were in most cases absent. Ethiopia was one of the countries where we had sponsorship program. From 1994 to 1996, I was sent to work in the EECMY under the Addis Ababa Synod as an adviser to the sponsorship program and women's department. This gave me a unique opportunity to see the magnitude of work the church had to cope with trying to help and organize the women in the various congregations in different parts of the city. The Challenges were enormous with bureaucratic problems, limited resources and shortage of qualified personnel. I am ever grateful for this opportunity to have seen and experienced the life and the struggles of the church so closely.

The lot of women in poor countries are basically the same, no matter where. The Ethiopian woman carrying heavy loads of wood to breaking point; the Brazilian woman running around in the extreme Brazilian heat to find work; both to earn few coins to feed their hungry children. In Brazil their meal of the poor consisted only of rice and beans and in Ethiopia perhaps a bit of injera with shiro without fat. Wherever we came, within and outside the church, the subordinate place of the women was but too obvious.

I have lived longer in Sweden than in my own country, now for 48 years. When we came in 1970 the plan was to return after four years. The revolution came and our hope for return was jeopardized. We stayed on. To write about the life of a long sojourn in a foreign country would require at least a volume. Here, I would only share few thoughts and reflections which perhaps tells a little of what people residing in other countries have to struggle with.

It is the reality in our time that so many people willingly or otherwise live outside their own countries. Whether by choice or otherwise, it has its price. All immigrants have their own history to tell, as it is different. We, as a family, have nothing to complain about. We have actually come to a country where we had many, many good friends, former missionaries, who took good care of us. They made life easier for us to integrate in the church and society. Our children benefited from the wonderful system Sweden offers for all people living in the country.

However, there is also the existential side of life which cannot be neglected. The Bible says, "One cannot live by bread alone." Whether or not the adjustment to the life in foreign countries is difficult or easy, one cannot just turn off the switch and forget one's own origin so easily. Absolutely not! There is more to us humans than the physical comfort. Like the Jewish people, all of us living outside our countries of origin are referred to as Diasporas.

Ethiopia has recognized this reality by baptizing a square by that name "Diaspora Square." Strange as it may seem, it felt good to me when I first saw it! We are not forgotten! We also exist here even if we are elsewhere.

One misses everything that has to do with the country of origin, one's own culture and language. A foreign language and culture are like unfitting garments that sit on the outside uncomfortably. No matter how long one stays in a foreign country, one is always, for the rest of one's live, considered as a foreigner. Unfortunately, the Swedish word for foreigner is "främling" which means a stranger. Am I a stranger in Sweden after 48 years? In a way, yes I am. Even if I am not consciously and uncomfortably thinking about it in everyday life, deep down I am in a continuous unsettled existence.

The longing for my origin, for my language, for my food, culture, my identity, my natural contextual existence which knows what to say when and how to behave without having to think twice, is ever present in me.

Do I mean that which is mine is better than the one I have elsewhere? Definitely, not! On the contrary Sweden is a very nice, just, fair, human, orderly and democratic country. Nonetheless, one misses ones origin! I am sure this would be true of all people residing outside their own country. It is human. Deeply sited childhood feelings cannot be extinguished easily, if ever.

When I have said that however, I would like to add that the whole world is in the hands of the Lord and He has promised to be with us wherever we are. (Is. 41, 10)

I hope and pray that the women's work in this congregation will get new wings and inspirations to widen its visions and develop its skills in every possible way to meet the need of the ever growing membership and of the new generation to come.

I love the AAMYC and am very grateful for all the spiritual nurture I have received there throughout my long life even from a distance. I am thankful for the many spiritual teachers and mentors, fathers and mothers, sisters and brothers and friends who have enriched my life in many different ways.

Gennet is married to Kes Ezra Gebremedhin. They have three children, seven grandchildren and two great grandchildren.

318

# Bibliography

(Ethiopian authors are listed under their first names.)

Arén, Gustav: *Envoys of the Gospel in Ethiopia*, EFS förlaget, Stockholm 1999

Arén, Gustav: *Evangelical Pioneers in Ethiopia*, EFS förlaget, Stockholm 1978

Bakke, Jonny: *Christian Ministry, Patterns and Functions within the EECMY*, Oslo/New Jersey 1987

Bauerochse, Ernst: *A Vision Finds Fulfillment*, LIT Verlag, Muenster 2008

Belletech Deressa: *Oromtitti – The Forgotten Women in Ethiopian History*, Raleigh 2003

Böll, Verena et al: *Ethiopia and the Missions*, LIT Verlag, Muenster 2005

Debela Birri: *Divine Plan Unfolding*, Lutheran University Press,, 2014

Eide, Øyvind M.: *Revolution and Religion in Ethiopia*, Ohio University Press, 2000

Emmanuel Abraham: *Reminiscences of my Life*, lunde forlag, Oslo 1983

Fekadu Gurmessa: *Evangelical Faith Movement in Ethiopia*, Lutheran Univ. Press, Minnesoata 2009

Gadaa Melbaa: *Oromia An Introduction to the history of the Oromo people*, Uni. Hs. Publisher, 1999

Gammachuu Danuu: *How did we get the Gospel of Christ?* (1866–1991), YDCS, Addis Ababa 2012

Gidada Solen: *The other Side of Darkness*, Friendship Press, New York 1972

Harms, Hartwig F.: *Concerned for the Unreached, Life and Work of Louis Harms*, 1999

Lambie, Thomas: *A Doctor Without a Country*, Fleming H. Revell Company, New York, London 1939

Launhardt, Johannes: *Evangelicals in Addis Ababa (1919–1991)*, LIT Verlag, Muenster 2004

Levine, Donalt: *Wax and Gold, Tradition and Innovation in Ethiopian culture*, Chicago U. Press, 1965

Lundstroem, Karl J. & Ezra Gebremedhin: *Kenisha, The Evangelical Church of Eritrea*, Red Sea Press 2011

Merkuria Bulcha: *The Making of the Oromo Diaspora*, Kirk House Publisher, Minneapolis 2002

Saeveras, Aud: *Der lange Schatten der Macht*, Giessen/Basel, 1993

Samuel Yonas Deressa, ed.: *The Life, Works, and Witness of Tsehay Tolessa & Gudina Tumsa*, Lutheran Quarterly Books, June 2017

Shell, Sandra Rowoldt: *Children of Hope*, Ohio University Press, 2018

Tasgaraa Hirphoo: *Abbaa Gammachis (Onesimos Nasib)*, Biographie, Ethiopia 2007

Tasgaraa Hirphoo: *Short Biographies of Oromoo Women Evangelical Pioneers*, Addis Ababa 2013

Tessama Zewde: *The Seed bore Fruit, the beginnings of Evangelistic work in Sidama*, Oslo 2010

Uhlig et al.: *Ethiopia, History, Culture and Challenges*, LIT Verlag, Muenster 2017

Wassmann, Dietrich (sen): *Der Durchbruch des Evangeliums im Gallaland*, Hermannsburg 1948

# The editors

**Christel Ahrens**, a health professional of German nationality, came to Ethiopia in 1988. She is a nurse midwife and holds a Masters in Mother and Child Health from the University College London, UK. For the last ten years she has been organizing people with podoconiosis in self-help groups in more than 200 communities. Christel is a member of the EECMY and has a keen interest in women and history.

**Ebise Ashana** is from Aira, West Wollega and working for the EECMY since 1974. She has a Masters in Poverty Reduction and Development Management from Birmingham University, UK and is the Gender and Development officer of the Development and Social Services Commission/EECMY. "ተሐድሶአዊ የልማት ሥራ መግቢያ", an introduction to transformational development is the title of her first book. Ebise is passionate about the promotion of gender equality and human rights issues.

# Beiträge zur Missionswissenschaft / Interkulturellen Theologie
hrsg. von Henning Wrogemann und John G. Flett

Francis Abdelmassieh
**Egyptian-Islamic Views on the Comparison of Religions**
Positions of Al-Azhar University Scholars on Muslim-Christian Relations
Bd. 49, 2020, 184 S., 29,90 €, br., ISBN 978-3-643-91280-0

Josef Estermann
**Befreiung oder Unterdrückung?**
Mission und Theologie in der wechselvollen Geschichte von Kolonialismus und Dekolonisation
Bd. 47, 2019, 194 S., 29,90 €, br., ISBN 978-3-643-80313-9

Dirk Puder
**Die Welt verändern**
Transformatives Potential in Heilung und Mission der pentekostalen Religionsformation in den Entwürfen von Amos Yong, Veli-Matti Kärkkäinen und Opoku Onyinah
Bd. 46, 2020, 298 S., 34,90 €, br., ISBN 978-3-643-14481-2

John O'Brien
**The QUR'AN and the CROSS**
A study of al-Nisa (4):157. 'and they did not kill him and did not crucify him, but it was made to appear so to them'
Bd. 45, 2020, 296 S., 49,90 €, br., ISBN 978-3-643-91082-0

Tobias Schuckert
**Auf der Suche nach Verbundenheit**
Der japanische Umgang mit der Tsunamikatastrophe 3.11 und eine Implikation der Theologie des Kuschelns
Bd. 44, 2018, 294 S., 39,90 €, br., ISBN 978-3-643-14222-1

Adolphus Chikezie Anuka
**Mmanwu and Mission among the Igbo People of Nigeria**
An Inculturative Dialogue
Bd. 43, 2018, 344 S., 34,90 €, br., ISBN 978-3-643-91063-9

Dyah Ayu Krismawati
**Reformdenken indonesischer Muslime in der era Reformasi**
Religionswechsel und Religionsfreiheit im Denken von Gelehrten der Muhammadiyah und der Nahdlatul Ulama
Bd. 42, 2018, 296 S., 34,90 €, br., ISBN 978-3-643-14166-8

Riley Edwards-Raudonat; Uwe Gräbe; Kerstin Neumann (Eds.)
**Mission in Solidarity – Life in Abundance for All**
Proceedings of the EMS Mission Moves Symposium in Bad Boll 2017
Bd. 41, 2018, 144 S., 29,90 €, br., ISBN 978-3-643-90952-7

Barbara Gierull
**„Evangelisch-in-Jerusalem" im interreligiösen Dialog**
Fragen bezüglich des interreligiösen Dialogs vor Ort – gewollt, gebraucht oder entbehrlich?
Bd. 40, 2017, 444 S., 49,90 €, br., ISBN 978-3-643-13854-5

Heinrich Balz
**Warum Robinson nicht zu Hause blieb**
Europäische Expansion, Welterkundung und Mission
Bd. 39, 2017, 144 S., 29,90 €, br., ISBN 978-3-643-13836-1

LIT Verlag Berlin – Münster – Wien – Zürich – London
Auslieferung Deutschland / Österreich / Schweiz: siehe Impressumsseite

# Afrikanische Studien / African Studies

Siegbert Uhlig; David Appleyard; Alessandro Bausi; Wolfgang Hahn;
Steven Kaplan (Eds.)
**Ethiopia**
History, Culture and Challenges
ETHIOPIA is a compendium on Ethiopia and Northeast Africa for travellers, students, businessmen,
people interested in Africa, policymakers and organisations.
In this book 85 specialists from 15 countries write about the land of our fossil ancestor 'Lucy', about
its rock-hewn churches and national parks, about the coexistence of Christians and Muslims, and
about strange cultures, but also about contemporary developments and major challenges to the region.
Across ten chapters they describe the land and people, its history, cultures, religions, society and politics, as well as recent issues and unique destinations, documented with tables, maps, further reading
suggestions and photos.
Bd. 58, 2017, 380 S., 34,90 €, br., ISBN 978-3-643-90892-6

LIT Verlag Berlin – Münster – Wien – Zürich – London
Auslieferung Deutschland / Österreich / Schweiz: siehe Impressumsseite